MW00989006

Boris Godunov

and

Little Tragedies

Alexander Pushkin

Translated by Roger Clarke

ALMA CLASSICS

ALMA CLASSICS
is an imprint of

ALMA BOOKS LTD
3 Castle Yard
Richmond
Surrey TW10 6TF
United Kingdom
www.almaclassics.com

Boris Godunov first published in Russian in 1831
The Mean-Spirited Knight first published in Russian in 1836
Mozart and Salieri first published in Russian in 1831
The Stone Guest first published in Russian in 1839
A Feast during the Plague first published in Russian in 1832
This translation first published by Alma Classics in 2010
This new edition published by Alma Classics in 2017
English translations, introductions, notes, extra material and appendices
© Roger Clarke, 2010
Cover design by William Dady

Printed by CreateSpace

ISBN: 978-1-84749-691-1

Contents

Publisher's Foreword

This is one of a series of volumes, to be published by Alma Classics during the coming years, that will present the complete works of Alexander Pushkin in English. The series will be a successor to the fifteen-volume Complete Works of Alexander Pushkin published by Milner and Company between 1999 and 2003, the rights to which have been acquired by Alma Classics. Some of the translations contained in the new volumes will, as here, be reprints of those in the Milner edition (corrected as necessary); others will be reworkings of the earlier translations; others again will be entirely new. The aim of the series is to build on the Milner edition's work in giving readers in the English-speaking world access to the entire corpus of Pushkin's writings in readable modern versions that are faithful to Pushkin's meaning and spirit.

In publishing this series, Alma Classics wishes to pay a warm tribute to the initiative and drive of Iain Sproat, managing director and owner of Milner and Company and chairman of the original project's editorial board, in achieving the publication of Pushkin's complete works in English for the first time. Scholars, lovers of Pushkin and general readers wishing to gain knowledge of one of Europe's finest writers owe him the heartiest gratitude.

– Alessandro Gallenzi

OTHER WORKS OF ALEXANDER PUSHKIN AVAILABLE
FROM ALMA CLASSICS

Ruslan and Lyudmila, a dual-language text
trans. Roger Clarke

The Queen of Spades and Other Stories
trans. Paul Debreczeny

Eugene Onegin, a dual-language text
trans. Roger Clarke

The Captain's Daughter and A History of Pugachov
trans. Paul Debreczeny and Roger Clarke

Love Poems
trans. Roger Clarke

Belkin's Stories
trans. Roger Clarke

Alexander Pushkin (1799–1837)

Abrám Petróvich Gannibál,
Pushkin's great-grandfather

Sergéy Lvovich Pushkin,
Pushkin's father

Nadézhda Ósipovna Púshkina,
Pushkin's mother

Natálya Nikoláyevna Pushkina,
Pushkin's wife

The Imperial Lyceum in Tsárskoye Seló,
which Pushkin entered in 1811

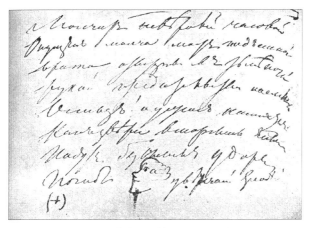

Fragment from Pushkin's manuscript
of the ode 'Liberty'

БОРИСЪ ГОДУНОВЪ,

СОЧИНЕНІЕ

АЛЕКСАНДРА ПУШКИНА.

САНКТПЕТЕРБУРГЪ.
1831.

Title page of the 1831 edition
of *Boris Godunov*

A selection of Vladímir Favórsky's woodcuts for *Boris Godunov*:
Pimen and Grigóry (*Boris Godunov*, Sc. 5)

Borís Godunóv
(*c*.1551–1605)

Boris Godunov

Introduction

Who has fathomed, who has understood, Boris Godunov, *that lofty and profound work, enclosed in a private and inaccessible poetry, a work that has rid itself of all crude and garish adornment of the kind that normally fascinates the masses?...*
– N. V. Gogol, 'Some Remarks about Pushkin' (1832)

Boris Godunov is Alexander Pushkin's only full-length drama and one with which he was particularly pleased. It is a historical play, in the manner of the historical plays of Shakespeare, whom Pushkin greatly admired. The circumstances of its composition, its unique structure and literary significance and the historical background to the action are described more fully in the Extra Material and Appendices at the back of this volume.

Pushkin completed work on *Boris Godunov* on 7th November 1825. The authorities withheld permission for its publication for several years. When it was eventually approved for publication at the beginning of 1831 Pushkin incorporated a number of significant changes, ranging from the alteration or omission of odd words to a more drastic curtailing of certain passages, a reversal of the order of two scenes, and the deletion of three scenes in their entirety. The reason for particular changes is not always clear. Some Pushkin was obliged to make to meet the objections of the censorship; others were consequences of these; others he made of his own accord to correct mistakes or improve drafting. A few of the minor differences in the 1831 edition may have been printing errors. The subject is discussed in more detail later in this volume.

The approach of subsequent editors has varied. But strangely, until the last few years *Boris Godunov* has hardly ever been published in either of the versions sanctioned by Pushkin during his lifetime. Normally Pushkin's 1831 text has been taken as a basis, but with some reinstatement of deleted material, notably of Scene 3. The 1831 text itself seems never till recently to have been republished; and it was not until 2004 that the University of Wisconsin Press did Pushkin scholarship a service by bringing out for the first time the full text of the play, in Russian and English, as Pushkin had originally composed it. Subsequently, in 2008, a new Russian edition has appeared giving both a facsimile of the 1831 edition and the 1825 text.

In this volume I have followed almost entirely Pushkin's 1825 text, as given in the 2008 Russian edition. The few divergences are noted in the commentary. This is the version that seems to me to represent, very largely, the author's unconstrained conception and aspiration for the play. I have also examined the 1831 edition directly and have identified and listed in Appendix 2 – for the first time in an English edition – all the significant differences between the 1825 and 1831 versions. Scholars, readers and directors in the English-speaking world are therefore now able to make their own fully informed judgements on which text to use.

There are a few other editorial decisions I have made of which the reader should be made aware at this stage. The first concerns the numbering of scenes. Pushkin's play consists of a continuous succession of twenty-five scenes, ungrouped into acts. Pushkin did not number the scenes; but for ease of reference I have assigned them numbers in this volume. My numbers coincide with those in the University of Wisconsin Press edition. Secondly, although neither Pushkin's original text nor the 1831 edition contained a list of scenes or of the dramatis personae, I have drawn up lists of both in the pages immediately following this introduction for the convenience of readers, scholars and directors.

The last point relates to metre. Pushkin followed Shakespeare in composing *Boris Godunov* for the most part in blank verse – unrhymed lines of ten or eleven syllables, stressed normally on the even syllables. A few scenes and shorter passages are in prose. Two whole scenes and other brief passages he composed in other metres. This translation largely reproduces Pushkin's metres (or their absence).

For the treatment of Russian and Polish names see the Translator's Note at the end of the Extra Material. Asterisks have been placed in the text after words that are the subject of an endnote.

– Roger Clarke

List of Scenes

Characters

Russians

The Tsar and His Household

Borís Godunóv, Regent, and later Tsar of Russia
María Godunóva, his wife (*silent part*)
Feódor, his son
Xénia, his daughter
Xénia's nurse
Stewards in the palace
Court servants and officials

Russian Orthodox Churchmen

Patriarch of All Russia
Superior of the Monastery of the Miracle
Father Pimen, an elderly monk at the Monastery of the Miracle and
a chronicler
Grigóry ("Grishka") Otrépyev, a young monk at the same monastery;
later the Pretender Dimítry
Older monk at the same monastery
Varlaám and Misaíl, vagrant monks
Other church dignitaries

Boyars, Nobles and Officials in Moscow or in the Service of Tsar
Borís

Prince Vasíly Ivánovich Shúysky, a boyar
Prince Vorotýnsky, a boyar
Afanásy Mikháylovich Pushkin, a boyar
Mosálsky, a boyar
Shchelkálov, secretary to the Tsar's Council

7

Semyón Nikítich Godunóv, relative of Borís and head of his secret police
Rozhnóv, a nobleman, a prisoner of the Pretender
Basmánov, a nobleman of low rank and general in Tsar Borís's army
Captain Margeret, a Frenchman in Tsar Borís's army
Captain Walther Rosen, a German in Tsar Borís's army
Other boyars
Guests of Prince Shúysky

Others

 Landlady of an inn on the Polish frontier
 Boy, servant in the house of Prince Shúysky
 Other servants of Prince Shúysky
 Andréy Karéla, a Cossack chieftain
 Nikólka, a holy fool
 Urchins
 Beggar
 People of Moscow, police, soldiers

Boyars, Nobles, etc. in Exile in Poland

 Gavríla Pushkin, nephew of Afanásy Pushkin
 Prince Kurbsky, son of a boyar exiled by Tsar Iván the Terrible
 Khrushchóv, a nobleman
 Other Russian exiles and adventurers

Poles

 Mniszech (*Mníshek*), Governor of Sandomierz
 Maryna Mniszech, his daughter
 Róża (*Ruzha*), Maryna's maid
 Wiśniowiecki (*Vishnevétsky*), a nobleman, friend of Mniszech
 Sobański (*Sobánsky*), a nobleman
 Father Czernikowski (*Chernikóvsky*), a Jesuit
 A poet
 Adventurers in the Pretender's service
 Ladies
 Soldiers, menservants, maidservants

To the memory
precious to Russians
of
Nikoláy Mikháylovich Karamzín
this work,
inspired by his genius,
is dedicated
with veneration and gratitude
by
*Alexander Pushkin**

A Comedy
concerning
Tsar Borís
and
Grishka Otrépyev.
1825.*

Scene 1*
Moscow, the Kremlin Palace – 20th February 1598

*Princes Shúysky and Vorotýnsky.**

VOROTÝNSKY

    Our orders are to keep an eye on Moscow;
    it seems, though, that there's no one left to watch:
    the city's empty; everyone's gone off
    after the Patriarch* towards the convent.
    What's your assessment? How'll this turmoil end?

SHÚYSKY

    How will it end? It isn't hard to tell –
    the mob will howl and wail a bit again,
    Borís will frown a bit more in reply
    (how like a drunkard pressed to take some wine!),
    till, overcome at last by his compassion,   10
    he'll humbly condescend to take the crown.
    Then... then he'll be our ruler once again,
    just as before.

VOROTÝNSKY

                But it's a month now since
    he shut himself up in his sister's convent
    and seemingly renounced all worldly business.
    The Patriarch, the boyar-councillors* –
    none of them's got him yet to change his mind;
    Borís won't listen to their tearful protests:
    their prayers, the lamentations of all Moscow,
    the Grand Assembly's* voice – he's deaf to all.   20
    His sister too they've begged and begged in vain
    to give her blessing* to Borís' accession;
    but the Tsarítsa, widow now and nun,
    is firm as he and equally unyielding –

under Borís's influence, no doubt.
What if the Regent really has grown weary
of the anxieties of sovereign power
and won't agree to ascend the vacant throne?
What'll you say then?

SHÚYSKY

                  I'll say that it was pointless,
if so, to shed the young Crown Prince's blood;   30
Dimítry could have then remained alive.

VOROTÝNSKY

A shocking crime was that! But is it true
Borís put the Crown Prince to death?

SHÚYSKY

                       Who else?
Who offered bribes in vain to Chepchugóv?
Who charged the Bityagóvskys and Kachálov
with their mysterious mission? I was sent
to Uglich to make on-the-spot enquiries
into the affair; I found the clues still fresh:
the whole town had been witness of the outrage;
the evidence of all the townsfolk tallied;   40
on my return a single word of mine
could have exposed the wretch for what he was.

VOROTÝNSKY

Then why did you not bring about his downfall?

SHÚYSKY

I must confess that at the time his calmness,
his unexpected shamelessness confused me.
He looked me in the eye with perfect candour
and questioned me on each particular –
and face to face with him I just repeated
the nonsense that he'd primed me with himself.

VOROTÝNSKY
    Shame on you, Prince.

SHÚYSKY
                      What *else* could I have done?   50
    Revealed all to Feódor? But the Tsar
    saw all things through the eyes of Godunóv,
    heard all things with the ears of Godunóv.
    Suppose that I'd convinced him of it all,
    Borís would soon have unconvinced the Tsar,
    and then I'd have been placed under detention,
    and in good time in some dark prison cell
    I'd have been quietly strangled, like my uncle.*
    I do not mean to boast, but this is certain –
    when the time comes no death will make me flinch;   60
    I am no coward, but nor am I a fool,
    and I'll not volunteer for execution.

VOROTÝNSKY
    A shocking crime! Mark what I say: I'm sure
    the murderer must be tortured by remorse –
    that innocent boy's blood's no doubt the reason
    that keeps him now from mounting Russia's throne.

SHÚYSKY
    He'll not be stopped by that: he's not so squeamish!
    Think what an honour for us and for Russia:
    yesterday's slave, a Tatar, son-in-law of
    butcher Malyúta, butcher at heart himself –   70
    this man will take the monarch's crown and mantle…*

VOROTÝNSKY
    Yes, he's not nobly born; *we* are more noble.

SHÚYSKY
    So one would think.

VOROTÝNSKY

               We Shúyskys, Vorotýnskys…
princes by birth, and let us not forget it!

SHÚYSKY

Princes by birth, and of the line of Ryúrik.

VOROTÝNSKY

You know, Prince, we ourselves would have a right to
succeed the late tsar.

SHÚYSKY

               Yes, a better right
than Godunóv's.

VOROTÝNSKY

          Indeed that's so.

SHÚYSKY

                  Well then,
if Godunóv keeps up these crafty tactics,
why don't we rouse the people to our own ends?   80
If we can once detach them from Borís,
they've real princes in abundance: they can
choose which of us they like to be their tsar.*

VOROTÝNSKY

It's strange: we heirs of Ryúrik* are not few,
but we can't well contend with Godunóv.
No longer do the people see in us
the sons and grandsons of their warrior-chieftains.
We long ago were stripped of our domains;
it's long we've served the tsars as lowly vassals;
while *he* by fear and love and his prestige   90
has had the wit to hold the people spellbound.

SHÚYSKY *(looking out of the window)*
He's had the nerve, that's all, while we… But stop,

16

d'you see? – they've all dispersed, they're coming back.
Let's hurry and find out if it's been settled.

Scene 2*
Red Square

The populace.

FIRST MAN
He'll not be moved. He's driven from his presence
boyars and bishops, even the Patriarch.
They fell prostrate before him, but – no use:
the majesty of the tsarship overawes him.

SECOND MAN
Good heavens! Who'll we have then for our ruler?
That's bad for us!

THIRD MAN
                    The Secretary of State –
look! – coming out to announce the Council's verdict!

POPULACE
Quiet! Quiet! The Council Secretary's* speaking;
shsh – listen!

SHCHELKÁLOV *(from the Grand Steps)*
                    It has been resolved in Council
to strive one last time to convince the Regent   10
to put aside his grief and change his heart.
Tomorrow the most holy Patriarch,
after a solemn service in the Kremlin,
preceded by the banners of the saints,
with the icons of Vladímir and the Don,*
will go forth; with him too will go the Council,
the boyars, court officials, delegates
from other towns,* and all Moscow's believers –
we'll all go to petition the Tsarítsa

at last to pity Muscovy's bereavement   20
and give her blessing to Borís' accession.
Go back now to your homes, and God be with you;
pray earnestly – and may the earnest prayer
of Moscow's faithful reach up to the heavens.

(The people disperse.)

Scene 3*
Maidens' Field,* the Novodévichy Convent

The populace.

A MAN

They've just gone into the Tsarítsa's cell;
Borís, the Patriarch and all the boyars
went in together.

ANOTHER MAN

What's the news?

THIRD MAN

He's still
as obstinate; but nonetheless there's hope.

PEASANT WOMAN *(with baby)*

Goo, goo! Don't cry, don't cry! Watch out, there's bogey –
bogey will get you! Goo, goo!… Oh, stop crying!

A MAN

Couldn't we find some way inside the walls?

ANOTHER MAN

What! Not a chance. There's crush enough out here,
don't mention inside. It's no trifling matter.
All Moscow's squeezed together; look: walls, roofs,   10
all the cathedral belfry's galleries,

18

domes of the churches, even their very crosses
are studded thick with people.

FIRST MAN

It's quite something!

A MAN
Hey! What's that noise?

ANOTHER MAN

Shsh, listen! What's that noise?
People have started wailing. Look, like waves
they're dropping row on row... more... more... Well, friend,
it's our turn now; be quick! get on your knees!

POPULACE *(on their knees; wailing and crying)*
Have pity, Father! Take the crown; become
our Tsar, our father!

A MAN *(softly)*

What's this crying for?

ANOTHER MAN
How're we to know? The boyars' business, this is –   20
above *our* heads.

PEASANT WOMAN *(with baby)*

Well, what a!... Now it's time
to yell, he's shut up! You just wait! Here's bogey!
You spoilt brat, cry!

*(She drops the baby on the ground; the baby squeals.)**

That's better.

A MAN

They're all crying.
We'd better cry too, friend.

19

ANOTHER MAN
                              I'm trying, friend,
    but I can't.

FIRST MAN
                    Nor can I. No onions on you
    to rub our eyes with?*

SECOND MAN
                              No, I'll use my spittle.
    What's happening now?

FIRST MAN
                              I just can't make it out.

POPULACE
    He'll take the crown! He's tsar now! He's consented!
    Borís is tsar! Long live our Tsar Borís!

Scene 4*
The Kremlin Palace

Borís, the Patriarch, boyars.

BORÍS
    My Father Patriarch and all you boyars,
    I have laid bare to you my inmost feelings:
    you've seen with what humility and awe
    I'm now accepting high authority –
    so burdensome the duties it imposes.
    I now succeed those mighty Tsars Iván,* and
    Feódor too, my angelic predecessor...
    O saintly one, my father-sovereign!
    From heaven regard the tears your loyal servants
    have shed, and send down on the man you loved,   10
    the man you raised here to such splendid honours –
    send down upon his reign your holy blessing:
    grant that I rule my people gloriously

and show myself as just and good as you.
Boyars, I look for your cooperation.
Give me the service you gave Tsar Feódor,
when I, not yet elected by the people,
myself was sharing with you in your tasks.

BOYARS

We shall not break the oath that we have given.

BORÍS

Now come with me and let's salute the tombs*   20
of Russia's monarchs who now lie at rest,
and then call to a banquet all our people –
yes, noble lords, blind beggars, everyone;
an open house to all, all guests are welcome!

(He leaves; the boyars follow.)

VOROTÝNSKY *(detaining Shúysky)*
Your guess was right.

SHÚYSKY

                    What's that?

VOROTÝNSKY

                                        The other day,
just here. Remember?

SHÚYSKY

                    No, I don't remember.

VOROTÝNSKY

When all the people went to Maidens' Field,
you said—

SHÚYSKY

                    Today is no day for remembering;
sometimes I recommend forgetfulness.

Besides, my slanderous talk then was a sham;   30
I had no other purpose but to test you,
better to know your private cast of mind.
But listen! – that's the cheering populace
greeting the Tsar – my absence might be noticed –
I'll catch him up.

VOROTÝNSKY

    You crafty sycophant!

Scene 5*
A Cell in the Monastery of the Miracle at Night – 1603

Father Pimen; Grigóry* asleep.*

PIMEN *(writing in front of an icon lamp)*
 Just one more entry, one last episode –
 and then my chronicle will be complete;
 the task assigned by God to this poor sinner
 will be discharged. No, not in vain did God
 appoint me witness of these many years
 and grant me knowledge in the art of writing;
 one day some studious monk will come across
 this conscientious, unnamed work of mine;
 like me, he'll light his icon lamp, then shake
 the centuries-old dust from off the parchments   10
 and copy out my faithful chronicles –
 so Christian Russia's future generations
 shall learn the story of their native land
 and call to mind the great tsars of the past
 for their hard work, their glory and their goodness;
 but for their misdeeds, for their darker doings –
 for these they'll humbly pray to Christ for mercy.
 In my old age I live my life anew,
 the expired years pass before me in procession –
 was it so long ago that they swept by,   20
 full of events, tempestuous as the ocean?
 Now they are calm and silent; just a few

of the main actors live on in my mind,
just a few words of theirs I still recall,
all else has perished irretrievably...
But day is near, the lamp is burning low –
just one more entry, one last episode. *(Writes.)*

GRIGÓRY *(awaking)*
Always the same dream! Can it be? A third time!
Infernal dream!... And the old man's still sitting
by the icon candle, writing – then he can't   30
have closed his eyes in sleep the whole night long.
How much I love that tranquil look of his,
when, heart and soul immersed deep in the past,
he's working on his chronicle; and often
I've tried to guess the events he's writing of –
the dark ages of Tatar domination?
Or Tsar Iván's bloodthirsty executions?
The factious parliaments of Nóvgorod?*
The glory of our homeland? But – no use.
That lofty brow, those eyes, are hard to read,   40
one can't make out the old man's hidden thoughts:
always that same aloof, yet humble look.
Just like a clerk, grey-haired with years in court,
he views good men and bad without emotion,
listening impassively to right and wrong,
immune alike to pity and to anger.

PIMEN
Awake, then, brother?

GRIGÓRY
                    Please give me your blessing,
Reverend Father.

PIMEN
                    May the good Lord bless you
both this day and for evermore. Amen.

GRIGÓRY

All night you've been awake busily writing;   50
but, though I've slept, my sleep's kept being troubled
by a hellish dream the Devil's sent to vex me.
I dreamt that I was climbing a steep staircase
up a high tower,* and looking from the top
I saw the whole of Moscow like an ant heap;
below, a crowd was seething in the square;
they kept on pointing up at me and jeering,
and made me feel ashamed and terrified –
and then I tumbled headlong, and woke up…
and three times now I've dreamt this selfsame dream.   60
Isn't it weird?

PIMEN

        Your young blood's overheated.
Strengthen your self-control with prayer and fasting;
then there'll be nothing to your nightly dreams
but harmless visions. Even now, if I
give way against my will to drowsiness
and fail to finish my long evening prayers –
old as I am my sleep's not calm and sinless:
I see before me sometimes rowdy feasts,
at other times a soldiers' camp, or else
armed battles – mindless pastimes of my youth!   70

GRIGÓRY

What a great time you had when you were young!
You fought beneath the towers of Kazán,
you rescued Pskov from Poland under Shúysky,*
you saw the sumptuous court of Tsar Iván!
Lucky one! As for me, from boyhood years
a poor young monk, I've roamed from cell to cell.
Why shouldn't I too have some fun in battle,
why shouldn't I go feasting with the Tsar?
Like you, in old age I'd have time enough
to lay aside those worldly vanities,   80
pronounce my strict monastic vows, and shut
myself at last within a quiet cloister.

24

PIMEN

    Brother, don't fret because you've so soon left
    the sinful world; be glad the Almighty's sent you
    so few temptations. You mark what I say:
    wealth, honour, and the treacherous love of women
    can even from afar lead us astray;
    in my long life I've tasted many pleasures;
    but I'd not known true bliss until the time
    that I was led by God to be a monk.   90
    My son, consider our great Russian tsars.
    There's no one higher – only God – and no one
    ever dares act against them. Well, quite often
    they've found the golden crown too burdensome,
    and they've exchanged it for a friar's hood.
    Our Tsar Iván used to seek peace of mind
    through copying monastic disciplines.
    His court, full of proud favourites though it was,
    took on the novel aspect of a cloister:
    the dreaded bodyguard, dressed in hair shirts   100
    and skullcaps, used to appear as docile monks,
    Iván the Terrible their meek superior.
    I saw them right here – in this very cell.
    (Kiríll* – the good Kiríll, who'd suffered much –
    he lived here then. That was the time I came
    to realize, by God's grace, the emptiness
    of worldly show.) Yes, here I saw the Tsar,
    wearied of angry thoughts and vengeful deeds.
    The Terrible was sitting in our midst
    reflective, quiet; we stood by transfixed;   110
    then softly he began to talk with us.
    To brothers and Superior he said:
    "Fathers-in-Christ, the longed-for day will dawn –
    I'll come before you yearning for salvation.
    You, Nikodím, you, Sergy, you, Kiríll,
    all of you here, accept my solemn pledge:
    I'll come to you, vile sinner that I am,
    and falling here at your feet, holy father,
    I'll vow obedience to the strictest rule."*

So said our mighty sovereign, Tsar Iván;   120
sweetly the words kept pouring from his lips –
and he was weeping. We wept too, and prayed
that God would send tranquillity and love
into that storm-swept, suffering soul of his.
As for his son Feódor, though he reigned
as tsar, he craved the calm untroubled life
of a monk vowed to silence. He transformed
his state rooms into a retreat for prayer,
where even the grievous burdens of his rank
ceased to disrupt his saintly meditations.   130
The Lord was well pleased with Feódor's meekness
and Russia under him enjoyed a respite
of peaceful glory – and in the hour he died
there took place an unheard-of miracle:
a figure of extraordinary brightness,
seen only by the Tsar, approached the deathbed.
Feódor started to converse with him
and to address him as "great Patriarch".
All who were in the room were gripped with fear,
perceiving that he'd seen a heavenly vision –   140
you see, the holy Primate at that time
chanced to be absent from the royal chamber.
And when the Tsar had passed away, the palace
was permeated with a holy fragrance;
his face too shone out brightly like the sun –
we'll never see a tsar like that again.
Oh terrible, unparalleled disaster!
We've angered God, we have indeed transgressed:
for we appointed then as our new tsar
the killer of a tsar.

GRIGÓRY
                    Reverend Father,   150
I've long wanted to question you about
the death of Prince Dimítry; at the time,
I'm told, you were in Uglich.

PIMEN
>   Don't I know it:
> God led me there to witness the evil deed,
> that crime of blood. At that time I'd been sent
> all the long way to Uglich on some mission.
> I arrived at night. Next day at early Mass
> I heard a sudden clang – the alarm was sounding;
> then screams and bedlam; people running to the
> Tsarítsa's court.* I followed; all the town   160
> was there by then. I looked: the Prince lay murdered;
> over her son crouched the Tsarítsa, senseless
> with grief; one nursemaid sobbed in desperation;
> the furious crowd were dragging the other off
> (she was the godless woman who'd betrayed him)…
> Then in their midst that Judas, Bityagóvsky,
> appeared, his frenzied visage white with malice.
> "Quick, there's the villain!" howled the mob at once,
> and in a trice they'd lynched him. Then the crowd
> chased three more of the killers as they fled;   170
> they caught the wretches where they'd taken refuge,
> and hauled them back before the boy's warm corpse;
> and then a miracle! – the body shuddered.
> "Confess, confess!" the people yelled at them:
> and in their dread at summary execution
> the villains did confess – and named Borís.

GRIGÓRY
> What was the Prince's age when he was killed?

PIMEN
> Oh, seven perhaps;* and that would make him now…
> (ten years have passed since then… no, more than that:
> twelve years) – he'd be the same age as yourself,   180
> and tsar! But God determined otherwise.
> This sorry episode will be the last
> I'll enter in my chronicle; since then
> I've not delved much in politics. Grigóry,
> brother, you've taught yourself to read and write:

to you I'll hand my work on. In the hours
unoccupied by spiritual tasks
write down quite simply and impartially
all the events you live to see unfold:
both war and peace, the actions of our rulers,   190
the godly miracles of holy men,
prophecies, heavenly phenomena…
It's time though now, high time, for me to rest
and put the candle out… But ah!… They're ringing
the bell for matins… grant your blessing, Lord,
on us your servants!… Pass my stick, Grigóry. *(He goes out.)*

GRIGÓRY

Borís, Borís! At your name Russia trembles,
no one so much as dares bring to your mind
the thought of wretched Prince Dimítry's fate –
yet meanwhile in this dark cell here a hermit's   200
writing his grim indictment of your crime:
you'll not escape from judgement here on earth,
no more than you'll escape from Heaven's judgement.

Scene 6*
Within the Monastery Walls

Grigóry and a malicious monk.

GRIGÓRY

What a bore, oh what a pain, this squalid life a young monk leads!
One day passes, then another; still the same old sights and sounds:
all you see's the same black cassocks, all you hear's the same dull
bell.
All day you meander yawning; doing nothing makes you nod;
all night long, though, up to daybreak, there's no sleeping for a
monk.
When at last sleep overwhelms you, gloomy dreams torment your
soul;
then you're glad the bell starts tolling, glad they wake you with a stick.
No, I won't – I can't – abide it. Climb the wall and off I'll run!

It's a big world; I can travel north or south or east or west,
I'll get clean away.

MONK

        That's right, son: all you feisty novices –   10
it's an irksome life you lead here, you're too lively to be monks.

GRIGÓRY

Oh that Poland would attack us, or the Tatars mount a raid!
What a prospect! Off I'd go then, draw my sword and beat them back.
What if our Crown Prince Dimítry were to rise up from the grave
and cry out: "Where are you, youngsters, you, my loyal men-at-arms?
Rise against my adversary, rise against that rogue Borís,
take that man who wronged me prisoner, bring the scoundrel here to
             me!..."

MONK

That's enough: don't blather nonsense. Our dead don't come back
            to life!
No, it's clear that fate determined something else for that Crown
            Prince.
Listen, though: if it's a matter of taking action, take it then...   20

GRIGÓRY

What d'you mean?

MONK

        Well, if I were a bright young lad like you are,
             friend,
if my whiskers weren't so speckled with these damnable grey hairs...
Got my message?

GRIGÓRY

        No, I haven't.

MONK

           Listen: stupid Russian folk
gladly swallow all you tell them – marvels, anything that's new;

and the boyars, they still reckon Godunóv as one of them;
everyone remains nostalgic for the Ryúrik dynasty.
You're the same age as the Crown Prince... If you're shrewd and
                                                      resolute...

Get me now?

(a silence)

GRIGÓRY

        Yes, now I get you.

MONK

                Well then?

GRIGÓRY

                      Right, I'll go for it!
I'm Dimítry, I'm the Crown Prince.

MONK

                   I salute you: you'll be tsar.

Scene 7*
The Patriarch's Palace

The Patriarch; the Superior of the Monastery of the Miracle.

PATRIARCH
And he's run away, Father Superior?

SUPERIOR
Yes, run away, Your Holiness. Two days ago now.

PATRIARCH
The ungodly scoundrel! And what family is he from?

SUPERIOR
From the Otrépyev family, lesser nobility from Gálich. He took his
vows as a boy (I don't know where), and lived in Suzdal* in St Yefím's

monastery; then he left there, wandered from one friary to another, and ended up with my community of the Miracle. I saw that he was still young and immature and placed him under the authority of Father Pimen, a venerable old man of mild and unassuming disposition. He was very good at reading and writing: he used to read our chronicles and compose canticles to the saints; but clearly his gift for letters was not from the Lord God…

PATRIARCH
Oh, these literates!… What other ideas have got into his head? "I shall be Tsar of Muscovy"! Ugh, he's possessed of the Devil! All the same, there's nothing here to report to the Tsar; why bother our Sovereign Father? It'll be sufficient to notify one of the secretaries of state of the defection – Smirnóv or Yefímyev. Such heresy! "I shall be Tsar of Muscovy"!… He must be caught, this disciple of Satan – caught and banished to Solovétsky* for a perpetual penance. This is heresy indeed, Father Superior.

SUPERIOR
Heresy, Your Holiness, downright heresy.

Scene 8*
The Tsar's Palace

Two stewards.

FIRST STEWARD
So where's the Tsar?

SECOND STEWARD
              He's shut himself inside
his bedchamber with one of those magicians.*

FIRST STEWARD
Yes, that's his favourite company these days:
clairvoyants, fortune-tellers, those wise women.
No pretty girl could do more crystal-gazing.
I wonder what he's trying to find out?

SECOND STEWARD
   Well, here he comes. Perhaps you'd like to ask him?

FIRST STEWARD
   How grim he looks!

(They go off.)

BORÍS *(entering)*
                    I've reached the height of power:
   this is the sixth year of my peaceful reign.
   But I've no inner happiness. It's like   10
   when in our youth we fall in love and crave its
   gratification: just when we've appeased
   our hungry hearts with momentary possession,
   immediately we're cold and bored and tired...
   It's no good these magicians promising
   that I'll enjoy long years of quiet rule –
   I take no joy in power or life itself;
   I dread some bolt from heaven, some disaster.
   No happiness for me! I'd planned to soothe
   my people with contentment and with splendour,   20
   to win their love with generous largesse –
   but now I've given up the useless effort:
   the rabble always hates a living ruler;
   affection they'll show only to the dead.
   We're mad if we permit the people's cheers
   or angry howls to spoil our peace of mind.
   When God began to afflict our land with famine,
   the people, suffering, dying, cried for help;
   I opened up the granaries for them,
   I gave them gold, I found them work to do.   30
   My thanks? – they cursed me: they'd the Devil in them.
   Some lost their homes in the great conflagration,*
   and so I built them new ones. In return
   they even blamed the blazes onto *me*.
   There's the mob's justice: try to win their love – huh!
   So I sought comfort in my family:

I tried to find my daughter a good husband –
but, like a storm, death swept the man away...
and then dishonest rumour made it out that
the culprit for my daughter's widowhood   40
was me, yes me, her own unhappy father!
Whoever dies, I am their secret killer:
I hastened Tsar Feódor's death, they said;
I poisoned my own sister the Tsarítsa,*
a harmless nun... For everything I'm blamed!
I understand now: nothing in this world
of misery can give us peace of mind,
no, nothing, nothing... save an easy conscience.
Our conscience, if it's sound, will ride in triumph
over black calumny and spitefulness...   50
but if by some unlucky chance a blemish,
one single blemish, should have lodged in it,
then – trouble! For the soul becomes inflamed
as with the plague, the heart swells up with poison,
reproaches ring in the ears like hammer blows,
there's constant nausea and dizziness,
and visions of young boys streaming with blood...
one longs to escape; there's nowhere, though... ugh, ghastly!
Yes, pity one whose conscience is unclean.

Scene 9*
An Inn on the Polish Frontier

Misaíl and Varlaám, vagrant monks; Grigóry Otrépyev, dressed as a layman; landlady.*

LANDLADY
What can I offer you, reverend sirs?

VARLAÁM
Whatever God provides, little lady. There isn't any liquor?

LANDLADY
Of course there is, fathers! I'll fetch it this minute.

33

(She goes off.)

MISAÍL

Why so downcast, friend? You've been hankering so to get to the Polish frontier, and here it is now.

GRIGÓRY

I shan't be comfortable till I'm inside Poland.

VARLAÁM

Why this passion for Poland? Look at us – Father Misaíl, and me, sinner that I am – ever since we said goodbye to the monastery we've taken no thought for anything at all. Living with Russians, living with Poles: listening to zithers or listening to viols: for us it's all fine, so long as there's wine... and here it comes, I opine!

MISAÍL

Fine turn of phrase, Father Varlaám.

LANDLADY *(enters)*

Here you are, fathers. Drink to your health.

MISAÍL

Thank you, darling; God bless you.

(The monks sing: Varlaám strikes up the song 'Dear girl, you are passing my cell...'* etc.)

(To Grigóry)

Why aren't you whining with us... or even wining with us?*

GRIGÓRY

I don't wish to.

MISAÍL

Free will for those who want it, as they say, and paradise for the saved.*

34

VARLAÁM

Paradise for the sozzled, you mean, Father Misaíl! So let's drink a
little toast – to our little lady-host!...

("Where a fine young lad against his will..." etc.)*

All the same, Father Misaíl, when I have a booze, sober company's
not what I choose; it's one thing to drink big, but quite another to
think big. D'you want to live like us? Then the pleasure's ours. You
don't? Then pack up and get moving: a fool's no friend for a friar.

GRIGÓRY

Drink yourself drunk, and don't be a meddlesome monk, Father
Varlaám... You see, I've got a fine turn of phrase too, sometimes.

VARLAÁM

And why shouldn't I be a "meddlesome monk", eh?

MISAÍL

Leave him alone, Father Varlaám.

VARLAÁM

Vowed himself to abstinence, has he? It was him pushed himself
on our company; we don't know who he is, don't know where he's
from – and now *he* turns the cold shoulder; p'rhaps he's smelt the
filly...*

(Drinks and sings.)

GRIGÓRY *(to the landlady)*

Where does this road lead to?

LANDLADY

Into Poland, good sir; to the Luyóv Hills.*

GRIGÓRY

And is it far to the Luyóv Hills?

LANDLADY

No, not far. You could get there by evening time if it wasn't for the Tsar's roadblocks and the police on patrol.

GRIGÓRY

Roadblocks, eh! What does that mean?

LANDLADY

Someone's on the run from Moscow, and there's orders to stop everyone and examine them.

GRIGÓRY *(to himself)*

That puts paid to your little bid for freedom, granny!*

VARLAÁM

Hi, friend! Cosying up to the landlady, I see. So it's the wenches, not the wine, that's your weakness: very well, brother, very well! To each man his own ways. But me and Father Misaíl, we've only one care: we drink up what's there, we drink it right up, then we upend our tankard and its bottom we spank 'ard.

MISAÍL

Fine turn of phrase, Father Varlaám...

GRIGÓRY

But who on earth are they after? Who's on the run from Moscow?

LANDLADY

Lord knows who it is – thief, or bandit maybe... All I can say is that here at the moment there's not even decent folk being let through. And what'll come of it? Nothing; they'll not catch a bare-faced devil: as though there weren't no other way to Poland beside the high road! Look, you just turn off here to the left and walk along the footpath through the fir wood till you get to the chapel, the one on the Chekán brook, and then straight across the marsh to Khlópino, and from there to Zakháryevo, and from then on any young lad can show the way to the Luyóv Hills. All these policemen are good for is roughing up travellers and robbing us poor folk.

(A noise is heard.)

Now what's there? Ugh, here they are, curse them! They're doing their rounds.

GRIGÓRY
Wait! Isn't there some other little hidey-hole in this shack?

LANDLADY
No, dear. I'd be glad to hide somewhere myself. This doing of rounds – it's only an excuse; they make me serve them liquor, and bread, and I don't know what – I wish they'd drop dead, the godless wretches! I wish they'd—

(Enter police.)

OFFICER
Good day, lady!

LANDLADY
Welcome, my dear sirs, make yourselves at home.

ONE OFFICER *(to a second)*
Well, well, so there's a binge going on here; we'll make the most of this. *(To the monks)* What people are you?

VARLAÁM
We're reverend men of God, humble friars, on our way from village to village and collecting alms from Christian folk for the monastery.

OFFICER *(to Grigóry)*
And you?

MISAÍL
Our companion...

GRIGÓRY
A layman from the local town. I've been showing these holy men the way to the border; from here I'm going back home.

MISAÍL

So you've changed your mind.

GRIGÓRY *(in a whisper)*

Quiet!

OFFICER

Come on then, lady; bring out some more liquor, and we'll stay and have a little drink and a little chat with the reverends.

SECOND OFFICER *(in a whisper)*

The young chap's got nothing on him by the look of it; there'll be no takings there. But the reverends...

FIRST OFFICER

Hush, we'll come to them now... Well, fathers? How's business?

VARLAÁM

Bad, oh mine son, bad!* These latter days Christian folks are become miserly; they love their money, so they hide their money. It's little they give to God. Great sin hath come upon the nations of earth. Men have turned every one to trafficking, to extortion; their thoughts are for worldly riches, not for the salvation of the soul. You walk and walk, and beg and beg, and sometimes not make three quarter-copecks in three days. Such sinfulness! A week'll pass, and another; and when you peep into your purse, there's so little there you're ashamed to show up at the monastery. What's to be done? To drown your grief you'll drink away what little you've got; trouble, naught but trouble! Oh, it's bad; our last days must have come...

LANDLADY *(in tears)*

Lord, have mercy and save us!

(In the course of Varlaám's speech the first officer has been staring meaningfully at Misaíl.)

FIRST OFFICER
Alyókha! Have you got the Tsar's decree with you?

SECOND OFFICER
Yes, I have.

FIRST OFFICER
Quick, pass it over here.

MISAÍL
Why are you staring at me like that?

FIRST OFFICER
I'll tell you why: a certain wicked heretic, Grishka Otrépyev, is on the run from Moscow; have you heard that?

MISAÍL
No, I've not.

OFFICER
You haven't heard? Very well. And the Tsar has ordered that this runaway heretic is to be caught and hanged. Did you know that?

MISAÍL
No, I didn't.

OFFICER *(to Varlaám)*
Can you read?

VARLAÁM
I learnt when I was young, but I've forgotten.

OFFICER *(to Misaíl)*
And you?

MISAÍL
The Lord's not gifted me that way.

OFFICER

Well anyway, here's the Tsar's decree for you.

MISAÍL

What's it got to do with me?

OFFICER

It's my impression that this runaway heretic, fraud and trickster is you.

MISAÍL

Me! Mercy! What can you mean?

OFFICER

Stay where you are! Guard the doors. Now we'll find out if we're right.

LANDLADY

Oh, these fiends from hell! They won't even leave a holy man in peace!

OFFICER

Who here can read?

GRIGÓRY *(stepping forward)*

I can.

OFFICER

Well I never! And who on earth did you learn from?

GRIGÓRY

From our sacristan.

OFFICER *(giving him the decree)*

Come on then, read it aloud.

GRIGÓRY *(reading)*

"An unworthy monk of the Monastery of the Miracle, by name Grigóry, of the family of the Otrépyevs, has fallen into heresy, and, instructed by the devil, has made bold to confound the holy brotherhood with divers temptations and impieties. Enquiries have established that the said ungodly Grishka has fled in the direction of the Polish frontier—"

OFFICER *(to Misaíl)*
It *must* be you.

GRIGÓRY
"… and the Tsar has commanded that he be caught—"

OFFICER
And hanged.

GRIGÓRY
It doesn't say "hanged" here.

OFFICER
Rubbish: some words are written between the lines. Read "caught and hanged".

GRIGÓRY
"… and hanged. And the age of the said fraud Grishka is… *(looking at Varlaám)* over fifty. He is of medium height; he has a bald pate, grey beard, fat paunch…"

(All look at Varlaám.)

FIRST OFFICER
Lads, Grishka's here! Hold him, tie him up! This is something I didn't think, didn't imagine.

VARLAÁM *(snatching the paper)*
Keep off, you sons of a whore! What kind of Grishka am I? What! Fifty years old, grey beard, fat paunch! No, brother! You're too young to be playing practical jokes on me. It's a long time since I did any reading and I'm not good at making it out, but I'll make it out this time for sure, now it's coming to the gallows. *(Reading syllable*

41

by syllable) "And the age of the said fraud Grish-ka is... twen-ty."
Well, brother? Where's the "fifty" here? You see? Twenty.

SECOND OFFICER
Yes, it's coming back: twenty. That's what we were told too.

FIRST OFFICER
So it seems that you're a jester, brother.

(During the reading Grigóry stands with lowered head, one hand inside his coat.)

VARLAÁM *(continuing)*
"He is small in stature,* broad-chested, one arm shorter than the other, blue eyes, ginger hair, a wart on the cheek and another on the forehead." But surely this is you, friend?

(Grigóry suddenly draws a dagger; all step back from him: he springs to the window and leaps out.)

POLICE
Stop him! Stop him!

(All run about in confusion.)

Scene 10*
Moscow, Shúysky's House

Shúysky, numerous guests, supper.

SHÚYSKY
Another cup of wine.

(He stands up, and the company do the same.)

Well now, dear guests,
the final round of drinks! Boy, read the prayer.*

BOY

O Tsar of heaven, all-present, everlasting,
give ear to the petition of Thy servants,
as we now pray for our great sovereign,
for the god-fearing man that Thou hast chosen
to reign as mighty tsar of Christendom.
Preserve him in his home and on the field,
preserve him on the road and in his bed.
Grant him to triumph o'er his enemies;   10
may his renown extend from shore to shore;
may all his family be strong and flourish,
and may its precious branches spread to o'ershadow
the earth's wide bounds; and towards us, his servants,
may he be as benign as in the past,
and as beneficent and as forbearing;
and may his never-failing fount of wisdom
well up and bathe us in its bounteous flood.
Now, as we raise our wine cups to the Tsar,
so rise our prayers to Thee, O Tsar of heaven.   20

SHUÝSKY *(drinks)*

Long life and health to our great sovereign!
And now, dear friends, I bid you all goodbye;
I'm grateful that you've not seen fit to spurn
my hospitality. Goodbye. Sleep well.

(The guests leave; he sees them to the door.)

AFANÁSY MIKHÁYLOVICH PUSHKIN*

At last they've gone; well, Prince Vasíly Ivánovich, I was beginning
to think we'd get no chance at all to talk things over.

SHÚYSKY *(to the servants)*

Why do you all stand there gaping? You're forever trying to eavesdrop
on your masters. Clear the table and be off... What is it, Afanásy
Mikháylovich?

43

A.M. PUSHKIN
Miracles, no less.
Today a courier reached me from Cracow,*
sent by my brother's son, Gavríla Pushkin.*

SHÚYSKY
Well?

A.M. PUSHKIN
It's strange news my nephew's letter brings.
The son of Tsar Iván... Wait.

(He goes to the door and looks.)

The Crown Prince,
the boy they murdered on Borís's orders—

SHÚYSKY
There's nothing new in this.

A.M. PUSHKIN
Just wait a minute:
Dimítry's living.

SHÚYSKY
Well, well! What a story!
The Crown Prince living! Miracles indeed.
Is that all?

A.M. PUSHKIN
No, I haven't finished. Listen.
Whoever he may be – the Crown Prince rescued,   40
a spirit, perhaps, who's taken on his form, or
some brazen rogue and impudent impostor –
the fact is that Dimítry has appeared there.

SHÚYSKY
He can't have.

A.M. PUSHKIN

            Pushkin saw the Prince himself;
he saw him ride into the royal palace,
then walk straight through the ranks of Polish lords
into the King of Poland's private chamber.

SHÚYSKY

Who is he, then? And where's he from?

A.M. PUSHKIN

                     We're baffled.
Here's all that's known for sure: he was a page
of Wiśniowiecki's*; one day on his sickbed*   50
he mentioned who he was to his confessor;
and when Lord Wiśniowiecki learnt the secret
he nursed him, set him once more on his feet,
and then rode off with him to see King Zygmunt.*

SHÚYSKY

But how do they describe the cheeky fellow?

A.M. PUSHKIN

By all accounts he's clever, friendly, quick –
to everybody's liking. He's bewitched
our exiled Muscovites. The Roman priests
support him. And the King shows him great favour
and, so it's said, has promised Polish aid.   60

SHÚYSKY

Friend, these events bewilder me so much –
despite myself my head will soon be spinning.
He's an impostor – there's no doubt of that;
but, I admit, he poses quite a threat.
Important news! And if the common people
get ear of it, there'll be a mighty storm.

A.M. PUSHKIN

So fierce a storm, Borís will be hard put
to keep the tsar's crown* on his clever head.

And serve him right! His government reminds one
of the nightmarish reign of Tsar Iván.*   70
What good's the lack of public executions –
that we're no more impaled for all to see,
singing Christ's praises as we bleed to death –
that we're not burnt alive now in Red Square,
while Tsar Iván stokes the embers with his staff?
Our poor lives – are they safer now than then?
Each day we face the threat of banishment,
monastery life, chains, prison or Siberia,
and then – a secret death, by strangling, starving...
Our most illustrious families – where are they?   80
Where are the Princes Shestunóv or Sitsky,
or the Románovs, Russia's hope and pride?*
Some, locked away; some crushed in savage exile.
Just give him time, and *you* will meet the same fate.
An easy life, huh? We're beset at home
by treacherous serfs as though by Polish armies –
tongues primed to talk at any time for money,
dastardly sneaks the Government has bribed.
We're at the mercy of the first rogue-serf
we catch out cheating and decide to punish.   90
And he's resolved to end St George's Day:*
we're not even masters now of our estates.
"Thou shalt not sack a sluggard." Willy-nilly
you have to feed him. "Thou shalt not recruit
thy neighbour's workman" – or to court with you!
Well, did you even under Tsar Iván
hear of such mischief? And the people – ask them
if *they* are better off. Let this pretender
try offering to restore St George's Day –
yes, then the fun will start!

SHÚYSKY
                              Pushkin, you're right.   100
But do you know what I think? We'll do best
to hold our tongues about all this for now.

A.M. PUSHKIN

True;

say nothing, I agree. You're sensible;
I'm always glad to have a talk with you;
if something worries me at any time,
I can't bear not to let you know about it.
Besides, your mead and velvety-smooth beer
have loosened up my tongue tonight, for sure...
Goodbye, then, Prince.

SHÚYSKY

Goodbye, friend; see you soon.

(He shows Pushkin out.)

Scene 11*
The Tsar's Palace

The Crown Prince drawing a map; the Princess; the Princess's nurse.*

XÉNIA *(holding a portrait)*

Why have your lips
not called me?
your smiling eyes
not looked at me?
Or are your lips
fast shut for ever,
your smiling eyes,
grown dim for ever?

Brother – dear brother! Did the Prince look like my little picture?

FEÓDOR

I keep telling you, he did.*   10

XÉNIA *(kissing the portrait)*

My darling fiancé, my handsome Prince, I didn't win you after all,
even though I was your bride-to-be; no, it was death that won you,

47

a dark and wretched death in a wretched foreign land. I shall never
be happy again; I'll weep for you for ever.

NURSE

Tush, Princess! A lassie's tears are like the dew that falls; the sun will
rise and dry the dew.* You'll have another suitor, a handsome and a
kindly one. You'll take to loving him, you pretty child of ours; you'll
forget Prince John.

XÉNIA

No, Nanna; even though he's dead I'll still be true to him.

(Enter Borís.)

TSAR

What is it, Xénia? What is it, dear?   20
A girl still, and a tearful little widow,
forever weeping for a dead fiancé!
My child, it's not been granted me by fate
to bring the pair of you the joy I planned.
Maybe it's because I've made the heavens angry
that I've so failed to make you a good match.
You shouldn't suffer though, poor innocent –
But you, son – what's engrossing you? What's this?

FEÓDOR

A map of Muscovy;* it's our own empire
from one end to the other. Look, here's Moscow,   30
here's Nóvgorod, here's Ástrakhan. That's sea;
those are the deep, dark forests around Perm;*
and that's Siberia.*

TSAR

               But what's this here,
this twisty line?

FEÓDOR

              Ah, that's the River Volga.

TSAR

    How splendid! Here's rich fruit of education!
    You can survey at once, as from the clouds,
    the whole of the empire – rivers, towns and frontiers.
    Keep studying, my boy; learning curtails
    the lessons brief life needs itself to teach us –
    one of these days, quite soon perhaps (who knows?),   40
    all the domains that you've just now been sketching
    so cleverly upon this piece of paper –
    all these will pass beneath your own control.
    Keep studying, my boy, so as to grasp
    with surer ease the duties of a sovereign.

(Enter Semyón Godunóv.*)

    Here's Godunóv with a report for me.
    (To Xénia) My darling, will you go off to your room;
    goodbye, my dear. May God assuage your grief.

(Xénia and the nurse go off.)

    What news, Semyón Nikítich?

SEMYÓN GODUNÓV

                      At first light   50
    today Prince Shúysky's steward and a servant
    of Pushkin's came to me with information.

TSAR

    Well?

SEMYÓN GODUNÓV

        Pushkin's servant told his story first:
    yesterday morning there reached Pushkin's house
    a courier from Cracow; one hour later
    he was sent back without a written message.

TSAR

    Arrest the man.

SEMYÓN GODUNÓV
> We're after him already.

TSAR
> What about Shúysky?

SEMYÓN GODUNÓV
> He was entertaining
> his friends last evening – both the Miloslávskys,
> Mikhaíl Saltykóv, the Buturlíns,*   60
> and Afanásy Pushkin – and some others;
> they didn't leave till late; and Pushkin stayed
> behind alone together with his host
> and had another lengthy talk with him—

TSAR
> Then send immediately for Shúysky.

SEMYÓN GODUNÓV
> Sire,
> he's here already.

TSAR
> Call him here to me.

(Semyón Godunóv goes off.)

> Dealings with Poland, eh? What does this mean?
> I can't abide this treacherous clan of Pushkins;*
> and neither is Prince Shúysky to be trusted:
> he seems obedient, but he's bold and cunning...   70

(Enter Shúysky.)

> Ah, Prince! I want to have a word with you.
> But you yourself, it seems, have come on business:
> so first I'll hear what you have got to say.

SHÚYSKY

    Yes, sire: it is my duty to acquaint you
    with some important news.

TSAR

                  I'm listening.

SHÚYSKY *(quietly pointing to Feódor)*
    But, sire...

TSAR

          Crown Prince Feódor is entitled
    to know all that Prince Shúysky knows. Speak on.

SHÚYSKY

    Tsar, we've had news from Poland...

TSAR

                    Not the news
    that Pushkin's courier brought him yesterday?

SHÚYSKY

    He knows it all! – Forgive me, sire: I thought   80
    that you'd not yet have heard that secret message.

TSAR

    Never mind, Prince. I'd like now to compare
    our two accounts. In this way we'll find out
    the true facts.

SHÚYSKY

            Well, I only know this, that
    in Cracow a pretender has appeared
    and that the Polish King and lords are for him.

TSAR

    Who's this pretender? What do people say?

SHÚYSKY
    I don't know.

TSAR
              But... in what way is he dangerous?

SHÚYSKY
    Unquestionably, sire, your power's secure;
    your clemency, munificence and zeal   90
    have won you the devotion of your subjects.
    But as you know yourself, the unreasoning mob
    is superstitious, fickle and unruly,
    too ready to indulge in idle hope,
    too prone to obey the impulse of the moment;
    they neither hear the truth nor wish to hear it;
    pure fabrication – that's what they thrive best on.
    They like a man to show brazen bravado;
    and if this unknown vagabond in Cracow
    should cross the Polish frontier into Russia,   100
    the idiots will flock to him, attracted
    by the revival of Dimítry's name.

TSAR
    Dimítry's... What? You mean that little child?
    Dimítry's name!... Crown Prince, please leave the room.

SHÚYSKY
    His face is flushed: here comes the storm!...

FEÓDOR
                      But, sire,
    won't you allow me...

TSAR
             No, my son; be off.

(Feódor goes off.)

    Dimítry!...

SHÚYSKY

        He knew nothing after all, then.

TSAR

Now listen, Prince: take steps this very hour
to close and seal the Polish frontier
with roadblocks; not a single soul must pass   110
across this border; not even a hare
must run to us from Poland; not a raven
must fly from Cracow into Russia. Go.

SHÚYSKY

I'm on my way.

TSAR

        Wait! Far-fetched, isn't it,
this tale from Poland? Have you ever heard
of dead men coming back from out the grave
to check a tsar's, a lawful tsar's, credentials –
a tsar proposed and chosen by the people,
solemnly crowned by our great Patriarch?
Funny, eh? Well, why is it you're not laughing?   120

SHÚYSKY

Me, sire?...

TSAR

        Listen a moment, Prince Vasíly:*
when I learnt that that young lad had been... er...
that somehow that young lad had lost his life,
you were dispatched to investigate; and now
I charge you by the Cross, by God in heaven –
tell me the truth as in your heart you know it:
you recognized the boy that had been killed?
you're sure there'd been no substitution? Answer.

SHÚYSKY

I swear to you—

TSAR

No, Shúysky, do not swear,
just answer: *was* it the Crown Prince?

SHÚYSKY

It was.   130

TSAR

Prince, think with care. I promise you forgiveness;
a lie of years back I don't mean to punish
by pointless banishment. But if today
you try to fool me, then I swear to you
by my son's head – you'll meet an evil death,
a death to make Iván the Terrible
himself shudder with horror in his grave.

SHÚYSKY

I don't fear death, but I fear your displeasure.
Will I dare play you false here in your presence?
And could I have been so blind, so deluded,   140
as to mistake Dimítry? Over three days
I visited his corpse in the cathedral,
and each time all of Uglich came there with me.
Around him lay another thirteen bodies,
those that the crowd had torn apart, and they'd
plainly by now begun to decompose;
the young face of the Crown Prince, though, was radiant,*
fresh and serene, just like a child asleep;
the deep wound hadn't started to congeal;
in fact, his features hadn't changed at all.   150
No, sire, there is no room for doubt. Dimítry
sleeps in his grave.

TSAR *(calmly)*

Enough then. You may go.

(Shúysky goes off.)

A heavy blow, ugh… Let me get my breath back…
I felt as though my blood had all at once
rushed to my face, then took long to subside…
So this is why for thirteen years on end
I've not stopped dreaming of the murdered child!
Yes, yes – that's what it is. I understand now.
Who *is* he, though, my fearsome adversary?
Who's threatening me? An empty name, a shadow –   160
surely a shadow can't depose the tsar,
a sound can't disinherit his two children?
I am a fool! What made me so afraid?
Puff at this apparition – and it's gone!
That's settled, then: I'll show no sign of fear;
yet I shall need to take every precaution…
Oh, it's a heavy crown we tsars must wear!*

Scene 12*
Cracow, Wiśniowiecki's* House

The Pretender and Father Czernikowski.

PRETENDER

No, father, there will not be any problem;
I know my people's spiritual outlook;
they're not fanatical in their religion:
they treat their tsar's example as God's law.
Such passiveness invariably means indifference.
I promise that within the next two years
all of my people, all the Eastern Church,*
will recognize the primacy of Rome.*

FATHER

I pray that St Ignatius* may vouchsafe you
his aid, when matters reach the proper stage.   10
Till then, though, Crown Prince, deep within your soul
bury these precious seeds of heavenly grace.
To hide from lay folk our true aspirations
is sometimes what our sacred task demands:

men judge us by our words and by our actions;
our inner motives God alone regards.

PRETENDER
Amen. Who's there now?

(A servant enters.)

Tell them we are ready.

(The doors open; a crowd of Russians and Poles enter.)

Comrades-in-arms! Tomorrow we march out
from Cracow. I propose to stop three days
in Sambor,* Mniszech,* at your residence.   20
Your hospitable castle, I well know,
not only dazzles with its lordly wealth
but is far-famed as well for its young mistress,
the beautiful Maryna, whom I hope
to see while I am there. And as for you, friends,
Russians and Poles, your kindred banners raised
in one accord against the common foe,
against this wily villain who has wronged me –
you sons of Slavs, before long I shall lead
your fearsome ranks into the longed-for battle...   30
But I can see new faces here among you.

GAVRÍLA PUSHKIN
Yes: they have come to ask Your Grace if they
might fight for you and serve you.

PRETENDER
                                        Welcome, men:
join me, my friends. But tell me, Pushkin, who is
this fine young man?

GAVRÍLA PUSHKIN
                        Prince Kurbsky.*

PRETENDER *(to Kurbsky)*

Famous name!
You're kinsman to the hero of Kazán?

KURBSKY
I am his son.

PRETENDER

He's still alive?

KURBSKY

No, dead.

PRETENDER
A great mind! Good at fighting and in counsel!
But since the days when he used to appear
with Polish troops beneath the old walls of Pskov*   40
avenging cruelly the wrongs he'd suffered –
since then we've heard no news of him.

KURBSKY

My father
spent his remaining lifetime in Volhynia*
on the estates that King Stefan Batory*
had granted him. There, quiet and remote,
he hoped in study to find consolation;
he found, though, no relief in peaceful work:
thoughts of the country where he'd spent his youth
caused him to pine for it until he died.

PRETENDER
Unlucky prince! His stormy life of clamour   50
dawned with a sunrise of such glorious promise.
How pleased I am that in you, noble knight,
his blood is reconciled now with his homeland.
But let us not dwell on our fathers' errors;
peace to their graves! Kurbsky, approach. Your hand!
How strange – the son of Kurbsky leads to power
none other than the son of Tsar Iván…

All is on my side – men and fate alike.
Now you're?…

A POLE

        Sobański, a nobleman freeborn.*

PRETENDER

A son of freedom! Praise and honour to you!   60
Pay him up front one third of his allowance…
But who are these? I recognize their clothes
as those of Russia. They must be our own men.

KHRUSHCHÓV *(bowing to the ground)*

Yes, sire, our father, you are right: we are
your own devoted, persecuted slaves.
We fled from Moscow under banishment
to join you, our true Tsar: for you we're ready
to suffer death, to make our bodies steps
by which you may ascend the throne of Russia.*

PRETENDER

Take heart: you suffer through no fault of yours;   70
just wait for me to get to Moscow – then
Borís will have to settle up his debts*
with all of us. What news is there in Moscow?

KHRUSHCHÓV

All's quiet there still. But the people lately
have got wind of their Crown Prince's deliverance;
now everywhere they're reading your announcement.
They all await you. Recently two boyars
were executed by Borís because
at meals they drank a secret toast to you.

PRETENDER

How loyal in adversity, you boyars!   80
But blood for blood! And woe to Godunóv!
What do they say about him?

KHRUSHCHÓV

                      He's withdrawn
into his gloomy palace. Menacing
and grim he looks. Men fear more murders. But
some ailment's gnawing him.* He's hardly able
to crawl about! It's thought that his last hour
may now be near.

PRETENDER

                 Well I'm a generous foe:
I wish Borís a quick death. Otherwise
he'll meet a fate still worse, the villain. Whom, though,
does he intend to name as his successor?   90

KHRUSHCHÓV

He keeps his ideas to himself, you know,
but seemingly he's grooming his young son,
Feódor, as the heir to Russia's throne.

PRETENDER

Perhaps his calculations will prove wrong.
And who are you?

KARÉLA

              A Cossack from the Don,
sent to you from the free troops, their brave chieftains –
indeed from all the Cossacks of the Don* –
to glimpse your eyes, the clear eyes of a tsar,
and put their very lives at your disposal.

PRETENDER

There speaks a Don man! I was sure I'd see   100
some Cossack standards here in my battalions.
We thank our Cossack army of the Don.
We are aware the Cossacks at this time
are wrongfully oppressed and persecuted;
but if with God's help we ascend the throne
of our forefathers, then we shall restore
the ancient freedoms to our faithful Don.

POET *(approaches, bowing low and catching Grishka by the skirt of his coat)*
    Great Prince, son of a king, illustrious Highness!

PRETENDER
    What do you want?

POET *(handing him a manuscript)*
               Be gracious to accept
    this paltry product of my earnest labours.   110

PRETENDER
    What's this I see? Why, lines of Latin verse!
    Blessings abound when sword and lyre combine;
    both share one prize, a single crown of laurel.
    Though I was born beneath the midnight sky,
    the Latin Muse's voice is known to me:
    I love the flowers she culls from Mount Parnassus.*

(reads to himself)

KHRUSHCHÓV *(quietly to Pushkin)*
    Who's this?

GAVRÍLA PUSHKIN
        A poet.

KHRUSHCHÓV
        What on earth is that?

GAVRÍLA PUSHKIN
    How to explain? In Russian we'd say "rhymester"
    or maybe "jester".*

PRETENDER
        These are splendid verses!
    I've great faith in a poet's prophecies;   120
    the rapture seething in his fervent breast

is not in vain: for when he celebrates
deeds in advance he thereby sanctifies them.
Approach, my friend: in token of our meeting
accept this gift.

(He gives him a ring.)

          And when fate has fulfilled
its purposes in me, when I put on
my ancestral crown – I hope once more to hear
this pleasant voice of yours, this splendid ode.
Musa gloriam coronat, gloriaque Musam.*
And so, my friends, goodbye until tomorrow.   130

ALL

  To war, to war! Long may Dimítry live,
  long may he reign Grand Prince of Muscovy!

Scene 13*

Governor Mniszech's Castle at Sambor, Maryna's Dressing Room

Maryna; Róża, dressing her and doing her hair; maidservants.

MARYNA *(in front of a mirror)*
  Well, is it finished yet? Why can't you hurry up?

RÓŻA

  Excuse me – you must first resolve a tricky problem:
  what do you want to wear – perhaps a rope of pearls?
      or maybe this half-moon of em'rald?

MARYNA

      My diamond diadem.

RÓŻA

  An excellent idea! You wore it, you remember,
  when you were pleased to pay that visit to the court.
  They say that at the ball you glittered like the sunlight;

You made the menfolk gasp, and set the girls a-whisp'ring…
Then it was, I suppose, that young Chodkiewicz first   10
set eyes on you – the one who shot himself dead later.
    Indeed, they say, each man that caught
    a glimpse of you, at once adored you.

MARYNA

    Can't you be quicker?

RÓŻA

              Nearly done.
Your father has his hopes centred on you today.
    You've certainly impressed Dimítry:
he's found it past his strength to hide his fond delight;
    he's wounded now; the time has come for you
        decisively to overpow'r him.
        Indeed, my lady, he's in love.   20
        A month now, since he came from Cracow,
        forgot the war, the Russian throne,
        and lived it up here as your guest:
    he's made his Poles and Russians furious…
    Lord, shall I really see the day?…
    Can you imagine?… When Dimítry calls you
to Moscow to be crowned as Russia's new tsarítsa,
    I hope you won't leave me behind!

MARYNA

    Tsarítsa – do you think that's really what I'll be?

RÓŻA

But who else, if not you? Who else in all of Poland   30
    would dare compare herself with you for beauty?
The Mniszech family takes second place to none;
    your intellect surpasses praise…
Lucky the man your eyes count worthy of attention,
lucky the man at last to win your heart's affection –
    be he what may, our Polish King
    or the French monarch's royal successor,

not just your beggar-prince from Russia –
that God-knows-who from God-knows-where.

MARYNA

He *is* son of a tsar – the whole world's recognized him. 40

RÓŻA

But even so last winter he was just
a page in Wiśniowiecki's house.

MARYNA

Yes, lying low.

RÓŻA

I won't argue about it;
but there's just one thing: do you know
what common people say about him? –
that he's a sacristan from Moscow on the run,
a rogue well-known in his own parish.

MARYNA

What an absurd idea!

RÓŻA

Oh, it is not true, I'm sure.
But all I say is this: that he ought, there's no question,
to thank his lucky star because with your affection 50
you've favoured him above the rest.

MAIDSERVANT *(running in)*

The guests have now arrived.

MARYNA

You see now: you'd be ready
to spin your stupid chatter out
till dawn, while I sit here half-dressed still.

RÓŻA
In no time we'll be done.

(Maids bustle about.)

MARYNA

I must find out the truth…

Scene 14*
A Suite of Brightly Lit Rooms – Music

Wiśniowiecki, Mniszech.

MNISZECH
He talks to nobody but my Maryna,
with my Maryna he spends all his time…
you know, it all looks awf'lly like a marriage;
well, did you think – be frank now, Wiśniowiecki –
that my own daughter'd be tsarítsa? Eh?

WIŚNIOWIECKI
Yes, it's miraculous… and did you, Mniszech,
imagine that my pageboy would be tsar?

MNISZECH
But, I say, what a girl is my Maryna!
I just dropped her the hint: "Now, mind!" I said.
"Don't let Dimítry go…" And there you are: 10
the whole job's done. She's netted him already.
Look, here he comes – and with her ladyship!*

(A polonaise is played; the pretender and Maryna come forward as the leading couple.)

MARYNA *(quietly to Dimítry)*
All right, tomorrow evening at eleven,
I'll be there, in the lime walk, by the fountain.

(They separate. Another couple.)

OFFICER
What *does* Dimítry see in her?

LADY

Why, she's

so lovely.

OFFICER
Yes, a nymph chiselled from marble:
her eyes, her lips are lifeless and unsmiling...

(new couple)

LADY
He isn't handsome, but his face is pleasant,
and you can see that he's of royal blood.

(A new couple.)

LADY
When *do* you march?

OFFICER
When the Crown Prince commands.   20
We're ready; but, it seems, the lady Mniszech
persuades Dimítry to detain us here.

LADY
Pleasant detention.

OFFICER
Yes, indeed if you...

(They separate. The rooms empty.)

MNISZECH

    We old men now no longer join the dancing,
    we're not drawn on by a mazurka's din,
    we no more squeeze and kiss those pretty fingers –
    Oh, when I think what pranks we revelled in!
    No: things are not the same now as they once were –
    youth now, for sure, lacks our audacity,
    and beauty's lost its former gaiety –   30
    you must confess, it's all grown rather dreary.
    Come, friend, let's leave them; let's go off and ask
    my men to dig us up a vintage flask
    of Magyar wine* all overgrown with herbage,
    and in some nook we'll make our two hearts glow
    with liquor, thick like oil, with fragrant nectar,
    and, as we drink, discuss – what? I don't know...
    Let's go then, friend.*

WIŚNIOWIECKI

                 That's right, old friend, let's go.

Scene 15
Night-time, a Garden, a Fountain*

PRETENDER *(enters)*

    Ah, here's the fountain: this is where she'll meet me.
    I've never thought that I was born a faint-heart:
    I've looked death in the eye from close at hand,
    but death has never made my spirit flinch.
    At times I've risked imprisonment for life,
    I've been a wanted man – but I've not faltered
    and through bold action I've escaped arrest.
    But what is this that now constricts my breathing?
    What do these helpless palpitations mean?
    Is it the trembling of intense desire?   10
    Oh, no – it's fear. So what is it I fear?
    I don't myself know. All day I've been waiting
    for this clandestine meeting with Maryna;
    the whole day I've been thinking what I'd tell her,

how I'd win round that haughty mind of hers,
how I'd address her as Moscow's tsarítsa –
but now the time's come I remember nothing.
Gone are the speeches that I learnt by heart:
my love's befuddling my imagination...
But something glistened then... a rustling... ceased now...   20
No, it was just the moonlight playing tricks,
the noise a breeze made in the leaves.

MARYNA *(enters)*

                              Crown Prince!

PRETENDER
    She's here!... My pulse has failed, my heart's stopped beating.

MARYNA
    Dimítry! Is it you?

PRETENDER
                    Bewitching voice!

(going to her)

    It's you at last? It's really you I see
    alone with me, night's silent screen around us?
    How slowly did the tedious day roll by!
    How slowly did the sunset's glow die down!
    How long the night has seemed while I've been waiting!

MARYNA
    The hours race by too fast: I've none to waste –   30
    I didn't make this assignation with you
    so as to spend time listening to a lover's
    soft speeches. Words aren't needed. I believe
    that you're in love. But listen: I've decided
    to couple my own destiny with yours,
    stormy and dangerous though it be; so I've
    the right, Dimítry, to insist on one thing:

    yes, I insist you now disclose to me
the secret hopes you've stored up in your heart,
the plans you've laid, and even your forebodings –   40
that I may start my life with you in boldness
close by your side – not blindly, like a child;
not as a slave to a husband's every whim,
a concubine with never a word to say –
but as your wife, a wife who's worthy of you,
worthy to help you reign as Russia's tsar.

PRETENDER

    O please let me forget just for one hour
the trials and troubles of my future life!
And *you* forget that he who stands before you
is a crown prince. Maryna, see in me   50
your lover, yes, the lover you've now chosen,
for whom a single glance from you means bliss –
Oh, listen to the pleadings of my love,
let me say all that wells up in my heart.

MARYNA

    It's not the time, Prince. While you temporize
your army's loyalty begins to cool;
each hour the difficulties and the dangers
become more difficult and dangerous still;
already doubting talk is in the air
and each new rumour gives way to another.   60
And Godunóv meanwhile is taking steps...

PRETENDER

    Why "Godunóv"? Does Godunóv control
your love, my only source of happiness?
No, no. The throne of Godunóv, the tsardom –
I now regard them with indifference.
Your love... without that what is glory to me,
what is the Russian crown, or life itself?
In lonely steppe lands, in a poor hut you...
you will make good for me the power I forfeit;
your love...

MARYNA

        Shame on you! You must not forget   70
the sanctity of your sublime commission:
to you your rank should be more precious than
all the alluring pleasures life can offer –
nothing can be equated with your rank.
Mark well: this solemn offer of my hand
I make not to an over-excited youth
half-crazed by an obsession with my beauty,
but to the man who's heir to Russia's throne,
the Crown Prince saved from death by Providence.

PRETENDER

Maryna, you're so lovely – don't torment me;   80
don't speak as though it were my rank, not me,
that you have chosen. You don't know, Maryna,
how painfully your words have stung my heart –
What! Just supposing... oh, horrendous doubt! –
tell me: if Fate, blind Fate, had not assigned me
my faultless pedigree of Russian tsars,
if I were not the son of Tsar Iván,
not the young prince the world had long forgotten:
then... then would you have loved me just the same?

MARYNA

You *are* Dimítry – him and no one else;   90
I cannot love another man.

PRETENDER

          No, stop!
I have no wish to share the one I love
with the dead man that she by rights belongs to.
No: I must stop pretending. I will tell
the whole truth; mark it well, then: your Dimítry's
dead, buried long since, and won't rise again.
But then, who *am* I? Do you want to know?
Very well, I will tell you: a poor monk.
But I grew tired of monastery restrictions,

69

and so beneath my cowl I hatched a scheme,   100
a bold scheme – yes, I planned to amaze the world.
I finally absconded from my cell,
fled to the camps of wild Ukrainian Cossacks
and learnt the mastery of horse and sabre;
and then I came here, called myself Dimítry
and passed myself off on these brainless Poles.
What will you say now, eh, my proud Maryna?
I hope you're satisfied with my confession.
Why don't you speak?

MARYNA

                    Oh, shame! Oh, shattered hopes!

(silence)

PRETENDER *(aside)*

My fit of anger's made me go too far.   110
My brilliant prospects, built up with such effort,
I now maybe have ruined past repair.
Madman! What have I done?... *(aloud)* I see, I see.
You are ashamed your lover's not a prince.
Well, say the word then, say the fateful word;
my future's in your hands now, so decide:
I'm waiting.

(He falls to his knees.)

MARYNA

                    You pathetic charlatan!
Get up! Do you suppose your grovelling
will soften this proud heart of mine, as if
I were some weak and credulous young girl?   120
You're so wrong, friend: already at my feet
I have had knights and counts – yes, noblemen;
but when I coolly waved aside their pleas
it wasn't so that some vagabond monk—

PRETENDER *(stands up)*
> Don't underestimate this young pretender;
> maybe in him great qualities lie hidden,
> qualities worthy of the throne of Russia,
> worthy of your hand, priceless though it be—

MARYNA
> Worthy of death and infamy, you upstart!

PRETENDER
> Yes, I'm at fault; possessed by arrogance   130
> I've tried to dupe both God and earthly rulers,
> I've told the world lies; but, Maryna, *you* have
> no right to punish me; I've not wronged *you*.
> No, I could never have duped you, Maryna.
> You've been the only object of my worship,
> with you at least I've not dared to pretend.
> It was my love, my blind and jealous love,
> it was love only, that just now compelled me
> to tell you all.

MARYNA
>   The madman – what a boast!
> Did anyone demand your full confession?   140
> If you, a nameless vagabond, have managed
> till now against all odds to hoax two nations,
> then at the very least it was your duty
> to prove that you were worthy of your success
> and safeguard your presumptuous imposture
> by careful, close and constant secrecy.
> I ask you, can I give myself to you,
> can I forget my birth, my modesty,
> and link my destiny to yours, when you
> have shown that you are so ingenuous,   150
> so flippant, as to expose your own dishonour?
> He blurted it all out to me from love!
> Indeed, I'm so surprised that you've not yet
> opened your heart to Father out of friendship,

71

or to the King from joy and gratitude,
or, come to that, to the Lord Wiśniowiecki
out of your loyal devotion as his page.

PRETENDER

I swear to you that you and you alone
could have wrung that admission from my heart.
I swear to you that nowhere, never again –   160
not at a feast when drink befuddles brains,
not in a chat with intimate companions,
nor under torture nor beneath the knife
will my tongue give away these dangerous secrets.

MARYNA

You swear! Then, I suppose I must believe you –
believe I do! – but what, may I enquire,
do you swear by? By God's name, possibly,
as a devout disciple of the Jesuits?
Or by your honour, as a noble warrior?
Or, maybe, simply by your word as Tsar   170
or a tsar's son? Well, aren't I right? Go on then.

DIMÍTRY *(proudly)*

Know this: the ghost of Tsar Iván's proclaimed me
Dimítry from the tomb, his son and heir;
nations he's gathered round me; and he's named me
as his avenger – so, Borís, beware!
I *am* the Crown Prince. But enough: it shames me
to cringe before a Polish woman's scorn.
Goodbye for ever. War's bloodthirsty sport,
and the endless troubles fate is bound to bring me
will soon engulf, I hope, this painful love –   180
oh, I shall come to feel such hatred for you,
as soon as passion's shameful fever passes.
I'm leaving now. In Russia there awaits me
either annihilation or the crown.
Whether I die in battle as a hero
or, criminal-like, on a public scaffold,

you'll have no portion in my destiny.
You could have had my friendship – but forget it!
The splendid role you might have played in Russia
you've now renounced – maybe, though, you'll regret it.*   190

MARYNA

But what if first I took steps to expose
to everyone your impudent imposture?

PRETENDER

You surely don't think I'm afraid of you?
or that men will believe a Polish girl
more than the Russian Crown Prince? – But mark this:
neither your king, nor Pope, nor Polish lords
care one iota if my story's true.
What's it to them if I am *not* Dimítry?
I *am* a pretext for dispute and war –
that's all they want; and should you interfere   200
they'll find some way to silence you, be sure.
Goodbye.

MARYNA

                    Stop, Crown Prince. Now at last I hear
the words not of a pageboy, but a man.
Yes, Prince: they bring back my regard for you.
Already I'm forgetting your mad outburst;
I see Dimítry once again. But listen:
it's time to act! Wake up, don't dawdle longer;
lead out your forces quickly against Moscow.
First purge the Kremlin, occupy the throne,
then send a marriage envoy here to fetch me;   210
but – God be witness – until you have set
your foot upon the steps of Russia's throne,
until you've overthrown that Godunóv,
I'll listen to no speeches about love.

(She goes off.)

73

PRETENDER
    No: easier to fight with Godunóv,
    or to outwit a Jesuit courtier,
    than deal with women, damn them: I've no strength left.
    They entangle you, they twist and writhe and squirm,
    slip from your fingers, hiss, rear up, then strike.
    Snakes, snakes! I know now why at first I trembled: 220
    she's very nearly been my ruination.
    But now it's settled: we shall march at dawn.

Scene 16*
The Polish Frontier – 16th October 1604

Prince Kurbsky and the Pretender, both on horseback; the troops are approaching the frontier.

KURBSKY *(galloping up first)*
    Look, here it is! It's here – the Russian frontier!
    Yes, holy Russia, fatherland, my home!
    Contemptuously I shake the foreign dust
    from off my clothes; I gulp in the new air,
    my native air... O Father, now your soul
    will have its consolation; in the grave
    your exiled bones can rest at last in gladness!*
    Once more it's flashed forth, our ancestral sword,
    this famous sword, the scourge of grim Kazán,
    this faithful sword that's long served Russian tsars!   10
    Today's its day of feasting and carousing
    in honour of its sovereign and its hope!...

PRETENDER *(riding quietly with lowered head)*
    How happy he is! Open-heartedly
    he's bubbling with idealism and joy!
    You champion of mine, I envy you.
    You're Kurbsky's son, brought up in banishment:
    the wrongs your father suffered you've forgotten,
    his errors you've made good, though he's now dead
    and you're preparing to pour out your blood
    for Tsar Iván's son; you mean to restore   20

your fatherland's true tsar... You're doing right,
your spirit *should* be ablaze with radiant joy.

KURBSKY

Surely, though, your heart too is full of joy?
Here is our Russia: she is yours, Crown Prince.
Your people wait there eagerly for you:
Moscow, the Kremlin, Russia's throne are yours.

PRETENDER

But, Kurbsky, Russian blood must first be shed.
You're fighting for your Tsar: you're innocent;
but *I* lead you against your brothers; I have
called Poland against Russia; yes, I'm showing   30
our foes the sacred road to our dear Moscow...*
But may my sin fall not upon my head –
but upon yours, Borís, tsar-murderer!
Advance!

KURBSKY

                    Advance – to Godunóv's destruction!

(They gallop forward. The troops cross the frontier.)

Scene 17*
Moscow, the Tsar's Council

Tsar, Patriarch and boyars.

TSAR

Can it be true? A monk who's been unfrocked,
a runaway, leads lawless gangs against us,
dares write to us with threats! This is outrageous;
it's time to teach the madman sense! Set out, then,
you, Trubetskóy, and you, Basmánov; help
is needed by my loyal generals.
Chernígov* is besieged by the insurgents.
Try and save town and townsfolk.

BASMÁNOV

Sire, I promise:
in three months' time from now, not more than that,
there'll be no further talk of this pretender;   10
we'll bring him in an iron cage to Moscow,*
like some outlandish animal. In God's name
I swear to you.

(He goes off with Trubetskóy.)

TSAR

The Swedish King has sent me
word by his envoys, offering his alliance;
but we do not have need of foreign help;
we have sufficient fighting men ourselves
to beat off the invading Poles and turncoats.
I have declined. Shchelkálov,* send out orders
to every part of Russia to our warlords:
tell them to mount their horses and dispatch   20
their men for army service in the old way;
and in the monasteries commandeer
the clergy's servants likewise. Years ago
whenever trouble threatened Russian lands
the holy men themselves came out to battle –
but this time we have no wish to disturb them;
their duty is to pray for – this is
the Tsar's command, the boyars' resolution.
Now we must settle an important question:
this impudent impostor, you know,   ()
has spread his artful stories everywhere;
yes, everywhere the letter he has sent
have sown the seeds of unrest and suspicion,
the mob's in ferment with seditious whispering,
men's minds are on the boil: they must be cooled;
I should prefer to avert the need for bloodshed,
but how? Let us decide now. Holy Father,
you be the first to tell us what you think.

PATRIARCH
    Praise be to God most high, who has implanted
    within your soul, great sovereign, a spirit   40
    of mild forbearance and of clemency;
    it is not your wish that the sinner perish;
    you wait in quietness till error pass,
    and pass it will: eternal truth's bright sun
    will lighten all men. Well, your loyal priest,
    albeit no wise judge in worldly matters,
    is bold this day to offer you his counsel.
    This demon's son, this godless renegade,
    has made the crowd believe that he's Dimítry;
    with the Crown Prince's name he's shamelessly   50
    arrayed himself, as in a stolen vestment:
    but just you strip it off – and nakedness
    will plunge him in confusion and disgrace.
    Now, God himself sends means unto this end.
    Listen to this, sire: once, six years ago –
    it was the very year in which the Lord
    blessed you and led you to accept the tsardom –
    one day at eventide a simple shepherd,
    ancient and venerable, came to see me;
    he brought me strange, mysterious information.   60
    "In my young years," he said, "I lost my sight,
    and from that time I knew no day, no night-time
    till I grew old. Vainly I tried to cure
    myself with herbs and magic incantations;
    vainly I used to visit monasteries
    and pay my homage to great wonder-workers;
    vainly I used to bathe my darkened eyes
    with healing water drawn from holy wells;
    but God would not vouchsafe me a recovery.
    And so, you see, at length I lost all hope,   70
    I grew accustomed to my gloom; no more
    did I so much as dream of objects seen;
    I only dreamt of sounds. Then once, when I
    was fast asleep, I heard a young child's voice
    saying to me: 'Get up, old man – be off

to Uglich town, to the Transfiguration
Cathedral; say a prayer there by my grave:
the Lord is merciful – and I'll forgive you.'
'Who *are* you, though?' I asked the boyish voice.
'I am Crown Prince Dimítry. God in heaven   80
has numbered me among his angel host,
and I am now a great worker of wonders.
Be on your way, old man.' I woke and thought,
'Well, maybe in reality the Lord
is granting me an overdue recovery.
I'll go.' And off I went. The way was long.
Once in the town I stepped inside the holy
cathedral and stood listening to the Mass,
and, heart ablaze with piety, I wept
so sweetly that it seemed as though my blindness   90
was trickling with the tears from out my eyes.
In due course folk began to leave; I then
said to Iván, my grandson: 'Take me to
the tomb of Prince Dimítry.' And the boy
took me there. I'd no sooner reached the tomb
and, standing by it, said my silent prayer
than I regained my sight; and I could see
God's gift of light, my grandson, and the grave."
This is the story, sire, the old man told me.

*(General agitation. In the course of this speech Borís several times
wipes his face with a handkerchief.)*

I made express enquiries then in Uglich,   100
and it transpired that many sufferers
had been vouchsafed a similar recovery
at the memorial stone of the Crown Prince.
Here's my advice: transfer the sacred relics
to the Archangel Cathedral* in the Kremlin;
install them there; then people will see clearly
how the ungodly villain has misled them,
and then, like dust, his fiendish host will vanish.

(silence)

PRINCE SHÚYSKY

    But, Holy Father, who can know the ways
    of the Most High? It's not for me to judge him.   110
    God *can* grant to a child's remains a death-sleep
    free of decay, and wonder-working powers;
    but common rumours ought to be examined
    dispassionately and with thoroughness.
    I wonder, should we really contemplate
    such a great step in stormy and troubled times?
    Won't men be saying that we're brazenly
    making a saint our tool for worldly ends?
    The crowd's already unsettled and unruly;
    already there's enough loud talk out there: 120
    this is no time to startle people's minds
    with such a grave and sudden innovation.
    I too can see that it's of prime importance
    to quash the rumour spread by this ex-monk;
    but there are other – simpler – ways to do it.
    I'm ready, therefore, sire, if you consent,
    to appear myself in public in the square:
    I'll talk the people round, reprove their madness,
    expose that vagrant's impious fraudulence.

TSAR

    Yes, be it so. Now, my Lord Patriarch,   130
    I pray you come with me into the palace:
    I need to have a talk with you today.

(He goes off. All the boyars follow after him.)

A BOYAR *(quietly to another)*

    Did you observe how pale the Tsar became
    and how great beads of sweat ran down his face?

SECOND BOYAR

    I must confess, I didn't dare look up;
    I didn't dare to breathe, far less to move.

FIRST BOYAR
Prince Shúysky saved the day though – good for him!

Scene 18*
A Square in front of a Cathedral in Moscow

The populace.

A MAN
Is the Tsar going to come out of the cathedral soon?

ANOTHER MAN
The Mass has finished; it's the prayers now.

FIRST MAN
What? Have they already called down curses on you-know-who?

SECOND MAN
I was standing in the porch and heard the deacon wailing out: "Grishka Otrépyev... anathema!"

FIRST MAN
Then they can call down all the curses they like; the Crown Prince hasn't anything to do with Otrépyev.

SECOND MAN
Well, now they're chanting the "everlasting remembrance" for the Crown Prince.

FIRST MAN
The "everlasting remembrance" for someone who's alive! They'll pay for this, the blasphemers.

THIRD MAN
Listen! A noise. Isn't it the Tsar?

FOURTH MAN
No; it's the holy man, the fool.*

(The holy fool enters wearing a cap of iron and draped with chains; he is surrounded by urchins.)

URCHINS
Nikólka, Nikólka! Iron numbskull!… Tr-r-r-r…

OLD WOMAN
Let the holy man alone, you little fiends. – Say a prayer for me, Nikólka; I'm such a sinner.

HOLY FOOL
Give me, give me, give me a little copeck.

OLD WOMAN
There's a little copeck for you; do pray for me.

HOLY FOOL *(sitting down on the ground and singing)*

> Moon is rising,
> kitten's crying;
> on your feet, holy fool,
> ba-y, ba-y, ba-y…
> pray to God our Father!

(The urchins surround him again.)

AN URCHIN
Hullo, Nikólka; why don't you take your cap off? *(rapping him on his iron cap.)* Wow, what a ring!

HOLY FOOL
But I've got a little copeck.

URCHIN
You're fibbing. All right, show it.

(He snatches the copeck and runs away.)

HOLY FOOL *(crying)*
They've taken my poor copeck; they're being cruel to Nikólka!

POPULACE
The Tsar, the Tsar's coming.

(The Tsar comes out of the cathedral. A boyar in front distributes alms to the beggars. Other boyars follow.)

HOLY FOOL
Borís! Borís! The kids are being cruel to Nikólka.

TSAR
Give him money. What's he crying about?

HOLY FOOL
The little children are being cruel to Nikólka... Have their throats cut, like you cut the throat of the little Prince.

BOYARS
Get away, idiot! Seize the idiot!

TSAR
Leave him. God's fool, pray for me.

(He goes off.)

HOLY FOOL *(calling after him)*
No, no! Mustn't pray for Tsar Herod* – Our Lady won't have it.

Scene 19*
A Plain near Nóvgorod-Séversky – 21st December 1604

A battle.

SOLDIERS *(running in disorder)*
Look out! Look out! The Crown Prince! Polish troops! They're there! They're there!

(Enter Captains Margeret and Walther Rosen.*)

MARGERET

Ver, ver do you go? *Allons**... get back zer!

ONE OF THE DESERTERS

"Get zer" yourself, if that's what you want, you damned heathen.*

MARGERET

Quoi? Quoi?*

ANOTHER

Co-aa, co-aa, co-aa! Foreign crow! *You* can croak at the Russian Crown Prince, if you like; but *we* are orthodox, you know.

MARGERET

Qu'est-ce à dire "osodox"?... Sacrés gueux, maudite canaille! Mordieu, mein Herr, j'enrage: on dirait que ça n'a pas de bras pour frapper, ça n'a que des jambes pour foutre le camp.*

W. ROSEN

Es ist Schande.*

MARGERET

Ventre-saint-gris! Je ne bouge plus d'un pas – puisque le vin est tiré, il faut le boire. Qu'en dites-vous, mein Herr?*

W. ROSEN

Sie haben Recht.*

MARGERET

Tudieu, il y fait chaud! Ce diable de "Pri-tenn-der", comme ils l'appellent, est un bougre qui a du poil au cul. Qu'en pensez-vous, mein Herr?*

W. ROSEN
   Ja.*

MARGERET
   Hé! Voyez donc, voyez donc! L'action s'engage sur les derrières
   de l'ennemi. Ce doit être le brave Basmanoff, qui aurait fait une
   sortie.*

W. ROSEN
   Ich glaube das.*

(Enter Germans.)

MARGERET
   Ha, ha! Voici nos Allemands. – Messieurs!... Mein Herr, dites-leur
   donc de se rallier et, sacrebleu, chargeons!*

W. ROSEN
   Sehr gut. Halt!

(The Germans take up formation.)

   Marsch!

GERMANS *(marching)*
   Hilf Gott!*

(An engagement.* *The Russians again run away.*

POLES
   Victory, victory! Hurrah for Tsar Dimítry!

DIMÍTRY *(on horseback)*
   Sound the withdrawal! The victory's ours. That's enough; spare
   Russian blood. Withdraw!

(Trumpets; drums.)

Scene 20*
Sevsk

The Pretender, surrounded by his men.

PRETENDER
Where is the prisoner?

POLE
                          Here.

PRETENDER
                    Call him to me.

(A Russian prisoner enters.)

Your name?

PRISONER
          Rozhnóv,* a nobleman of Moscow.

PRETENDER
You've been a soldier long?

PRISONER
                    About a month.

PRETENDER
Aren't you ashamed, Rozhnóv, that you've upraised
your sword against me?

PRISONER
                    Why? It wasn't our wish.

PRETENDER
You fought, did you, at Nóvgorod?

PRISONER

I reached here
a couple of weeks too late, coming from Moscow.

PRETENDER

What's Godunóv been up to?

PRISONER

He was deeply
shaken to hear he'd lost the battle and that
Mstislávsky had been wounded; now he's sent   10
Shúysky to take command of the army.

PRETENDER

Why, though,
has he recalled Basmánov home to Moscow?

PRISONER

The Tsar's rewarded his good services
with gold and honours. Now Basmánov sits
on the Tsar's council.

PRETENDER

He'd be more use fighting.
Well, how are things in Moscow?

PRISONER

Quiet, thank God.

PRETENDER

What? Are they expecting me?

PRISONER

God knows; these days
no one there dares to talk too much of you.
One man may have his tongue cut off; the next
his head as well. "An execution daily" –   20
that's what they're saying. Prisons are chock-full;

and in the square as soon as three or four men
meet up, you'll see an agent hovering near;
and in his leisure time the Tsar himself
conducts the interrogation of his spies.
One's soon in trouble; better to keep mum.

PRETENDER
Enviable lives Borís's subjects lead!
Well – and the army?

PRISONER
                    The army's fine. Well-clothed,
well-fed, quite happy.

PRETENDER
                    But how big is it?

PRISONER
God only knows.

PRETENDER
                    But are there – thirty thousand?   30

PRISONER
Oh, it'll be more likely fifty thousand.

(The Pretender pauses for reflection. The bystanders look at one another.)

PRETENDER
Well, well! How do they judge me in your camp?

PRISONER
Oh, when they talk about Your Grace they say
that you're – I quote (don't take offence) – a fraudster,
a brave one though.

PRETENDER *(laughing)*
                    Then I shall prove it to them
    in action. Comrades, we'll not wait around
    for Shúysky; here's some news to hearten you:
    tomorrow, battle!

(He goes off.)

ALL
                    Long live Prince Dimítry!

A POLE
    Battle tomorrow! They are fifty thousand,
    and we, all told, are hardly fifteen thousand.   40
    He must be crazy.

ANOTHER POLE
                    Nonsense, friend; one Pole can
    challenge five hundred Muscovitish weaklings.

PRISONER
    You'll challenge, yes. But when it comes to fighting
    you'll run away from *one* of us, you braggart.

SECOND POLE
    If you, my cheeky prisoner, were with sabre,
    I'd use mine here *(pointing to his own sabre)* to put you in your place.

PRISONER
    We Russian lads can do without a sabre:
    maybe you'd like to fight with this *(shows his fist)*, you dolt!

(The Pole eyes him superciliously and walks off in silence. All laugh.)

Scene 21*
A Forest

False Dimítry, Gavríla Pushkin

(In the background lies a dying horse.)

FALSE DIMÍTRY*
My poor old charger! He showed so much spirit,
galloping off today to his last battle;
and, even wounded, he still bore me swiftly.
My poor old comrade.

G. PUSHKIN *(to himself)*
There's a thing to fret for –
his horse! When our whole army has been pounded
to dust!

PRETENDER
Listen, I wonder if perhaps
it's just that he's exhausted from his wound
and he'll revive.

G. PUSHKIN
Of course he won't. He's dying.

PRETENDER *(going to his horse)*
My poor old charger!... What to do? Unrein him,
undo his saddle girth. We'll let him die   10
at liberty.

(He unbridles and unsaddles the horse. Several Poles enter.)

Good evening, gentlemen.
I do not see Prince Kurbsky with you – why?
Today I watched him as he slashed his way
into the thick of battle; countless sabres
closed the young warrior round like waving corn;

89

but his sword was raised higher than the rest
and his grim war cry drowned all other cries.
Where *is* my champion?

A POLE

                  He lies with the dead.

PRETENDER

Peace to his soul, and honour to his valour.
How few are we survivors of the battle!   20
The traitors! Cossack villains from the Dnieper,
damnation on them! *They* have been our ruin –
not to hold out against three minutes' pressure!
Just let them wait! I'll hang one man in ten,
the brigands!

G. PUSHKIN

              But whoever was at fault there,
the fact is we've been utterly defeated,
annihilated.

PRETENDER

             But the day was ours.
I'd almost crushed their leading companies –
but then the Germans beat us back – and how!
My! They are fighters: good G ! th are fight s: 30
I love them for it: I shall certai
recruit my guard of honour fr   the German

G. PUSHKIN

But may I ask where we're to s nd t   night?

PRETENDER

Why, in the forest, here. What's wrong with this?
At dawn we'll move off; we'll make Rylsk by lunchtime.
Good night.

(He lies down, puts the saddle beneath his head and goes to sleep.)

G. PUSHKIN

       Good night. A pleasant sleep, Crown Prince.
Smashed, pulverized and fleeing for his life –
as unconcerned, though, as a placid child!
Providence is protecting him, that's clear;
then nor must we, friends, give way to despair.   40

Scene 22*
Moscow, the Tsar's Palace

Borís, Basmánov.

TSAR

  Yes, he's defeated, but what good is that?
The victor's crown we've won is valueless.
His scattered army he's now reassembled;
he holds Putívl and threatens us from there.
And meanwhile what are our war heroes doing?
Standing at Kromy, whilst a few odd Cossacks
laugh at them from behind a crumbling rampart.
There's glory for you! No, they've let me down;
I'll send you out as their supreme commander;
I'll pick my generals for brains, not birth.   10
Let them bemoan their loss of precedence;
it's time I braved the titled rabble's anger
and put an end to a pernicious practice.

BASMÁNOV

  Ah, sire, a hundred times blessèd will be
the day in which the Registers of Rank* –
and all the strife and privilege they foster –
are fed into the flames!

TSAR

            That day's not far off;
just let me first suppress the Russian people's
rebellious instincts.

BASMÁNOV

Why regard the people?
At heart they're always minded to rebel: 20
so does a horse of mettle chew his bit,
and a young lad resent his father's power.
So what? The father manages the lad still;
the horseman, too, calmly controls his mount.

TSAR

But horses have been known to throw their riders,
and sons eventually defy their fathers.
Only by unrelenting harshness can we
hold down the people. So Iván the Great thought,
that clever monarch, who calmed many storms;
that was his savage grandson's* view as well.   30
The people are impervious to kindness:
be good to them, and they'll not thank you for it;
plunder and kill, and you'll be no worse off.

(A boyar comes in.)

Yes?

BOYAR

Sire, the foreign visitors are here.

TSAR

I'll come out to receive them. Wait, Basmánov.
Stay here: I need to talk a little more
with you.

(He goes out.)

BASMÁNOV

A spirit masterful and lofty!
If God will only grant him to succeed
against this damned Otrépyev, he'll accomplish
more good – yes, very much more good in Russia.   40

Important thoughts are stirring in his mind:
they must not be allowed to die. How great
the prospects that will open to me, once
he crushes the hereditary boyars!
In military matters I've no rival;
I shall be first beneath the Tsar himself...
and even p'rhaps... But what is that strange noise?

(Commotion. Boyars, court officials and servants run about in disorder, meet with one another and exchange whispers.)

FIRST MAN
  A doctor, quick!

SECOND MAN
          First get the Patriarch!

THIRD MAN
  He's calling for the Crown Prince, the Crown Prince!

FOURTH MAN
  Fetch his confessor.

BASMÁNOV
          What on earth has happened?   50

FIFTH MAN
  The Tsar is ill.

SIXTH MAN
          The Tsar is dying.

BASMÁNOV
          Good God!

FIFTH MAN
  Yes, he was seated on his throne, then slumped down –
  and blood streamed from his mouth and from his ears.

93

(The Tsar is carried in on a chair. All the Tsar's household, all the boyars.)

TSAR

Go, every one of you – let the Crown Prince
remain alone here with me. *(All withdraw.)* I am dying;
let us embrace. Goodbye, my son: soon now
you will begin to reign… O God, O God,
I'll soon appear before Thee – and there's no time
for me to cleanse my soul in penitence.
But as I feel – my son, you're dearer to me   60
than the salvation of my soul… so be it!
A common subject I was born: I should have
died, too, a common subject, unbeknown.
But I've attained supreme power… by what means?
Don't ask. It's all right: *you* are innocent,
you will commence your reign now rightfully,
and I alone shall answer before God
for everything*… My dear son, don't be fooled,
don't blind yourself deliberately to facts –
you're coming to the throne in troubled times: 70
he's dangerous, this mysterious pretender,
he's armed himself with an ill-omened name…
With my long years' experience of ruling
I've managed to check unrest and rebellion;
I've made men dread me and tremble in my presence;
here no one's dared give voice to thoughts of treason.
But you are young, unpractised as a monarch –
how will you govern, then, beneath this threat,
quash the rebellion, smother treachery?
But God is great! He teaches young men wisdom,   80
He gives strength to the weak… now listen to me:
choose someone first of all as your adviser,
a man of trust, cool and mature in years,
a favourite with the people – and the boyars
too must respect him for his birth or good name –
someone like Shúysky. You need for the army
a general with experience: send Basmánov

94

and bear with fortitude the boyars' protests.
Since you were small you've sat with me in Council,
you know the workings of the government;   90
don't change the run of things too much: the essence
of power is continuity. I've lately
had to bring banishments back and killings – you can
abolish them anew; then men will bless you
just as they blessed your uncle Tsar Feódor
when he replaced Tsar Iván the Terrible.
Little by little, as time passes, you should
draw tight once more the reins of sovereignty;
but now, without letting them go, relax them...
Give foreigners a welcome, show them favour,   100
always accept their services with trust.
Observe the Church's ordinances strictly.
Be slow to speak; it's wrong that a tsar's voice
should lose itself in the air to no good purpose;
no, it should only, like some holy bell chime,
proclaim some great grief or some great feast day.
My dear son, you're now entering those years
in which our blood is stirred by a woman's face.
Preserve in all its holy purity
your innocence, your modest dignity: 110
the man who's taken in his youth to drowning
his senses in voluptuousness and vice –
when he's mature he grows morose and cruel,
his mind becomes dull, too, before its time.
You're head now of your family: don't fail them.
Honour your mother, but be your own master –
you are a man and tsar. Cherish your sister –
you are the one protector she has left.

FEÓDOR *(on his knees)*
    No, no – live on, reign for a long, long time:
    without you Russia's lost, and so are we.   120

TSAR
    All's finished now – my eyes are growing dim.
    I feel the coldness of the tomb...

(Enter the Patriarch, church dignitaries, and behind them all the boyars. Also the Tsarítsa, supported on each side; and Princess Xénia, sobbing.)

         Who's there?
A monk's robe!*... ah, yes! now my holy vows...
The hour has struck; the Tsar becomes a monk –
my cell will be the darkness of the grave...
Patience a moment, my lord Patriarch;
I am still Tsar. Attend to me, you boyars:
here is the one to whom I leave the tsardom;
kiss the cross in Feódor's name... Basmánov,
my friends... upon death's threshold I entreat you   130
to serve him truly and devotedly.
He's still so young, he's still so innocent.
Do you swear?

BOYARS

    Yes, we swear.

TSAR

        Then I'm content.
Please pardon me my foibles, my mistakes,
and my deliberate and secret crimes...
Now, Holy Father, you may come: I'm ready.

(The rite for administering the monastic vows commences. The women faint and are carried out.)

Scene 23*
A Tent

Basmánov ushers in G. Pushkin.

BASMÁNOV

  Come you in here, and speak without reserve.
  So, he has sent you here to see me, has he?

G. PUSHKIN

He offers you his friendship and the highest
position under him in Muscovy.

BASMÁNOV

Feódor, though, has given me already
a high post. I'm commander of the army;
for my sake he's ignored the rules of rank
and braved the boyars' wrath. I've sworn allegiance.

G. PUSHKIN

You've sworn allegiance to the lawful heir
to Russia's throne; but what if there's still living   10
another heir *more* lawful?...

BASMÁNOV

                    Listen, Pushkin,
enough of that: don't talk such rubbish. *I* know
his real identity.

G. PUSHKIN

                    Russians and Poles
have long since recognized him as Dimítry.
But nonetheless I do not press the point.
Maybe he is the actual Dimítry,
or maybe he's a charlatan. The one thing
I know is this: Borís's son is bound
sooner or later to lose Moscow to him.

BASMÁNOV

So long as I stand by young Tsar Feódor,   20
for so long he'll remain upon the throne.
I thank the Lord that we have troops aplenty;
I mean to hearten them with victory.
And who do you propose to send against me?
Cossack Karéla? Surely not. Or Mniszech?
How many are you, eh? A mere eight thousand!

97

G. PUSHKIN

You're wrong: you'll find that we are less than that.
I'm telling you myself – our army's trash:
our Cossacks spend their time in raids on peasants;
our Poles spend their time showing off and drinking;   30
as for our Russians... but need I say more?
I'll not attempt to hide the truth from you.
Do you know, though, Basmánov, where our strength lies?
Not in the army, not in Polish aid,
but in the mind, yes, in the people's mind.
Do you recall Dimítry's march of triumph,
the peaceful manner of his victories,
when everywhere before a shot was fired
towns were surrendering to him in submission
as mobs seized stubborn garrison commanders?   40
You've seen yourself how little your troops like
to fight against him. *That* was in Borís' day!
What about now?... Basmánov, no! The time's past
for wrangling, for rekindling strife's cold embers.
For all your intellect and strength of will,
you won't hold out; surely you'd do far better
to be the first to set a wise example,
proclaim Dimítry as the lawful tsar
and thereby earn his gratitude for life.
Well, what's your view?

BASMÁNOV

                    Tomorrow you will know.   50

G. PUSHKIN

Don't haver!

BASMÁNOV

         Goodbye.

G. PUSHKIN

        Think on it, Basmánov!

(He goes out.)

BASMÁNOV

He's right, he's right. Everywhere treason's ripening.
And what can *I* do? – surely not just wait
for mutineers to seize me like the others
and hand me over to Otrépyev? Better
forestall the storm-filled torrent's furious onrush,
better myself to... But to break my oath,
to earn dishonour for all my descendants,
to pay back with horrendous treachery
the trust in which I'm held by my young monarch!...   60
It's easy for an exile in disgrace
to contemplate conspiracy, rebellion –
but I, can I, the favourite of the Tsar?...
But death... and power... my country's troubles, too...

(He reflects.)

Here! Who's around?

(He whistles.)

                    My horse! Summon the troops!*

Scene 24
Moscow, the Place of a Skull*

Gavríla Pushkin walking along, surrounded by people.

POPULACE

A boyar's come to us from the Crown Prince.
Let's hear, then, what the boyar has to tell us.
Let's listen to him.

G. PUSHKIN *(on the rostrum)*
                    Citizens of Moscow,
the Crown Prince bids me offer you his greeting.

99

(He makes a bow.)

You know already how God's providence
rescued the Crown Prince from a murderer's clutches.
He *was* on his way here to avenge the crime;
Heaven's judgement, though, has struck Borís down first.
All Russia has submitted to Dimítry;
even Basmánov in heartfelt remorse   10
has brought the army under his allegiance.
In love and peace Dimítry's coming to you:
will you, then, just to please the Godunóvs,
uplift your hands against the lawful Tsar,
sole heir to the long line of Russia's rulers?*

POPULACE
  Of course not, no.

G. PUSHKIN
                    You citizens of Moscow!
The whole world knows how much you've had to suffer
under the regime of that savage upstart:
banishment, death, dishonour, heavy taxes,
forced labour, famine – you've lived through it all.   20
Dimítry though intends to show you favour –
yes, boyars, nobles, civil servants, soldiers
foreign guests, merchants – and all you good people.
Will you react with senseless obduracy
and turn a proud back on these kindnesses?
He's marching at the head of awesome forces,
to claim the throne of his tsar ancestors.
I warn you, don't enrage the Tsar, but fear God,
Kiss the cross in your lawful monarch's name;
humble yourselves, and be quick to dispatch   30
the Archbishop,* boyars, clerks and delegates
to meet Dimítry in his camp and there
to do him homage as our father-sovereign.

(He comes down. Murmuring among the people.)

POPULACE
  Why all this talk? The boyar spoke the truth.
  Long live Dimítry, Tsar and father to us!

PEASANT *(on the rostrum)*
  Now, folks! Into the Kremlin, to the palace!
  Come on! Let's truss that puppy of Borís's!

POPULACE *(rushing forward in a mass)*
  Truss him up, drown him! Long live Tsar Dimítry!
  Death to the family of Godunóv!

Scene 25*
The Kremlin, Borís's Residence – Guards by the Steps

Feódor at a window.

BEGGAR
  Give a poor man something, for Christ's sake!

GUARD
  Get away; orders are that no one's to speak to the prisoners.

FEÓDOR
  Go along, old man; I'm poorer than you: at least you're free.

(Xénia, wearing a veil, also comes to the window.)

SOMEONE FROM THE CROWD
  Brother and sister! Poor children, like birds in a cage.

ANOTHER
  Fancy feeling sorry for them! Cursed brood!

FIRST MAN
  The father was a villain, but the youngsters aren't to blame.

ANOTHER
  The apple doesn't fall far from the tree.

XÉNIA

Brother, brother dear, it looks as though some boyars are coming.

FEÓDOR

That's Golítsyn, Mosálsky... The others I don't recognize.

XÉNIA

Ah, brother dear, my heart fails me.

(Enter Golítsyn, Mosálsky, Molchánov and Sherefédinov, followed by three of the Tsar's bodyguard.)

POPULACE

Make way, make way. Some boyars are coming.

(They go into the house.)

SOMEONE FROM THE CROWD

What have they come for?

ANOTHER

Oh, probably to make Feódor Godunóv take the oath of allegiance.

THIRD MAN

Really? – You hear what a noise there is in the house! Quite a commotion; there's fighting going on...

POPULACE

Let's go up! – The doors are locked – do you hear? Shrieking! That's a woman's voice – the shouts have died down. There's still a noise.*

(The doors open. Mosálsky appears on the steps.)

MOSÁLSKY

People! María Godunóva and her son Feódor have poisoned themselves. We have seen their dead bodies.

102

(The people stand in horrified silence.)

Why are you silent? Shout: "Long live Tsar Dimítry Ivánovich!"

POPULACE
Long live Tsar Dimítry Ivánovich!*

– 7th November 1825

End of the comedy,
in which the main character is
Tsar Borís Godunóv.

Glory be to the Father
and to the Son
and to the Holy Ghost,
AMEN.*

Little Tragedies

Introduction

Pushkin composed these four one-act plays in the autumn of 1830 at his country estate of Bóldino – or at least he completed them then. There is evidence that three of them had been on his mind for up to four years. Pushkin certainly envisaged the four plays as a cycle; but they were not published together until after his death. Three of the plays were published separately during his lifetime, between 1831 and 1836.

Except for two songs, Pushkin wrote the *Little Tragedies* in unrhymed iambic pentameters (lines of ten or eleven syllables with the stress on the even syllables), a freer version of the same blank-verse metre he had used for his full-length historical drama *Boris Godunov* a few years earlier. I have adopted the same metre in this translation.

All the *Little Tragedies* are short, one-act plays, ranging in length from one to four scenes. The subject matter is varied, but all have a Western-European setting and atmosphere. They have in common a driving obsession on the part of the leading character and its destructive effects. In each case the obsession is one of which Pushkin had himself had close experience.

My translation is based on the texts contained in volume IV of Sobránie Sochinéniy Púshkina (Moscow: Gosudárstvennoye Izdátelstvo Hudózhestvennoy Literatúry, 1959–62).

Pushkin provided no lists of scenes or of dramatis personae. I have, however, included lists at the start of each play for the convenience of readers and prospective directors.

Extra material on the *Little Tragedies* as a whole and on the individual plays is provided at the back of this volume. Asterisks have been placed in the text after words that are the subject of an endnote.

– Roger Clarke

The Mean-Spirited Knight*

*Scenes from Chenston's Tragicomedy: The Covetous Knight**

List of Scenes

Scene 1: In a tower
Scene 2: A vaulted cellar
Scene 3: In the ducal palace

Characters (in order of appearance)

Albert, a young knight
Jan, his manservant
Solomon, a Jewish moneylender
Baron Philippe, Albert's father
Duke

Scene 1
In a Tower

*Albert and Jan**

ALBERT

    I *will* be at the contest, come what may;
    I *will* take part. Show me my helmet, Jan.

(Jan hands him the helmet.)

    A hole right through it – ruined. No, I can't
    wear that. I need to get myself a new one.
    What a hard blow he struck! Damn Count Delorge!

JAN

    You got your own back on him well and good, sir,
    knocking him from his stirrups like you did;
    he lay for days as dead* – he's not yet really
    mended.

ALBERT

          For all that, though, he's no worse off;
    his splendid body armour's in one piece;   10
    his body too. It won't cost him a penny;
    no, *he* won't need to buy himself a new set.
    I should have seized his helmet there and then!
    I would have done, if I'd not been ashamed
    before the ladies and the Duke. Damned count!
    I wish he'd made a hole right through my head!
    I need a change of clothes as well. Last time
    the other knights were sitting there in satins
    and velvets. At the table of the Duke
    no one but me wore armour. I made out   20

that I'd come to the contest quite by chance.
But what can I say this time? To be poor
is hateful, hateful – it degrades one so!
Delorge – remember? – aimed his heavy lance
and pierced my helmet through, then galloped past,
while I, bareheaded now, spurred my Emir
and flew off like a whirlwind in pursuit.
I threw the Count the length of twenty paces,
like a small pageboy. *That* made all the ladies
jump from their seats! Even Clotilda too   30
covered her face and screamed despite herself.
The officials all acclaimed my winning blow.
But no one then dreamt of the reason for
the unnatural strength and bravery I showed.
It was the damaged helmet that enraged me.
What was the cause of those heroics? – Meanness,
yes! It's not hard to catch that illness here,
living beneath the same roof as my father.
And how's Emir, poor horse?

JAN

                              He's limping still.
You can't ride out on him yet, that's quite clear.   40

ALBERT
    Oh well, it can't be helped. I'll buy the bay.
    It's not a high price that they're asking for him.

JAN
    It's not a high price, but our money's gone.

ALBERT
    But what says Solomon, that idle rogue?

JAN
    He says that he can't lend you any more
    unless you give him good security.

112

ALBERT
Security! Where'll I find that? – the devil!

JAN
I said as much.

ALBERT
                    And he?…

JAN
                            He sighed and shrugged.

ALBERT
You should have told him that my father's rich as
a Jew himself and one day soon or later   50
the lot will come to me.

JAN
                    I did say that.

ALBERT
And he?…

JAN
                He shrugged and sighed.

ALBERT
                                Oh, how frustrating!

JAN
I think he meant to come himself.

ALBERT
                            Thank God!
I'll not let him go back without a ransom.

(a knocking at the door)

    Who's there?

(Solomon enters.)

SOLOMON

           Your humble servant.

ALBERT

                       Ah, my friend!
Damned Jew you are, but still a man of honour.
Do come in, Solomon. Well, do I hear
that you won't give me credit?

SOLOMON

                    Ah, kind knight,
I swear to you: I'd gladly… but I can't –
truly. I've not the cash. I'm broke, quite broke.   60
You see, I try so hard to help you knights,
but no one pays me back. I meant to ask you,
you can't repay a part of?…

ALBERT

                 You old bandit!
Do *you* think that if I had funds to spare
I'd bother to be talking here with you. No,
Solomon dear friend, don't be so stubborn;
let's have your guilders.* Dish me out a hundred
or else I'll have you frisked.

SOLOMON

                 You want a hundred!
As if I had a hundred guilders!

ALBERT

                 Listen!
aren't you ashamed not to be bailing out   70
your friends?

SOLOMON

          I swear to you—

ALBERT

Enough, enough!
You're calling for security? What nonsense!
What can I give to gain your trust? A pig's hide?
If I'd had anything to pawn, then I'd have
long ago sold it. Or d'you count a knight's
word of too little value, cur?

SOLOMON

Oh, *your* word
is worth a lot to me, while you're alive.
Your word's enough to open up for you,
like magic, every treasure chest in Flanders.
But if you were to give your word to me,   80
poor Hebrew that I am, and then you died
(may God preserve you, sir), well then
your word would be to me of no more use than
the key to a money box that's lost at sea.

ALBERT

But surely I'll outlive my father, won't I?

SOLOMON

Who knows? Our days aren't counted out by us.
One day a youngster thrives; the next he's dead,
and you'll see four old men who'll carry
the corpse on stooping shoulders to its grave.
The Baron's healthy. God grant that he'll live   90
ten, twenty, twenty-five or thirty years.

ALBERT

You're talking rubbish, Jew: in thirty years
I shall be knocking fifty; then what use
will money be to me?

SOLOMON

Money? Money
is always useful at whatever age;

> but young men want it for a willing servant
> to send out everywhere without a qualm,
> while old men see in money a true friend
> and tend it like the apple of their eye.

ALBERT

> Oh no! My father doesn't see in money   100
> a servant or a friend. He sees a master
> that he must serve himself, and how! Just like
> a Moorish slave – like a chained dog: he lives
> in a cold kennel, eats dry crusts, drinks water,
> awake all night he runs around and barks –
> his treasure, though, lies peacefully at rest
> in chests. Stop waffling! One day all that gold
> will be my servant, it'll rest no more.

SOLOMON

> Yes, at the Baron's funeral there'll be
> more money flowing than there will be tears.   110
> May God let you inherit soon.

ALBERT

> Amen.

SOLOMON
> Maybe…

ALBERT
> What

SOLOMON
> Yes – ⸱ ⸱ gh ⸱cur ed ⸱ me
> there's wa s ar l rnear s

ALBERT

> What ways and means?

SOLOMON
                                        Just this –
  there's an old man I know, a little fellow,
  Jew, pharmacist, a poor chap...

ALBERT
                        Moneylender,
  same sort as you, or slightly honester?

SOLOMON
  No, sir, Tobias has another trade –
  he mixes drops of liquid: it's amazing
  how powerful they are.

ALBERT
        What's this to me?

SOLOMON
  Add to a glass of water... just three drops;   120
  no taste, no colour – nothing to be noticed;
  the one who drinks suffers no stomach pains,
  no nausea, no headache, but just dies.

ALBERT
  Your little old man deals in poison, then.

SOLOMON
                                        Yes –
  poison, that's right.

ALBERT
          Well? Not to lend me money,
  you're offering to lend two hundred bottles
  of poison, one per guilder. Is that it?

SOLOMON
  I know you like to laugh at me – but no,
  I meant... perhaps you might... I was just thinking
  that maybe it was time the Baron died.   130

ALBERT

    What! Poison my own father! And you dared
    to his son's face... Jan, seize him... and you dared...
    You know what I'll now do, you treacherous Jew,
    you dog, you snake? Yes, without more ado
    I'll hang you from the gates.

SOLOMON

                       I'm wrong, I'm sorry!
    Forgive me, I was joking.

ALBERT

                Jan, the rope.

SOLOMON

    I... I was joking. I *have* brought some money.

ALBERT

    Get out, you dog! *(Solomon leaves.)* So this is what I've come to
    through Father's meanness! This is what a Jew
    has dared suggest to me! A glass of wine please,   140
    I'm all a-tremble... but, Jan, we still need
    the money. Run now, catch the damned Jew up,
    just take his guilders. But first bring me here
    the inkstand. I shall write you a receipt
    to give the villain: I don't want him here,
    the Judas... O ... no, don't go after all;
    those guilders that he brought will reek of poison,
    just as the silver pieces of his forebear...
    I asked you for a glass of wine.

JAN

                       Our wine –
    there's not a drop left.

ALBERT

                But the wine Ramón   150
    sent as a gift to me from Spain – where's that?

JAN
    Last night I took the final bottle down
    to the sick blacksmith.

ALBERT
                                Oh yes, I remember…
    Give me some water, then. This damned existence!
    No, I've decided: I shall go and ask
    the Duke for justice: Father must be forced
    to treat me as a son, not as a mouse
    born underneath the floorboards.

Scene 2*
A Vaulted Cellar

BARON
    Like a young playboy waiting for a date
    with some seductive creature who's bewitched him,
    or with a dumb girl he's led on – I too
    have waited all day long for now, when I
    can creep down to my vault, to my strong chests.
    This is a special day! Today I can
    spread a fresh layer of gold that I've amassed
    in my sixth chest, the one that's not yet full.
    Little it seems, but it's little by little
    that treasures grow. I'm sure that I've read somewhere   10
    about a king who once ordered his troops
    to gather earth by handfuls in a heap,
    until a lofty hill rose up, and then
    the king could from the top enjoy the view
    of white tents stretching far across the plain
    and of his fleet that rode at sea beyond.*
    Just so I too have brought by meagre handfuls
    regular contributions to this store
    until my hill has risen – and from its top
    I can view everything that I control.   20
    What do I *not* control? Now like some demon

I can be sovereign over all the world;
I need but wish – and palaces will rise;
in my magnificent gardens bands of nymphs
will gather playfully to bring me pleasure;
the goddesses of art will pay their dues;
free-ranging Genius will be my slave;
Virtue and never-sleeping Industry
will patiently await my recognition.
I'll only whistle, and obediently   30
the very Power of Evil will creep up,
cringe, lick my hand, then look into my eyes
and in them read the message of my will.
Everything's mine, but I am – nobody's;
I've risen above desire; I am untroubled;
I know my power. But that's enough from me
of introspection…

(He looks at his gold.)

                        Yes, it seems so little;
and yet with all its weight it represents
so many human worries, tears and lies,
so many prayers, so many curses! I've   40
a Spanish gold coin* – here it is. Just now
a widow paid it back to me; before that
she'd knelt for half the day outside my window
with three young children, wailing – what a scene!
The rain came down, and stopped, and came again;
she kept up her performance though. I could have
chased her away, but something said to me
that she had brought her husband's debt to pay me –
she didn't want to land in jail tomorrow.
And this one? This was brought me by Thibault –   50
where did he get it from, the lazy villain?
Stole it, I'll bet; or maybe he went down
one night to where the high road skirts the wood…
Yes! If the bowels of the earth were suddenly
to throw up all the tears and blood and sweat

shed for these precious treasures that lie here,
there'd be a second Flood – and I should drown
in these strongrooms of mine. But now's the moment!

(He makes as though to open a chest.)

Each time that I approach one of my chests
to open it, I flush and palpitate.   60
It isn't fear. (Oh no! – what should I fear?
I have my sword by me; my valiant blade
will answer for the treasure.) But a strange
sensation grips my heart that I can't fathom…
The medics tell us that some folk there are
who get a kick from murder. And when I
insert the key into the lock, I feel
the same sensation as they must when they
bury the dagger in their victim: pleasant,
but at the same time dreadful.

(He opens the chest.)

                        There! What joy!   70

(He pours the money in.)

In you go, no more roaming through the world
and pandering to human lusts and needs.
Here you shall sleep the deep sleep of the strong,
the sleep the gods sleep in the furthest heavens…
Today I want to give myself a treat:
I'll light a candle by each treasure chest;
I'll open all of them; and then I'll feast
my eyes on glistening heaps of gold all round me.

(He lights candles and opens each chest in turn.)

121

I reign supreme!… Oh what a magic glow!
My empire is obedient, secure;   80
it is my bliss, my honour, and my glory!
I reign supreme… But after me, then who'll
succeed to all this power? My son and heir!
That brainless youth, who sprinkles cash like water,
has playboys and good-timers for his friends!
I'll be no sooner dead than he – yes he! –
will come down to these peaceful, silent vaults
with his false friends and greedy hangers-on.
He'll filch the bunch of keys off my dead body
and with a smirk unlock my treasure chests.   90
And all my closely guarded wealth will then
stream into satin pockets full of holes.
He'll smash the sacred vessels; and the oil
kept for anointing kings will soak the floor.
He'll squander… By what rule of law, I ask?
I hardly gained all this without exertion,
or as a pastime, like a gambler who
rattles the dice and rakes in piles of money!
There's no one knows what bitter self-denials,
what passions held in check, what ruminations,   100
what anxious days and long nights without sleep
all this has cost me. Or will my son assert that
this heart of mine is overgrown with moss
and that I've never known desires, that I've
not even felt the bite of conscience? – conscience,
that sharp-clawed beast that tears the heart – yes, conscience,
that uninvited guest, relentless talker,
who gives you credit, then demands it back,
that witch, who makes the moon go dark and stirs
the graves and conjures up the dead!…   110
No: first of all, boy, toil to make your fortune –
and then let's see if the young good-for-nothing
wastes what he's earned with his own sweat and blood.
If only I could hide this vaulted cellar
from all unworthy eyes! If only I
could come back from the grave, a ghostly watchman,

and seated on a chest preserve my treasures
from living beings, just as I do now!...

Scene 3
In the Ducal Palace

Albert; the Duke.

ALBERT

My lord, believe me: I've endured the shame
of galling povery too long now. If I wasn't
at my wits' end, you wouldn't hear my protest.

DUKE

I do believe you, yes: a noble knight
like you would not accuse his father if he
were not at his wits' end. Few are so base...
Don't worry: I shall offer my advice
in private to your father, without fuss.
I'm waiting for him now. We haven't met
for ages. He was friends with grandfather.   10
I still remember: when I was a boy,
he used to sit me on his horse and then
he'd put his massive helmet over me
as though it were a bell.

(He looks out of the window.)

                But who is that?
That's not him, surely?

ALBERT

           Sir, it is.

DUKE

               Then go off
into that room. I'll call you.

(Albert leaves. The Baron enters.)

                    Baron, welcome!
I'm glad to see you well and in good shape.

BARON

    My Lord, I'm happy that I'm strong enough
    to come here now in answer to your summons.

DUKE

    We've not met, Baron, for a long, long time;   20
    do you remember me?

BARON

                 Remember, sir?
    As clearly as I see you now. Oh, you were
    a lively boy, you were. The Duke – the late Duke –
    "Philippe," he'd say to me (it was Philippe
    he always called me), "what d'you think of this, eh?
    In twenty years the two of us, you'll see,
    we shall be gaga in this youngster's eyes…"
    In yours, that is…

DUKE

             Well, let's become acquainted
    afresh. You've never visited my court.

BARON

    I'm old, sir, old these days: what's there for me   30
    to do at court? You're young, you're fond of
    sports and festivities. But I at my age –
    I don't enjoy them. But if God should send
    a war, then, wheezing, I'll remount my horse;
    there'll be enough strength left in my frail arm
    to draw my ancient sword from out its scabbard.

DUKE

    We're well aware of your devotion, Baron.

You were a friend of grandfather's; my father
held you in high regard; and I have always
thought you a loyal and gallant knight. Let's sit.   40
You have some children, Baron?

BARON

                              Just one son.

DUKE

Then why do I not see him at my court?
You're tired, I know, of court life, but it's proper
for him, a young knight, to be here with us.

BARON

My son dislikes a hectic social life;
he has a wild and sullen nature – always
wandering in the forests round my castle,
like a young deer.

DUKE

                    But it's not good for him
to shun folk. We must quickly bring some fun
into his life – some dancing, friendly sports.   50
Send him to me; and grant him an allowance
that's fitting for his station as a knight.
You're frowning. Has the journey made you tired
perhaps?

BARON

                No, sir, it's not that I am tired;
but you've embarrassed me. I'd rather not have
acknowledged this to you, but you compel me
to tell you things about my son that I
should greatly have preferred you not to know.
Unfortunately, sir, he's not deserving
of sympathy or of your kind attention.   60
His life's an orgy of unruliness
and of depravity…

DUKE

But, Baron, that's
because he's on his own. A lonely life
devoid of useful pastimes ruins youngsters.
Send him to us. I'm sure he'll give up here
the habits he's developed in the wilds.

BARON

Forgive me, sir, but really there is no way
I can agree to what you have suggested...

DUKE

But why so?

BARON

Please don't pressure an old man...

DUKE

I must insist that you tell me the reason
for your refusal.

70

BARON

Well, I'm... angry with
my son.

DUKE

For wh ?

BARON

A crime, a wicked crime.

DUKE

But tell me, what exactly has he done?

BARON

Don't press me, Duke...

DUKE

You *are* behaving strangely.
Or is it shame you feel for him?

BARON

Yes... shame.

DUKE

But what's he done, then?

BARON

He... well, he intended
to kill me.

DUKE

Kill you! Then I'll have him tried
in court for such a hideous offence.

BARON

I'd rather not bring charges, though I know
that for a fact he's thirsting for my death,   80
and though I know that he's already tried
to take my...

DUKE

What?

BARON

My money.*

(Albert bursts into the room.)

ALBERT

No, you're lying.

DUKE *(to the son)*
How dare you!...

127

BARON

You're here! *You*, you dare say that!
That you could use that word to your own father!
Me lying! In the hearing of the Duke too!
You'll answer!… I'm a knight still.

ALBERT

You're a liar.

BARON

O God of justice, where's your thunderbolt?
Take up my challenge; let this sword decide!

(He throws down his glove; his son quickly takes it up.)

ALBERT

I thank you. That's the first gift from my father.

DUKE

Have I seen right? What is it I've just witnessed?   90
A son accepts his agèd father's challenge!
What times are these in which I've taken up
my chain of office! Quiet now: you madman,
and you young tiger! No more! *(to the son)* Drop it now;
your father's glove, hand it to me. *(He takes it from him.)*

ALBERT *(aside)*

A pity.

DUKE

You've sunk your claws well into it! You monster!
Be off: and don't you dare to come again
into my presence till I summon you
myself. *(Albert leaves)* And as for you, poor wretch, at your age
aren't you ashamed?…

BARON

Excuse me please, my lord…   100
I cannot any longer stand… my knees

are giving way... Air! Give me air!... My keys,
where are my keys? My keys!...

DUKE

                    Good God, he's dead!
Grim times are these! And grim, too, human nature!*

*Mozart and Salieri**

List of Scenes

Scene 1: A room
Scene 2: A private room in a restaurant

Characters (in order of appearance)

Salieri
Mozart
A blind violinist

Scene 1
A Room

SALIERI

They all say there's no justice here on earth.
But there's no justice up in heaven either –
that's clear to me, as clear as do-re-mi.
I've had a love of art since I was born.
When I was just a child and high aloft
in our old church the organ notes resounded,
I listened with such rapture that I wept –
I couldn't help it – yes, I wept for pleasure.
I quickly gave up juvenile pursuits;
school subjects that weren't relevant to music   10
I hated; proud and stubborn as I was,
I wouldn't study them; I pledged myself
to music, nothing else. I found the first
step hard, the journey trying, but the early
problems I overcame. My hard-won skill*
I set up as a pedestal for art;
yes, skilled I made myself: I trained my fingers
to rattle briskly up and down the keys,
my ear to hear true pitch. I butchered music,
dissecting scores like corpses. I worked out   20
my harmonies by algebra. And then,
having perfected my technique, I dared
to indulge in dreams of creativity.
I started to compose; but on the quiet,
in secret, not yet nursing thoughts of fame.
Sometimes, alone in my retreat, I'd sit
for days on end, forgetting sleep and food, but
relishing inspiration's thrills and tears –
and then I'd burn my work and coldly watch

the musical ideas that I'd created   30
flare up, and disappear in puffs of smoke.
What next, then? When that great composer Gluck*
came and divulged to us his magic spells
(yes, deep and potent magic) – what did I do?
I threw aside all that I'd learnt before,
all that I'd loved, believed in, with such fervour;
I stepped out after Gluck* without a qualm,
unquestioning – just like a man who's lost
and someone sends him off the other way.
By strenuous and dogged perseverance   40
at last I made it to the top in music,
an art form without frontiers; and I won
a smiling reputation; with the public
my compositions struck an answering chord.
Now I was happy, and I could enjoy
my work, success and fame in peace – and, too,
the works and the successes of my friends,
comrades in the sublimest of the arts.
I never felt the slightest jealousy,
no, never! – not when Niccolò Piccini*   50
bewitched unruly Paris with his operas,
nor when my ears first heard the opening bars
of Gluck's great *Iphigénie en Tauride.*
Who'd say that I, with all my self-respect,
could stoop to be a jealous man, a snake
that's trampled underfoot, but still lives on,
biting the sand and dust in impotence?
No one could say that! Yet I'll tell you frankly –
I *am* now jealous with a jealousy
intense, excruciating. – heaven above!   60
Where is your justice, when you send your sacred
gift, your immortal spark, not to reward
fervent devotion, or self-abnegation,
or hard work, or enthusiasm, or prayer –
but as a halo for an idiot,
an idle good-for-nothing?... Mozart, Mozart!

(Enter Mozart.)

MOZART

You saw me coming, eh! And I was wanting
to give you a surprise and make you laugh.

SALIERI

You've been here... long?

MOZART

                   No. I was on my way here,
to bring you something that I wished to show you;   70
but, just as I walked past an eating house,
I heard a violin. No, dear Salieri,
you've never in your life heard anything
so funny... In the bar a blind old fiddler
was playing – guess what! – my *Voi che sapete!**
I couldn't help bringing the old man here
to treat you to a violin recital.
Come in!

(Enter an old blind man with a violin.)

          Play us some Mozart, if you please.

(The old man plays an aria from Don Giovanni*; Mozart bursts into laughter.)*

SALIERI

And you can laugh?

MOZART

                Oh yes. But you, Salieri –
I can't believe that you're not laughing.

SALIERI

                    No.   80
I can't laugh when some clumsy builder's painter

caricatures a Raphael Madonna;
I can't laugh when some pitiful buffoon
dishonours Dante with a parody.
Be off, old man.

MOZART

A moment, wait: take this,
drink to my health.

(The old man leaves.)

Salieri, my old friend,
You're out of sorts today. I'll visit you
another time.

SALIERI

What is it that you've brought me?

MOZART

No – let it be; it's nothing. The other night I
had an attack of my insomnia,   90
and two or three ideas came to my head.
I've scrawled them down today; and I just wanted
to take your view of them; but other things
are on your mind today.

SALIERI

Oh Mozart, Mozart!
When have I too much on my mind for you?
Sit down; I'm listening.

MOZART *(at the fortepiano)*

Think of someone... who?
Well, me perhaps – when I was rather younger;
in love – not too much, slightly – and I'm with
a pretty girl, or with a friend – like you –
I'm cheerful... Then, a ghostly apparition   100
and sudden murk, or something similar*...
Just listen, then.

(He plays.)

SALIERI

               And you were on your way
to me with this, then stopped off at a café
to listen to that blind old fiddler! – Good God!
Mozart, you are unworthy of yourself.

MOZART

You think it's good?

SALIERI

               There's such profundity,
such ingenuity, such elegance!
You are a god, Mozart, and you don't know it;
I know it though.

MOZART

               Pah! Really? I suppose…
You know, this god of yours is feeling hungry.   110

SALIERI

Well, listen: why don't we dine out together,
down at the Golden Lion.

MOZART

               By all means;
delighted. But just let me first go home
to tell my wife not to expect me back
to dinner.

(He goes out.)

SALIERI

               I'll be waiting; do take care.
No! It's beyond me further to resist
my calling: destiny has chosen me
to stop him; otherwise we're – all of us,
priests, servitors of music – we're all finished,

137

yes, not just me with my dull reputation…   120
What future's there for us, with Mozart living*
and rising ever upwards to new heights?
Will he thereby raise music's standing? No;
it'll slump again as soon as he's departed:
he'll leave us no enduring heritage.
What good will that do? Like some heavenly angel
he's brought us down a few ethereal anthems
only to rouse in us poor wraiths of dust
impotent aspirations – and fly off.
Well then, get flying! And good riddance to you.   130

Here's poison – the last gift of my Isora.
I've carried it with me these eighteen years –
and often since I've felt that life's no better
than a repulsive sore, and I have sat
at table with an unsuspecting foe,
and heard temptation whispering, but never
have I giv'n way to it – and I'm not squeamish;
indeed I'm one to nurse offences deeply,
and prize life little. Each time, though, I've paused.
Although I've been tormented by this death lust,   140
I've thought, "Why should I die? It may be life
will bring me nice surprises after all;
maybe I'll feel a new enthusiasm,
a new urge to create, new inspiration;
maybe a second Haydn* will compose
some masterpiece, one that'll give me pleasure…"
Or, as I've dined with my obnoxious guest,
I've thought, "Maybe I'll find another such
worse still; maybe, a worse offence
will strike me from an overpowering height" –   150
Isora's gift would not then go to waste.
And I was right! At last now I have found
my enemy. A second Haydn *has*
now brought me pleasures that have stirred my being!
The time has come! That potent gift love gave me
will pass today into a loving cup.*

Scene 2
A Private Room in a Restaurant; a Fortepiano

Mozart and Salieri at table.

SALIERI

You seem downcast today – why's that?

MOZART

       Me? No!

SALIERI

Something's upset you, Mozart, I can tell.
The dinner's good, the wine is marvellous;
but you keep frowning and don't talk.

MOZART

         It's true:
my *Requiem* is troubling me.

SALIERI

      Oh really?
A requiem you're writing then? Since when?

MOZART

For some time, three weeks. But a strange event…
Haven't I told you?

SALIERI

   No.

MOZART

      Well, listen then.*
It was three weeks ago; I came back home
quite late. They told me someone had kept calling,
asking to see me. Why, I can't think – but
I spent the whole night wondering who it was.
What could he want from me? The morning after
the same man came, and once again he missed me.

10

139

The third day I was playing on the floor
with my young son.* The servants called for me.
I went out. And a man dressed all in black
greeted me civilly, asked me to compose
a requiem, then vanished. There and then I
sat down and started writing. Since that time   20
my man in black has never been again.
But I'm quite happy: I'd be loath to part
with my new work, although it's now quite finished,
this requiem. But meantime I...

SALIERI

Yes, what?

MOZART
   I feel ashamed to tell you...

SALIERI

Tell me what?

MOZART
   My man in black troubles me day and night,
gives me no peace. He chases after me
like my own shadow. There! – I see him now,
or seem to see him, sitting at our table
with us.

SALIERI
       No more of this! These fears are childish.   30
Give up this fantasizing. Beaumarchais*
used to say this to me: "Salieri, listen,
my friend," he'd say, "when black thoughts come to you,
uncork a bottle of champagne, or else
reread my *Mariage de Figaro*."

MOZART
   Oh yes! You were a friend of Beaumarchais;
you wrote the music for his script *Tarare*,*

a splendid opera. There's one tune in it...
It goes round in my head when I am happy...
La la la la*... Oh, is it true, Salieri,   40
that Beaumarchais gave someone poison?*

SALIERI
I think not: he was far too fond of fun*
for any business such as that.

MOZART
                        A genius! –
like you, and me. And genius and murder
are surely two things that don't go together.

SALIERI
You think so?

(He drops the poison into Mozart's glass.)

                Have a drink now.

MOZART
                        To your health,
my friend, and to the real bond that joins us,
that joins together Mozart and Salieri,
brothers in harmony.

(He drinks.)

SALIERI
                Wait, Mozart, stop,
stop, stop!... You've drained the glass!... What about me?   50

MOZART *(throwing his napkin onto the table)*
Well, that's enough, I'm full.

(He goes to the fortepiano.)

                    Salieri, listen –
my *Requiem. (He plays)* You're crying?

SALIERI

                                        These are tears
I've never wept before – pain and relief,
as though I've just fulfilled a weighty duty,
as though the surgeon's knife has just cut off
an aching limb! Mozart, my friend, these tears...
ignore them. Go on playing; just get on
and fill my soul once more with gorgeous music...

MOZART

If only everyone felt music's power
like you! But no; if that were so,   60
the world could not go on; there would be no one
to take care of our lower human needs;
they'd all be artists, living lives of freedom.
But as it is we're few, we lucky idlers,
select band, who despise utility
and disregard it, priests in Beauty's service.
Isn't that so? But I am out of sorts now;
I feel worn out; I'll go; I'll have a sleep.
Goodbye, then!

SALIERI

                    Au revoir!

(alone)

                        You'll have a sleep,
a long sleep, Mozart! But he's surely wrong –   70
aren't I a genius? "Genius and murder
are two things that don't go together." Wrong:
take Michelangelo. Or is it just
a stupid tale the mindless rabble tell – and
the Vatican's architect was *not* a killer?*

*The Stone Guest**

List of Scenes

Scene 1: Outside the gates of Madrid, by a cemetery, towards evening
Scene 2: A room, a dinner a Laura's, later that evening
Scene 3: The Knight Commander's monument
Scene 4: A room of Doña Ana's, the following evening

Characters (in order of appearance)

Don Juan,* a Spanish nobleman, exiled by the King
Leporello, Don Juan's servant
A monk at St Anthony's monastery
Doña Ana de Solva, the Knight Commander's widow
Laura, an eighteen-year-old actress
Guests at Laura's dinner
Don Carlos, the Knight Commander's brother
Statue of the Knight Commander Don Alvaro, killed earlier in a fight
with Don Juan

LEPORELLO:
  O statua gentilissima
  del gran Commendatore…
  *Ah, Padrone!**

                        – *Don Giovanni*

Scene 1

Don Juan and Leporello.

DON JUAN

Let's wait for nightfall here. Phew, now at last
we've reached Madrid! Here are the gates. I'll soon go
flitting along those streets I know so well,
my cloak wrapped round my whiskers, and my hat
over my eyes. Well? Nobody must know me.*

LEPORELLO

Oh yes! No one will recognize Don Juan!
Thousands there are that look like him!

DON JUAN

                                    You're joking!
Well, who will recognize me?

LEPORELLO

                        The first one
you meet – night watchman, Gypsy girl, drunk singer,
or any brazen ladies' man like you,   10
with sword at ready underneath his cloak.

DON JUAN

So what if I am recognized? As long
as I don't meet the King. In any case
there's no one in Madrid that I'm afraid of.

LEPORELLO

Tomorrow news is sure to reach the King
that you, Don Juan, have turned up in Madrid,
jumping your banishment – so, tell me, what
will he do with you then?

DON JUAN

               Just send me back.
He won't cut off my head,* for sure. Oh no,
I'm not accused of crimes against the state.   20
The King sent me to exile as a kindness,
so that the murder victim's kith and kin
should leave me in peace...

LEPORELLO

              Yes, that's my point exactly!
You could have stayed there safe and undisturbed.

DON JUAN

Oh, very helpful! I quite nearly died
of boredom there. Abominable people!
And what a country! Skies as grey as smoke.*
The women? I can tell you, Leporello,
you dimwit, I would not exchange the last
girl from an Andalusian country village   30
for their best-looking creatures – that's the truth.
I liked them well enough at the beginning,
with those blue eyes of theirs, their pale complexions,
their shyness – most of all their novelty;
but thank the Lord, I soon got wise to them –
time spent with them's a wicked waste, I realized:
there's no life in them – waxworks, that's all they are.
But *our* girls!... Listen though, this place we're in,
it seems familiar; do you recognize it?

LEPORELLO

Of course I do! I know this monastery –   40
St Anthony's. You used to ride here often,
and I would mind our horses in those trees.
The devil of a job that was, you know.
Believe me, your time here was better spent
than mine.

DON JUAN *(reflectively)*
>   Yes, I remember. Poor Iñez!
> She's gone now; but I loved her then so much.

LEPORELLO
> Iñez!... Oh, that's the dark-eyed one... yes, I know.
> You traipsed round after her for three whole months,
> until at last the Devil lent a hand.

DON JUAN
> It was July... one night. Her mournful eyes,   50
> her lips so deathly pale – they had a strange
> attraction for me. Yes, it's very odd.
> You didn't find her beautiful at all,
> I think. And truth to tell, there wasn't much
> of real beauty in her. Just her eyes,
> those eyes. That look of hers – I've never once
> met such a look again. Her voice, though – that
> was soft and faint, just like an invalid's –
> her husband was an evil brute, you know,
> I found out later... Oh my poor Iñez!*   60

LEPORELLO
> Well, you've had plenty after her.

DON JUAN
>   That's right.

LEPORELLO
> And while we're living, there'll be more, I'm sure.

DON JUAN
> Yes, right again.

LEPORELLO
>   So in Madrid today
> which of them are we looking up?

DON JUAN

                             Oh, Laura.
I'll hurry straight to see her.

LEPORELLO

                            Carry on!

DON JUAN

I'll go straight in – and if there's anyone
already with her – I'll show them the window.

LEPORELLO

Why ever not? Well, we *have* brightened up.
Dead girls don't trouble us for very long.
But who's approaching now?

(Enter a monk.)

MONK

                        She'll soon be here.   70
Who're you? Would you be Doña Ana's people?

LEPORELLO

No, we are gentlemen here privately,
just to enjoy ourselves.

DON JUAN

                     Who're you expecting?

MONK

Well, Doña Ana should be here quite soon to
visit her husband's tomb.

DON JUAN

                    Oh, Doña Ana
de Solva? – well! – wife of the Knight Commander*
killed by... by whom? I can't think.

MONK

> By that godless
pervert without a conscience, called Don Juan.

LEPORELLO

Aha, that's something! Don Juan's reputation
has even reached this peaceful monastery;   80
even the monks have learnt to chant his praises!

MONK

You know him then it seems?

LEPORELLO

> Oh no, not us.
But where is he right now?

MONK

> He's not round here;
he's far away in exile.

LEPORELLO

> God be thanked.
The further off, the better. All these perverts,
into one sack, I say; then in the sea.

DON JUAN

What! What's that nonsense?

LEPORELLO

> Quiet! I'm purposely...

DON JUAN

So this is where the Knight Commander's buried?

MONK

Yes, here. His wife put up a monument;
she drives out here to visit it each day   90
and to say prayers for her poor husband's soul
and to shed tears.

151

DON JUAN

Strange conduct for a widow!
She's not bad looking, is she?

MONK

Monks like us
are not supposed to notice women's looks;
but lying is a sin – and there's no saint
who'd not grant she's a miracle of beauty.

DON JUAN

No wonder her late husband was so jealous.
He kept his poor wife under lock and key,
not one of us could get a glimpse of her.
I'd dearly like a brief word with the lady.   100

MONK

Oh, Doña Ana will not speak with men
at all.

DON JUAN

And you – what about you then, Father?

MONK

With me it's different. I am a monk.
But here she is.

(Enter Doña Ana.)

DOÑA ANA

My Father, open please.

MONK

Immediately, señora. I've been waiting.

(Doña Ana goes after the monk.)

LEPORELLO
  Well, what of her?

DON JUAN
              I couldn't see a thing
  beneath that long black widow's veil she wore;
  I just observed the slenderest little heel.

LEPORELLO
  Enough for you. Your rich imagination
  will picture all the rest of her in no time;   110
  it's speedier than any portrait painter;
  you've no concern at all which bit you start from,
  eyebrow or foot.*

DON JUAN
              Just listen, Leporello,
  I mean to get to know her.

LEPORELLO
              Not again!
  That's all we needed. First he fells the husband,
  and then he wants to watch the widow's tears.
  Incorrigible!

DON JUAN
              But it's dark already.
  Before the moonlight shines out high above us
  and turns the darkness back to glowing twilight,
  let's go into Madrid.

LEPORELLO
              A Spanish noble   120
  waits like a thief for night and shuns the moon –
  good God! A devil's life. For how much longer
  must I put up with him? Oh give me strength!

Scene 2
A Room; a Dinner at Laura's

FIRST GUEST
Laura, upon my oath I've never seen you
acting with such perfection as today.
You showed such understanding of your role!

SECOND GUEST
And you developed it so well, so strongly!

THIRD GUEST
And with such artistry!

LAURA
                Yes, every line
and every gesture came off as I wanted.
I just let inspiration take me over.
It didn't seem I'd slaved to memorize
each word, they flowed spontaneously...

FIRST GUEST
                      That's true.
And even now your eyes are still aglow,   10
your cheeks are burning, you've not lost the rapture
that fired your acting. Laura, don't allow it
to die down uselessly. Sing to us, Laura,
sing something.

LAURA
           All right, hand me my guitar

(*She sings.*)

EVERYONE
Oh, good for you! Amazing! Nothing like it!

FIRST GUEST
We thank you. You are magical – and you have
bewitched our inner beings. Of life's pleasures
music takes second place only to love.
And love too is a melody… Look there:
even your surly guest Carlos is moved.   20

SECOND GUEST
What lovely music! So much feeling in it!
But whose words are they, Laura?

LAURA
                              They're Don Juan's.

DON CARLOS
Don Juan's, you say?

LAURA
                    Yes, that true friend of mine,
my errant lover – he once wrote those words.

DON CARLOS
That friend of yours Don Juan's a godless villain,
and you, you are his dupe.

LAURA
                          Have you gone mad?
I've half a mind to ask my serving men
to cut your throat, despite your noble birth.

DON CARLOS *(standing up)*
Then call them in.

FIRST GUEST
                   Oh Laura, do give over.
Don Carlos, don't be angry. She forgot…   30

LAURA

Forgot what? That Don Juan killed that man's brother
in a fair duel? Yes, a shame it wasn't
him that Juan killed!

DON CARLOS

                I'm stupid to've been angry.

LAURA

Aha! Then you admit that you are stupid.
Let's make it up then.

DON CARLOS

            It was my fault, Laura,
forgive me. But you know, I simply cannot
hear that man's name and keep my self-control...

LAURA

And is it my fault that with every minute
that name keeps coming back onto my tongue?

GUEST

Now just to show that you're no longer angry,   40
Laura – another song.

LAURA

              To say goodbye,
all right. Time's up; it's night. What shall I sing?
Listen to this, then. (*She sings.*)

EVERYONE

           Charming! Quite superb!

LAURA

Goodbye, then, gentlemen.

GUESTS

          And goodbye, Laura.

(They go out. Laura detains Don Carlos.)

LAURA

You wicked fellow! Stay behind with me.
I've come to like you. You reminded me of
Don Juan, the way you picked a fight with me
and clenched your teeth and snarled.

DON CARLOS

                         The lucky man!

So you did love him?

(Laura makes a sign of affirmation.)

                Very much?

LAURA

                Yes, very.

DON CARLOS

You love him now?

LAURA

                You mean this very minute?   50
No, not now. I can't love two men at once.
Now I love you.

DON CARLOS

             So tell me this, then, Laura:
how old are you this year?

LAURA

               I'm eighteen now.

DON CARLOS

You're very young... and you will still be young
in five or six years' time. For six more years
or so the men will jostle close around you,

caress you, fondle you, load you with gifts,
amuse you with nocturnal serenades, and
to win your love kill one another off
at night-time by some crossroads. But those years   60
will pass, and then you'll find your eyes grown sunken,
your eyelids leaden grey and creased with wrinkles,
and your dark tresses showing streaks of white,
and they'll begin to call you an old hag,
then – what will you say then?

LAURA

                        Then? Why do I
need think about that? What a conversation!
Are these the things that always fill your mind?
Come here – onto the balcony. The sky's calm;
no movement in the warm air – and the night
breathes bay and lemon, and a brilliant moon   70
is shining in that deep, dark indigo –
I hear the watchmen drawling out, "Fine weather!"*...
But far away, up north – in Paris, say –
the sky may well be shrouded in dark clouds,
with cold rain falling, and a fierce wind blowing.
But what is that to us? Now listen, Carlos,
I order you to give me a nice smile;
ah, that's much better!

DON CARLOS

                    Lovely witch!

(Knocking.)

DON JUAN

                           Hey! Laura!

LAURA
Who's there? Whose voice is that?

DON JUAN

Just open up…

LAURA

It can't be!… Oh, my God!…

(She opens the doors; in comes Don Juan.)

DON JUAN

Hallo…

LAURA

Don Juan!   80

(Laura throws herself around his neck.)

DON CARLOS
What did you say? Don Juan!

DON JUAN

My Laura! Darling!… *(kisses her)*
But Laura, who's here with you?

DON CARLOS

It is me,
Don Carlos.

DON JUAN

Here's an unexpected meeting!
Tomorrow I'll be at your service.

DON CARLOS

No!
No, now – immediately.

LAURA

Don Carlos, stop!
You're not out in the street – you're in my house.
Please go outside.

159

DON CARLOS *(not listening to her)*
> I'm waiting. Well, your answer?
You've brought your sword along, of course.

DON JUAN
>   If you're so
impatient, then by all means. *(They fight.)*

LAURA
>   Hey! Hey! Juan!…

(She throws herself on the bed. Don Carlos falls.)

DON JUAN
Get up now, Laura, it's all over.

LAURA
>   Is he –   90
dead? There's a fine thing! And in my room too!
What shall I do now? – good-for-nothing, fiend!
Where can I dump him?

DON JUAN
>   Wait: maybe he's still
alive.

LAURA
>   Alive! Yes, damn you! Take a look,
you've run his heart through – you've not missed, don't worry;
the blood's not oozing from the rapier's hole,
and he's stopped breathing… Well?

DON JUAN
>   It can't be helped.
He asked for it, and got it.

LAURA
>   Ugh, Don Juan,
you really are a pest. Always in trouble –

and never *your* fault... So, where have you come from?   100
Have you been here for long?

DON JUAN

                      I've just arrived –
in secret, though – I've not yet got my pardon.

LAURA

And you thought of your Laura straightaway?
Oh, very nice! But don't you give me that,
I don't believe it. You were passing by,
and just spotted the house.

DON JUAN

                    No, Laura dear,
ask Leporello, I've been lying low
in dreadful lodgings* out of town. I'm in
Madrid just to find you. *(He kisses her.)*

LAURA

                    My darling Juan!...
But wait... the corpse!... what can we do with it?   110

DON JUAN

Just leave it – very early, before daybreak,
I'll take it out of here beneath my cloak
and drop it at a crossroads.

LAURA

                    Very well,
but do take care that no one sees you do it.
It was a good thing you came when you did,
and not a minute earlier. Your friends
were having dinner with me. They had only
just gone away. If you had met them here!...

DON JUAN
Laura, had this man been your lover long?

LAURA

Who, him? You must be joking!

DON JUAN

                          But confess now,   120
how many other men have you made love to
since I went off?

LAURA

               And you, how many women?

DON JUAN

Just tell me... No, let's talk about it later.

Scene 3
The Knight Commander's Monument

DON JUAN

All's for the best: I've unexpectedly
dispatched Don Carlos; now I'm hiding here,
dressed as a lowly monk – and I get daily
sight of my lovely widow; I think, too,
she's noticed me. Till now we've done no more
than trade formalities; but I intend today
to get her into conversation; time's up!
How to begin? "May I presume?..." P'rhaps not;
"Señora?..." Pah! I'll say whatever comes
into my head, without premeditation;   10
I'll improvise the music of my love...
It must be time for her to come. I think,
without her the Commander's getting tetchy.
What a gigantic statue they have made!
What massive shoulders – quite a Hercules!...
And yet in life the man was short and puny:
if he'd stood here on tiptoe he could not have
reached with his hand the tip of his own nose.
In our set-to behind the Escorial*

162

he ran onto my rapier and expired –   20
a dragonfly upon a pin! – yet he was
self-confident and plucky – and determined*...
But here she is!

DOÑA ANA

                    He's here again. Oh Father,
I've interrupted your deep contemplations –
I'm sorry.

DON JUAN

                    It's for me to apologize
to you, señora. I fear *I* am hindering
you from submitting wholly to your grief.

DOÑA ANA

No, Father, my grief lies deep down within me;
your presence is not hindering my prayers
from rising humbly heav'nwards – I just ask   30
you too to join your prayerful voice to mine.

DON JUAN

Me join my prayers with yours! – oh Doña Ana,
I am unworthy of so high a calling.
I should not dare, with these vile lips of mine,
even to say the same prayers after you.
I only watch in worship from afar
how when you bend low at the grave you let
your dark hair spill out on the marble's
whiteness. I tell myself that it's an angel
who in disguise is visiting this tomb,   40
and I'm so agitated down inside
that I can't pray then. I just marvel, tongue-tied,
and think – lucky's the man whose stone-cold tomb
is warmed by such a heavenly being's breath
and moistened by the tears that prove her love...

DOÑA ANA

These words – astonish me.

DON JUAN

              Why so, señora?

DOÑA ANA
  I... You've forgotten.

DON JUAN

            What? That all I am
  is an unworthy monk? That I, a sinner,
  am wrong to raise my voice so loudly here?

DOÑA ANA
  It seemed to me... I didn't realize...   50

DON JUAN
  Ah, now I see! You've grasped the situation!

DOÑA ANA
  Grasped what?

DON JUAN

        That – yes – I'm not a monk at all –
  I lie down at your feet to beg forgiveness.

DOÑA ANA
  Oh heaven above! Get up... Who are you then?

DON JUAN
  The wretched victim of a hopeless passion

DOÑA ANA
  Oh heaven! Here, too, even at this grave!
  Be off with you.

DON JUAN

          A minute, Doña Ana,
  one minute!

DOÑA ANA

No, there may be someone coming!...

DON JUAN

The iron gate is locked. Oh, just one minute!

DOÑA ANA

Well? What? What are you asking for?

DON JUAN

To die.   60

Oh let me die now at your very feet,
and let them bury my poor body here,
not right beside the body of your loved one,
not just here – not so near – but farther off,
there by the gates, right at the very entrance,
so that you'll touch my gravestone with your foot,
your slender foot, or with the dress you're wearing,
when you come here, to this imposing tomb,
to bow your lovely head of hair and weep.

DOÑA ANA

You are insane.

DON JUAN

Is this insanity,   70

to want to end my life here, Doña Ana?
No, if I *were* insane, I would be wanting
to stay among the living; I'd be hoping
that my devoted love might touch your heart;
no, if I were insane, I'd stay for nights
not moving from beneath your balcony,
singing you serenades to stop you sleeping;
I wouldn't wear disguises; far from that,
I'd try to attract your notice everywhere;
no, if I were insane, I'd not put up   80
with suffering in silence...

DOÑA ANA

                              Oh, you call this
  silence?

DON JUAN

          It was an accident, that's all,
    that led me to admit… if not, you'd never
    have learnt the secret of my misery.

DOÑA ANA

  And have you been in love with me for long?

DON JUAN

    I do not know myself how long it is; but
    it's only now I've come to value life
    in all its brevity; it's only now
    I've come to grasp what happiness must mean.

DOÑA ANA

  Be off with you – a dangerous fellow *you* are.   90

DON JUAN

  Dangerous? Why so?

DOÑA ANA

                            It frightens me to hear you.

DON JUAN

    I'll say no more then; but don't chase away
    someone whose only joy is gazing on you.
    I nurse no hopes of which you need be fearful,
    I ask for nothing; it's just that I need
    to look upon you, if I am condemned
    to live on.

DOÑA ANA

              No – go. This is not the place
    for talk and senseless conduct like this. Come to

my house tomorrow. If you swear that you'll
behave to me with the same self-restraint,   100
I'll let you in – but later – in the evening.
I've not been seeing anyone at home
since I was widowed...

DON JUAN

                Doña Ana, angel!
God grant you consolation, just as you've
today consoled this wretched, suffering soul.

DOÑA ANA

Do go away now.

DON JUAN

             Still one minute longer.

DOÑA ANA

No, I shall go, then... I'm in any case
not in the mood for prayer now. You've distracted
me with your worldly talk; I've long since been
unused to hearing that. Tomorrow you   110
may visit me at home.

DON JUAN

              I daren't believe it,
I daren't trust in my newfound happiness...
I'm to see you tomorrow! – and not here,
not in disguise!

DOÑA ANA

           Tomorrow, yes, tomorrow.
Your name – what is it?

DON JUAN

           Diego de Calvado.

DOÑA ANA
Goodbye, Don Diego. *(She leaves.)*

DON JUAN
Hey there, Leporello!

(Enter Leporello.)

LEPORELLO
What is your wish, sir?

DON JUAN
My dear Leporello!
Great news!... Tomorrow, "later in the evening"...
tomorrow, Leporello – get things ready...
I'm happy as a sandboy!

LEPORELLO
You've been talking
with Doña Ana, have you? I suppose
she spoke two condescending words to you,
or you gave her your benediction, eh?

DON JUAN
No, Leporello, no! She's promised me
a meeting, yes, a meeting.

LEPORELLO
You don't say!
They're all the same, these widows.

DON JUAN
I'm so happy!
I want to sing, to give the world a hug.

LEPORELLO
The Knight Commander? What will *he* make of it?

120

168

DON JUAN

    You think he's likely to be jealous, then?
    I'm sure not. He's a reasonable fellow,   130
    he'll certainly have calmed down since he died.

LEPORELLO

    Oh no, he hasn't. Just look at his statue.

DON JUAN

    Well, what of it?

LEPORELLO

                    I think it's eyeing you
    angrily.

DON JUAN

         Well, go on then, Leporello,
    ask it to kindly come down to my place –
    not mine, to Doña Ana's, yes, tomorrow.

LEPORELLO

    Invite a statue? Why on earth?

DON JUAN

                       Well not
    for me to have a chat with it, for sure!
    Just ask the statue down to Doña Ana's
    later tomorrow evening, to stand guard   140
    beside the door.

LEPORELLO

             I know you like a joke;
    with *him*, though!

DON JUAN

           Just go on.

LEPORELLO

But…

DON JUAN

Yes, go on.

LEPORELLO
Most handsome statue, most distinguished statue!
Don Juan my master humbly begs Your Grace
to kindly come… God help me! No, I can't,
I'm frightened.

DON JUAN

Ninny! I'll give you!…

LEPORELLO

I'm sorry.
Don Juan my master begs of you to come
later tomorrow down to your wife's house
and stand beside the door…

(The statue nods its head in assent.)

Aah!

DON JUAN

What's that?

LEPORELLO

Aa-ah!

Aa-ah!… I'm done for!

DON JUAN

What's got into you?   150

LEPORELLO *(nodding his head)*
The statue… aah!

DON JUAN

        You're nodding.

LEPORELLO

                    No, I'm not;
the *statue* is!

DON JUAN

        What stupid talk is this?

LEPORELLO

Just come yourself.

DON JUAN

           Now, you watch out, you rogue.
(To the statue) I ask you, Knight Commander, to come down
tomorrow to your widow's – I'll be there –
and to stand guard beside the doors. You'll come?

(The statue nods again.)

Good God!

LEPORELLO

        Well then? I told you...

DON JUAN

                Time to go.

Scene 4*
A Room of Doña Ana's

Don Juan and Doña Ana.

DOÑA ANA

Don Diego, I've allowed you in. I'm just
afraid that you'll find my glum conversation

too tedious: poor widow that I am,
I'm always mindful of my loss. I'm tears
and smiles mixed up together, just like April.*
But why are you so quiet?

DON JUAN

                                I'm enjoying
quietly, deep within, the thought of being
alone with lovely Doña Ana – here,
not by that lucky fellow's monument, but
here, where I see you no more on your knees   10
before your marble consort.

DOÑA ANA

                                You're so jealous,
Don Diego! – Does my husband needle you,
even though he's dead?

DON JUAN

                                I've no right to be jealous.
He was the one you chose.

DOÑA ANA

                                No, actually
my mother made me marry Don Alvaro;
our family was poor, and he was rich.*

DON JUAN

The lucky man! He laid his paltry treasures
at a goddess's feet, and in return
he won a taste of heavenly bliss. If I had
known you before, it would have been such rapture   20
for me to give up rank, and wealth, and all,
yes all, just for one kindly glance from you;
I'd have been your alert and loyal slave,
I would have made a study of your whims
to meet them in advance, so that your life

would have been an enchantment without end.
Alas! – My fate decided otherwise.

DOÑA ANA

Stop, Diego: as I listen to your words,
I'm being led astray – I must not love you.
A widow should remain true to the dead.   30
If you could know how Don Alvaro used
to love me! Oh, if I had died before him,
I'm sure he'd not have loved another woman
or formed any attachment; he'd have been,
I'm sure, true to his wife.

DON JUAN

                Please, Doña Ana,
don't cause me pain by constantly recalling
your husband. You have punished me enough,
though I've deserved it, maybe.

DOÑA ANA

                 How is that?
You are not bound by ties of marriage, are you,
to anyone? In feeling love for me   40
you're blameless both in Heaven's eyes and in mine.

DON JUAN

Blameless in your eyes? God!

DOÑA ANA

                But surely you've
done *me* no wrong? What is it? Tell me.

DON JUAN

                      No,
I'll not say. Never.

DOÑA ANA

             Diego, what's the matter?

So have you wronged me? Tell me, in what way?

DON JUAN
  No, not for anything.

DOÑA ANA
                    What strange behaviour!
  I beg you, Diego – I insist.

DON JUAN
                    No, no.

DOÑA ANA
  So that's how you anticipate my whims!
  What was it that you said to me just now?
  That you'd like to have been my "loyal slave".   50
  I shall get angry, Diego: answer me,
  how is it you have wronged me?

DON JUAN
                    I daren't say.
  You'd loathe me if I told you what I've done.

DOÑA ANA
  Oh no, no. I forgive you in advance,
  But I just wish to know—

DON JUAN
                    Don't wish to know –
  the secret is a dreadful, murderous one.

DOÑA ANA
  Dreadful and murderous! You're tormenting me.
  I desperately want to know – what is it?
  And how could you have done me injury?
  I didn't know you – I've no enemies,   60
  and never had. The murderer of my husband's
  the only one.

DON JUAN

    (To himself) We're coming to the crunch now!
    Tell me: Don Juan, the unfortunate Don Juan –
    d'you know him?

DOÑA ANA

               No, never in all my life
    have I seen him.

DON JUAN

              But in your heart you rate
    him as your enemy?

DOÑA ANA

              I'm honour bound
    to do so. But you're trying to distract me
    from what I've just been asking you, Don Diego –
    I do insist...

DON JUAN

             But what if you did meet
    Don Juan?

DOÑA ANA

           Why, then I'd plunge a dagger blade   70
    into the villain's heart.

DON JUAN

           Well, Doña Ana,
    where is your dagger? Here's my heart.*

DOÑA ANA

                   Don Diego!
    What *do* you?...

DON JUAN

          I'm not Diego, I am Juan.

DOÑA ANA

Good God! It can't be. No, I don't believe it.

DON JUAN

I *am* Don Juan.

DOÑA ANA

                You're not.

DON JUAN

                        I am the man
who killed your husband; and I've no regrets
about it – I don't feel the least remorse.

DOÑA ANA

What do you say? No, no, it cannot be.

DON JUAN

I am Don Juan, and I'm in love with you.

DOÑA ANA *(falling)*

Where am I?… Where?… I'm fainting, faint…

DON JUAN

                                    Oh heaven!   80
What's wrong with her? What is it, Doña Ana?
Get up, get up, come to, come round: your Diego,
your slave is at your feet.

DOÑA ANA

                      Leave me alone!
(faintly) Oh, you're my enemy – it's you that robbed me
of all I had in life…

DON JUAN

                My dearest creature!
Whatever would redeem my crime I'll do;

here at your feet I'm waiting for your orders:
at your command I'll die; at your command
I'll breathe again – for you.

DOÑA ANA

So here's Don Juan...

DON JUAN

I've been described to you – is it not so? –   90
as villain, monster, and – yes, Doña Ana –
maybe the rumour's not completely false;
maybe there is a heavy weight of evil
pressing my weary conscience. I have long
been a keen student of depravity.*
But ever since the time that I first saw you,
it seems to me that I've been born anew.
In love with you, I'm in love too with goodness,
and, for the first time, on my trembling knees
I worship goodness in humility.   100

DOÑA ANA

Oh, Don Juan's fine at talking – I know that,
I've heard them say – and expert at seduction.
You're said to be a godless debauchee, the
devil incarnate. How many poor women
have you destroyed?

DON JUAN

There's not been up to now
a single one I loved.

DOÑA ANA

Should I believe
that this is the first time Don Juan's in love,
that I'm not just the latest of his victims?

DON JUAN

If I had really wanted to deceive you,

177

would I have confessed, would I have voiced the name,   110
the very name that you can't bear to hear?
What sign's there here of deviousness, of cunning?

DOÑA ANA

Oh, who can know your mind?* – But how was it
you got here? People could have recognized you;
your death then would have been a certainty.

DON JUAN

What does death mean? For one brief, sweet reunion
I'd give up life without a murmur.

DOÑA ANA

                             How
careless you are! How will you get away?

DON JUAN (kissing her hands)

And you are anxious for the life of poor
Don Juan! So, is there after all no hatred   120
in my dear Doña Ana's heavenly soul?*

DOÑA ANA

Hatred, Don Juan! If only I could hate you!
But now we really must not stay together.

DON JUAN

When shall we meet again?

DOÑA ANA

                         I've no idea,
some time.

DON JUAN

        Tomorrow?

DOÑA ANA

                Where then?

DON JUAN

Why not here?

DOÑA ANA
Oh Don Juan, I am such a feeble soul.

DON JUAN
A kiss of peace, a sign that you forgive me…

DOÑA ANA
No time, dear. Go!

DON JUAN

One formal kiss of peace…

DOÑA ANA
You'll not accept the answer "no"! All right then. *(They kiss.)*
But what's that knocking? Quick, slip out, Don Juan.   130

DON JUAN
Goodbye, we'll meet tomorrow, dearest friend.

(He goes out and runs back in again.)

Ah!

DOÑA ANA
What's the matter? Ah!

(Enter the statue of the Knight Commander. Doña Ana faints.)

STATUE

I've come, as asked.

DON JUAN
My God! Oh Doña Ana!

STATUE

                    Let her go.
Everything's over now. Don Juan, you're trembling.

DON JUAN

  Me? No. I asked you here. I'm glad to see you.

STATUE

  Give me your hand.

DON JUAN

                  Here then… Oh, what a forceful
grip there is in this stone right arm of his!
Leave me alone; let go, let go my hand…
I'm dying – it's all over – Doña Ana!

(The earth swallows them up.)

A Feast during the Plague

*After John Wilson**

There is one scene:
A street in London during the summer of 1665

Characters (in order of appearance)

Young man
Edward Walsingham, President of the feast
Mary Gray, a Scottish prostitute
Louisa, another prostitute
A Negro
An elderly priest
Others attending the feast

A street. A table laid for a meal. A number of men and women feasting.

Young man

    With your leave, President, I rise to honour
    a man whom we all knew extremely well.
    He told good jokes; his stories made us laugh;
    his repartee was sharp-tongued; and his jibes
    were cutting in their sarcasm. All of this
    gave zest to conversation round our table
    and drove away the gloom with which these days
    the lady Pestilence, unwanted guest,
    smothers the very brightest wits among us.
    Only two days ago our bursts of laughter   10
    showed how we loved his anecdotes; there's no way,
    as we enjoy our food and drink, we can
    forget old Jackson!* Here's the chair he sat in,
    still empty, just as if it's waiting for
    our cheery friend – but he's now gone away
    to take new lodgings, underground and cold…
    It's true: no tongue more eloquent than his
    has yet been stilled in death's decomposition;
    but lots of us are still alive, so we've
    no cause to be downcast. And so I now   20
    propose a toast to Jackson's memory:
    be merry; clink your glasses; call his name,
    as though he were still with us.

President

                        He was first
    to leave our company. Let's drink his toast
    in silence.

Young man

              Very well, then. Let's do that.

(They all drink in silence.)

PRESIDENT
My dear girl, you've a lovely voice: you sing
your Scottish folk songs with such wild perfection;
sing us now, Mary, something slow and sombre,
so that we then can go back to our pleasures
with all the more abandon, just like someone   30
who's been transported by some dream, then wakes.*

MARY *(sings)*

1

*Time was when our peaceful village
was a happy, thriving place.
Every Sabbath thankful people
filled the kirk to laud God's grace;
in the schoolroom voices rang out –
ditties by our wee bairns sung;
and across the sunlit meadows
steel blades flashed as scythes were swung.*

2

Now the kirk has lost its people;   40
*school is silent, locked for good;
fields with uncut corn have ripened;
no one roams the darkened wood.
Derelict now stands the village,
like an empty burnt-out mill.
All is quiet; just the graveyard –
that's not empty, that's not still:*

3

*all the time they're bringing bodies;
and with wailing those who live*

pray in fear to their Creator 50
peace unto the dead to give.
All the time they need new spaces,
while the tombs of those who sleep
stand together crowding tightly,
like a flock of frightened sheep.

4

If my springtime's cut off early
blighted by a Fate too drear,
you, whom I have loved so dearly,
you, whose love's my only cheer,
keep away from your dead Jenny, 60
I implore you; don't come near;
don't press my cold lips with kisses;
follow far behind my bier.

5

Then depart this stricken village;
go away, go anywhere
where you may find rest and comfort
and relieve your soul's despair.
When the plague is past, then, Edmund,
come greet my poor dust so fond;
Jenny will stay true to Edmund 70
even in the world beyond.*

PRESIDENT
    We thank you, Mary, you're a thoughtful girl;
    we thank you for that melancholy song.
    It seems that long ago a plague like this
    swept through your local hills and valleys too,
    and that, like here, pathetic sobs were heard
    along the banks of brooks and rivers, which
    now flow in peace and cheerfulness amid
    those wild idyllic landscapes of your homeland.

185

And the dark year in which there fell so many   80
good folk and true as victims of the plague –
the only record that year's left behind
is in some simple shepherd's song, a sad one,
yet soothing too. No, there is really nothing
that so subdues our spirits during laughter
as a lament we can't drive from our minds.

MARY

If only I had never sung that song
outwith the croft where I dwelt with my parents!
They used to love to listen to their Mary;
even today I seem to hear myself   90
singing there by the house where I was born –
my voice was sweeter in those days: it was
a voice of innocence...

LOUISA

                         Oh, songs like that
are out of fashion now! But there are always
people naive enough to let themselves
be upset by a woman's tears – blind fools!
Mary's convinced that with a tear-stained face
she's irresistible – and if she thought the same
about her laugh, then to be sure she'd grin
the whole time. Walsingham told us he liked   100
plaintive girls from the north: so she obliged
with the right mournful noises. How I hate
these Scottish women's jaundice-yellow hair!

PRESIDENT

Shh! Listen: I can hear the noise of wheels!

(A cart trundles by, laden with dead bodies and steered by a Negro.)

Ah, look! Louisa's fainting; I had thought –
to judge her by her tongue – she had a man's heart.
Well, well – the harsh one's weaker than the gentle;

she's gripped with fear, despite her fierce emotions!
Mary, splash water in her face. That's better.

MARY

    My sister, we share sorrow and disgrace;   110
    rest yourself on my breast.*

LOUISA *(coming to)*

                          An awful demon
    appeared to me, all black, with staring eyes...
    He bade me climb into his barrow, where
    corpses were lying – and were jabbering
    away at me with strange and dreadful sounds*...
    Tell me: did I see all that in a dream?
    Did a cart just go past?

YOUNG MAN

                       Oh come, Louisa,
    cheer up. We have the whole street to ourselves;
    this is our quiet hideout from the plague,
    a place where we can dine out undisturbed.   120
    But even so, you surely know, that black cart
    has freedom to go anywhere it likes –
    we have to let it through. Now, Walsingham,
    please listen: we should cut our quarrels short
    and put these female fainting fits behind us,
    you sing to us, a free and lively song –
    not something prompted by Scots morbidness,
    but a rumbustious bacchanalian song,
    composed once you've imbibed some foaming wine.

PRESIDENT

    I don't know one like that. Instead I'll sing you   130
    a hymn in honour of the plague. I wrote it
    myself just last night, after we had parted.
    I felt a strange desire for words that rhyme,
    the first time in my life. So listen now:
    my voice is croaky, but it suits the song.*

MANY VOICES
    A hymn in honour of the plague! Let's hear it!
    Hymn to the plague! How splendid! Bravo, bravo!

PRESIDENT *(sings)**

1

> *When mighty Winter, like the head*
> *of a bold army boldly led,*
> *attacks us with her spiky squadrons*   140
> *of icicles and frost and snow –*
> *the fireplace parries with a crackle,*
> *the festive season's all aglow.*

2

> *But now the plague, that dreaded queen,*
> *is marching on us, feared, unseen,*
> *cocksure of an abundant harvest;*
> *and on our windows day and night*
> *she taps with her great graveyard shovel...*
> *we're trapped! Who'll help us in our plight?*

3

> *Just as on Winter's tricks before,*   150
> *so on Queen Plague let's lock our door!*
> *Let's light the torches, fill the glasses,*
> *and drown our minds in jollity,*
> *and, rousing feast and dance to frenzy,*
> *let's hail the Plague Queen's sovereignty!*

4

> *There is a thrill in waging war,*
> *or treading a dark chasm's door,*
> *or tossing on the ocean's fury*

'mid stormy gloom and seas that drench,
or braving an Arabian sandstorm,   160
or breathing in the plague's vile stench.

5

In anything that bids to kill
there lurks that strangely pleasing thrill
for mortal beings – could this offer
a pledge of immortality?
This thrill if man can find and savour
'mid all life's tempests, lucky he!

6

So – Plague, it's you we celebrate!
We've no dread of the tomb's dark gate;
your summons causes us no terror.   170
Let's breathe our girlfriends' fragrant breath,
and drink the foaming cup together –
what if we breathe, and drink, our death!

(Enter an old priest.)

PRIEST
These godless revels, godless revellers!
Death's sombre silence has spread everywhere;
yet you pollute it with your rowdyism –
this drinking, and these songs of blasphemy!
I've been at prayer in yonder churchyard, trying
to calm the mourners' horror, soothe their fears –
but your disgusting gaiety disturbs   180
the graveside's stillness; and it shakes down earth
in lumps over the bodies of the dead.
If the shared death pit had not been made holy
by old folk praying for the ones they'd lost,
I might have thought that it was demons now
tormenting the doomed souls of unbelievers
and jeering as they dragged them down to Hell.

SEVERAL VOICES
      The way he talks of Hell, he's quite an expert!
      Get going, fogey! Go and mind your business!*

PRIEST
      I do adjure you, by the holy blood   190
      of Christ our saviour, crucified for us:
      give up this monstrous revelry – that is,
      if you still wish to meet in heaven again
      the souls of all those loved ones you have lost.
      Go on, get going to your homes!

PRESIDENT
                              Our homes
      are full of sorrow – young folk relish fun.

PRIEST
      Is that you, Walsingham? And was it also you
      who, only three weeks back, upon your knees
      sobbed as you hugged your mother's lifeless body
      and wailed and writhed in anguish on her grave?*   200
      Do you imagine that she's not now weeping,
      yes, weeping bitterly in heaven itself,
      as she looks down and sees this orgy here
      with her son taking part, and hears your voice
      singing these frenzied songs, while all around
      folk gasp out prayers to God with desperate groans?
      Up, follow me!

PRESIDENT
                    Why is it you have come
      to trouble me?* I cannot follow you;
      you've no right to demand it. I'm kept here
      by my despair, by fearful memories,   210
      by consciousness of all the wrong I've done,
      by horror at that deathly emptiness
      that I encounter when I go back home –
      yes, and by these wild pleasures new to me,

the blessed poison of this drinking cup,
the gentle kisses (oh forgive me, Lord!)
of this poor ruined being that I love...
My mother's ghost will not call me away
from here – it's too late – I have heard your voice
appealing to me – I do recognize,   220
old priest, how you have tried to save me. Go now
in peace; but cursed be any that goes with you!*

MANY VOICES
    Good for our President! He's right; hear, hear!
    There's today's sermon for you! Now push off!

PRIEST
    Matilda's blameless soul is calling you!

PRESIDENT *(standing up)**
    No! Swear to me, your pale and wasted hand
    lifted to heaven – swear you'll leave that name
    beneath the grave, not mention it again!*
    If only I could stop her deathless eyes
    seeing this spectacle! Once she believed   230
    that I was faultless, noble, self-controlled –
    she felt herself so blissful in my arms...
    Where am I? Holy child of light, I see you
    up there, where with this fallen soul of mine
    I never now can come...

A WOMAN'S VOICE
                        He's lost his wits –
    he's babbling of his wife who's dead and buried!*

PRIEST
    Come on, let's go...

PRESIDENT
                    For God's sake, Father, please
    leave me alone!

Priest

>> The good Lord save you yet!
Goodbye, my son.

(He goes off. The feasting continues. The President is left plunged deep in contemplation.)*

Notes on Boris Godunov

p. 9, *To the memory... by Alexander Pushkin*: Pushkin added this dedication for the published 1831 edition, in memory of the dedicatee's death several years earlier. Nikoláy Mikháylovich Karamzín (1766–1826) was a Russian poet, *littérateur* and historian, who had recognized Pushkin's talent and befriended him from his schooldays. Karamzín's great work was a monumental *History of the Russian State* in twelve volumes. The first volumes were published in 1818, and were greeted with enormous interest and enthusiasm in Russia. Volumes x and xi, covering the period from 1598 to 1606, appeared in 1824. Although the two men's political views and moral outlook did not always coincide, Pushkin remained throughout a great admirer of Karamzín's work; Pushkin's play, written in 1825, follows Karamzín's account of events very closely, though he also made use of other sources.

p. 11, *A Comedy... 1825*: In the published 1831 edition Pushkin replaced this somewhat wordy and provocative title with the starkly featureless word *sochinéniye* ("composition", "work"). The change may in part indicate the author's private disappointment and frustration at the toning down of the comic-realistic element of certain scenes in response to the censors. However, I believe that Pushkin originally gave the play the tongue-in-cheek title of "comedy" primarily to mark that he intended it at one level as a covert satire on the reigning Emperor Alexander I – a purpose that, as well as being politically perilous, had become outdated by 1831. The issue is discussed more fully in the Extra Material (see pp. *259ff.*).

p. 13, *Scene 1*: For the situation at the start of the play and the events and personages mentioned throughout see Appendix 1.

The apparent spontaneity of the dialogue in this scene hides an artistry of structure and content. It opens with the departure of the populace from Moscow and the boyar's question "What will happen?"; and it ends with the populace returning and the boyar's question "What has happened?". In between we learn of the main factors that drive the action of the play: Borís's ambition, soon to be fulfilled, to receive the tsardom; his effectiveness as a ruler; the boyars' impotence, despite their contempt for his origins, to remove him during his lifetime; and, at the heart of the scene (as of the play), Borís's murder of Crown Prince Dimítry and his subsequent remorse.

p. 13, *Princes Shúysky and Vorotýnsky*: Vasíly Ivánovich Shúysky (1552–1612) was from a leading boyar family and played a major role in the history of this period. The Shúyskys, along with the Románovs and other princely families, regarded themselves as having a claim to the Russian throne, and Shúysky did indeed reign precariously as tsar in Moscow during the Time of Troubles from 1606 to 1610. In a draft preface to *Boris Godunov*, prepared in 1829 in the form of a letter in French, Pushkin characterizes him as follows: "*Il montre dans l'histoire un singulier mélange d'audace, de souplesse et de force de caractère.*" ("Historically, he shows a unique mixture of boldness, flexibility and strength of character.")

The Vorotýnskys were another princely boyar family. Later, at the end of Vasíly Shúysky's reign as tsar in 1610, one member of the family, Prince Iván M. Vorotýnsky, who was Shúysky's brother-in-law, took a leading role in deposing him.

p. 13, *the Patriarch*: Head of the Russian Orthodox Church. Patriarch Íov owed his office and his own appointment to Borís and remained his close ally.

p. 13, *the boyar-councillors*: The Boyars' Council, or Boyars' Duma, was the main organ of government supporting the tsar, normally meeting under his chairmanship. It was a council of nobles (boyars) who gave the tsar advice and performed various state functions under him, or in his absence. Individual members also undertook various offices in the administration and army.

p. 13, *the Grand Assembly*: That is, the Assembly of the Land (*Zemsky Sobór*), a wider "parliament" occasionally convened by tsars (or, as here, by the Patriarch in the absence of a tsar) to settle or advise on issues of the highest importance. Here the purpose was to give a broader validation to Borís's election than was available from the Boyars' Council. The Assembly was normally drawn from boyars, clergy, civil servants, imperial guard, merchants and delegates from other Muscovite towns.

p. 13, *His sister… give her blessing*: Borís's sister, the Tsarítsa Irína, was the legitimate heir to her husband Feódor I, so her consent was needed for another to take her place.

p. 15, *like my uncle*: Andréy Ivánovich Shúysky, Vasíly Ivánovich's great-uncle, had attempted to stir up opposition to Borís Godunóv in the early years of his regency. In 1587 he and other members of the family were exiled for plotting against the Regent; although Prince Vasíly was soon allowed to return to Moscow, his great-uncle Andréy and another relative died, allegedly murdered, in exile.

p. 15, *the monarch's crown and mantle*: Literally: "the cap and mantle of Monomákh". The cap of Monomákh is a sumptuous cap of gold filigree, trimmed with fur, studded with gems and surmounted with a pearl-tipped cross, still to be seen in the Kremlin treasury. With a shoulder cape decorated with enamelled medallions of saints, it formed part of the insignia of the Russian tsars and grand princes, and was used in coronation ceremonies until the time of Peter the Great. They were so called because according to legend they were presented to Grand Prince Vladímir II Monomákh of Kiev (b.1053, r.1113–25) by his grandfather the Emperor Constantine IX Monomachos of Byzantium (r.1042–55) (though their dates hardly match). They thus embodied the line of succession of the Russian tsars not only back to one of the greatest grand princes of Kiev but beyond him to the emperors of Byzantium and Rome.

p. 16, *If we can once detach… be their tsar*: Shúysky is speaking here with unconscious prescience: within little more than a year of Borís's removal from the scene the people (or some of them) did in fact choose Shúysky to be tsar.

p. 16, *we heirs of Ryúrik*: Literally: "heirs of the Varangian". "Varangian" was a Russian name for the Scandinavians or Vikings, one of whom, Ryúrik, was said in legend to have founded the Russian state and ruling dynasty in the ninth century. Those Russians in later centuries who traced their ancestry back to Ryúrik were entitled to call themselves "prince". There were around 130 prince-boyars in Muscovy by this time, from around forty families.

p. 17, *Scene 2*: The scene is set in *Krásnaya Ploshchad*, always translated today as "Red Square", the wide open space immediately outside the eastern walls of the Kremlin. Originally, however, the words meant "Beautiful Square", a name it took from the spectacular St Basil's Cathedral (built in the 1550s) at one end of the square, to which the adjective *krásnaya* was originally applied.

There is nonetheless a topographical puzzle in this scene. The Council Secretary Shchelkálov is described in Pushkin's stage direction as delivering his announcement from the *krásnoye kryltsó* ("beautiful steps"), usually identified in commentaries as the ceremonial steps outside the tsars' palace in the Kremlin. But these steps are several hundred metres from Red Square and separated from it by the massive Kremlin walls. There is no way that someone speaking from the steps of the tsars' palace could be seen or heard from Red Square. Pushkin, who had been born in Moscow and lived there till the age of eleven, and who also visited Moscow several times in the late 1820s, must have been aware of this. Possibly, therefore, in mentioning the *krásnoye kryltsó* Pushkin had in mind the steps of the *krásnaya tserkov* – St Basil's Cathedral – in the *Krásnaya Ploshchad* – Red Square. This is a much more plausible vantage point for making a public proclamation, and is close to the *Lóbnoye Mesto* ("Place of a Skull") on Red Square, from which official proclamations were regularly read – see Scene 24. It is to be noted Pushkin has surreptitiously designed Scenes 2 and 24 as a matching pair: both are set in Red Square, and both include a proclamation read from a rostrum or flight of steps.

The action in Scene 2 takes place immediately after that of Scene 1.

p. 17, *The Secretary of State... The Council Secretary*: Vasíly Shchelkálov was a high official who had been in charge of the business of the Boyars' Council for several years. He was an ally of Godunóv.

p. 17, *the icons of Vladímir and the Don*: Two of the most sacred icons in the possession of the Russian Church. The "Vladímir icon of the Mother of God" allegedly originated from Constantinople in the twelfth century or earlier; it was brought to Moscow in 1395 from the city of Vladímir, which had preceded Moscow as the centre of north Russian power and culture. (It was housed in the Assumption Cathedral in the Kremlin till Communist times when it was moved to Moscow's Tretyakóv Art Gallery.) The icon of the "Virgin of the Don" was famous for having allegedly been taken by Grand Prince Dimítry Donskóy of Muscovy to the battle of Kulikóvo Field on the upper Don in 1380, where it was believed to have inspired his decisive and historic victory over the Tatars. It was also credited during Borís Godunóv's regency in 1591 with having saved Moscow from a marauding army of Crimean Tatars, after which it was housed in the purpose-built Donskóy monastery a couple of kilometres south of the city, where the Russian army had fought. (It too was moved to the Tretyakóv Art Gallery in the 1930s.)

p. 17, *delegates / from other towns*: Although Pushkin's text does not say explicitly where the "delegates" are from, it is clear from Karamzín, from whom Pushkin drew the details of this passage, that they were delegates to the Assembly from other Muscovite towns.

p. 18, *Scene 3*: The Novodévichy Convent is about four kilometres from the Moscow Kremlin.

In this scene Pushkin continues to take a number of details from Karamzín's *History*, but he departs significantly from Karamzín's politically correct standpoint: whereas Karamzín positions himself, so to speak, with Borís, his sister and the national leaders within the convent, Pushkin views the scene from among the common crowd outside the convent walls. Moreover, although Karamzín depicts Borís Godunóv as a hypocrite, he also emphasizes the seriousness and sincerity of both the crowd and their leaders in desiring a new tsar and in welcoming Borís's eventual acceptance of the title. Pushkin, on the other hand, lays more stress on the stage-management of the demonstration and on the incomprehension or even indifference of many of the ordinary participants. It was this irreverent and sometimes comically realistic portrayal of the scene and its representation of the authorities' cynical manipulation of the common people that led the censor in 1826 to recommend the deletion of a large portion of the scene, a recommendation that drove Pushkin to drop the scene in its entirety. It was reinstated in the edition of the play published a few years after Pushkin's death and has regularly been included in subsequent editions. Musorgsky used it in his operatic version of the play.

The scene is formed of two matching halves; the first ends with the populace begging Borís to become tsar; the second ends with their acclamation of him as tsar. Before that in each case there is a dialogue among members of the crowd, punctuated by an intervention from a peasant woman with a child.

Scene 3 takes place on the day after Scenes 1 and 2, on 21st February 1598.

p. 18, *Maidens' Field*: An open space on the edge of Moscow, near the Novodévichy ("New Maidens") Convent, founded in 1524, where (according to tradition) in the days of Tatar rule Muscovite girls were assembled before being sent away to the Tatar authorities as tribute.

p. 19, *She drops the baby on the ground; the baby squeals*: This is one of the details originating with Karamzín. It is Pushkin, however, who has injected comedy into the episode. In Karamzín women drop babies on the ground and *disregard* their cries because they are carried away by the emotion of the occasion.

p. 20, *No onions on you / to rub our eyes with?*: See Shakespeare, *Antony and Cleopatra*, Act I, Sc. 2, where Enobarbus, hearing of the death of Antony's wife Fulvia, says: "This grief is crowned with consolation… indeed the tears live in an onion that should water this sorrow" – or in Letourneur's more plodding French version, which Pushkin would have used, "*pour verser des larmes sur un tel chagrin, il faudrait les faire couler avec de l'oignon.*"

p. 20, *Scene 4*: This scene represents Borís's first formal public appearance as tsar, dated by Karamzín to 26th February 1598, after which he rejoined his sister in the convent till Easter. He made his second entry to Moscow on 30th April, and Pushkin has incorporated some of the events of this second visit into the text of this scene. Borís was not crowned till 1st September.

p. 20, *those mighty Tsars Iván*: The reference is particularly to Iván III the Great and Iván IV the Terrible – see Appendix 1.

p. 21, *salute the tombs*: Up to the time of Peter the Great the grand princes of Muscovy and, later, the tsars were buried in the Archangel Cathedral in the Kremlin.

p. 22, *Scene 5*: The Monastery of the Miracle, founded in 1365, was situated inside the Kremlin, not far from the residences of Borís Godunóv and the Patriarch (under whose jurisdiction it came). In the sixteenth and seventeenth centuries educated monks there were engaged in the transcription and translation of religious works and in the compilation of chronicles. It housed a rich library and was influential in government and court circles. The monastery was demolished in the early 1930s.

Historically, according to Karamzín, Grigóry Otrépyev absconded from Moscow and fled into Poland in early 1602. Pushkin, however, has put Grigóry's defection back by a year or more, presumably to increase the dramatic momentum of the ensuing scenes.

The lengthy scene is framed by matching speeches by Pimen and Grigóry at beginning and end. Pimen's first and last speeches are about closing his work as a chronicler and handing it on to a successor. In the first he talks of lighting a future icon lamp; in the last he talks of extinguishing his present one. Grigóry's speeches contrast the inscrutable chronicler, viewing "good men and bad without emotion, / listening impassively to right and wrong, / immune alike to pity and to anger", with his own outrage at Borís's crime and determination to see it punished.

p. 22, *Pimen*: A fictional character based on the authors of the Russian monastic chronicles, whose work Pushkin much admired. In a draft letter to the press of 1828 about *Boris Godunov*, never published during his lifetime, Pushkin wrote of him: "The character of Pimen is not my fabrication. In him I have brought together traits that have enthralled me in our ancient chronicles: there breathes through these precious memorials of times long past a simple-heartedness, an endearing humility, something childlike but at the same time wise, an almost religious devotion to the God-given authority of the Tsar, a total absence of flippancy and partiality…"

p. 22, *Grigóry*: Grigóry or "Grishka" Otrépyev was a historical person. By birth he was Yury Bogdánovich Otrépyev of Galich, north-east of Moscow. His early history is obscure. However, according to Karamzín, in his teens he became a monk in Vyatka, further to the north-east, taking the name of Grigóry; then, after moving to Suzdal and elsewhere, he came to the Monastery of the Miracle in Moscow, where his grandfather was already a monk. There he became a deacon. Intelligent, quick-witted and well educated, he served for a time as a scribe to the Patriarch and distinguished himself by composing collects to the saints. The Patriarch used to take him to the Tsar's palace, where he gained some knowledge of state affairs and procedures. In due course, it seems, he grew dissatisfied with the monastic environment in Moscow and developed views that were regarded as heretical. At that stage or later he apparently formed the idea of impersonating the Crown Prince Dimítry, youngest son of Iván IV, who had died mysteriously in 1591. In any case he absconded from the monastery in 1602 and made his way, in the company of two other vagrant monks, a priest Varlaám Yatsky and a church singer Misaíl Povadin, to the Polish frontier and then into Poland, where in time he persuaded some of the leading Polish families to recognize him as the rightful heir to the Russian throne and give him their support.

p. 23, *factious parliaments of Nóvgorod*: Nóvgorod the Great, in western Russia, was one of its leading independent city states for several centuries, until it was subjugated and crushed successively by Iván III and Iván IV of Moscow. Previously it had been unusual among Russian cities in developing a democratic form of government controlled by a *veche* or assembly of citizens, which nonetheless sometimes broke apart into warring factions.

p. 24, *climbing a steep staircase / up a high tower*: The dream symbolizes the Pretender's rise to power in 1605 and violent overthrow a year later. During the Time of Troubles the throwing of victims from a high tower became a popular form of punishment for those that successive pretenders regarded as traitors. These executions were often witnessed by large crowds, who were sometimes given a say in who was to be killed and who reprieved.

p. 24, *Kazán... Pskov... Shúysky*: See Appendix 1.

p. 25, *Kiríll*: This may be a reference to Kiríll (Cyril) IV, Metropolitan of all Russia (head of the Russian church before the office of patriarch was created), who was appointed by Iván IV in 1568 and died in 1572.

p. 25, *I'll vow obedience to the strictest rule*: Literally: "I shall accept the honourable *skhima*." *Skhima* was a Greek word for a cassock-like gown worn by the most devout monks who took on the strictest vows. Traditionally a tsar when about to die would take strict monastic vows in an attempt to distance himself from his wrongdoings as a ruler and secure God's forgiveness before death. Once the tsar had taken these vows he lost his right to the throne. See also the close of Scene 22.

The University of Wisconsin team explain that the content and phraseology of Iván's account of his spiritual struggles and monastic aspirations are based on letters he wrote to senior monastic figures at the time.

p. 27, *the / Tsarítsa's court*: The Tsarítsa María Nagáya, seventh and last wife and widow of Iván IV.

p. 27, *Oh, seven perhaps*: Dimítry was in fact eight and a half years old when he died.

p. 28, *Scene 6*: Pushkin dropped this scene from the published 1831 text, probably because of the censor's objection to the portrayal of evil or disreputable behaviour on the part of monks. He may also have been content to leave it out because some of his friends had found fault with it and in order to dispense with a non-standard metre in the interest of greater unity of style. Later, however, he talked of reinstating the scene. The scene has rarely been included in subsequent editions, perhaps because it has not been considered essential to the coherence of the action. It does, however, bridge something of a gap between Grigóry's righteous anger at Borís's perceived crime at the end of Scene 5 and the reference to him in Scene 7 as a dangerous heretic on the run from the monastery.

The part played by a "malicious monk" in instigating Grigóry's escapade goes back to Karamzín and possibly to a historical disaffection with Tsar Borís or with Muscovite religious orthodoxy among certain monks of the Monastery of the Miracle.

Pushkin composed this scene in mostly unrhymed trochaic octameters, lines of fifteen syllables with the stress on the odd-numbered syllables and with a caesura after the eighth. I have preserved the rhythm of the original, without rhymes.

For the timing of this scene see first note to p. 22.

p. 30, *Scene 7*: The palace of the Patriarch was situated in the Moscow Kremlin, not far from the Monastery of the Miracle, which came under his personal control. For timing see first note to p. 22.

p. 30, *Galich... Suzdal*: Galich was a town about 400 kilometres north-east of Moscow. Suzdal was a town some 200 kilometres north-east of Moscow.

p. 31, *Solovétsky*: The Solovétsky monastery, on an island in the White Sea in the far north of Russia, was used as a place of banishment for delinquent monks and other dangerous people.

p. 31, *Scene 8*: This scene would have taken place during 1603.

p. 31, *with one of those magicians*: Borís Godunóv was known to have been very superstitious, and dabbling in magic was one of the charges that his enemies made against him.

p. 32, *the great conflagration*: In 1591, soon after the death of Prince Dimítry, there was a terrible blaze in Moscow that destroyed much of the city. Borís, as regent, gave assistance to the victims; but the rumour spread about that he had himself started the blaze in order to distract attention from the Prince's death and gain credit from the citizens for his relief measures.

p. 33, *poisoned my own sister the Tsarítsa*: The Tsarítsa Irína, Borís's sister and widow of Tsar Feódor I, died in 1603 in the convent where she had lived since her husband's death.

p. 33, *Scene 9*: For the timing of this scene see first note to p. 22.

p. 33, *Misaíl and Varlaám, vagrant monks*: The censor sought the deletion of a considerable portion of this scene on the grounds that it portrayed disreputable behaviour on the part of monks (see Extra Material p. 257 and Appendix 2). In order to preserve the integrity of the scene in the 1831 edition Pushkin therefore resorted to the tactical device of recasting the "vagrant monks" as "vagrants disguised as monks". Historically, however, as Karamzín made clear and Pushkin knew, Misaíl Povadin and Varlaám Yatsky really were runaway monks. According to the tradition accepted by Karamzín, they were monks from the Monastery of the Miracle in Moscow who absconded at the same time as Grigóry Otrépyev and accompanied him on his journey to and beyond the Polish frontier. Pushkin follows an alternative tradition, also reported by Karamzín in a note, according to which Grigóry met the pair en route for Poland.

Pushkin's Varlaám had a taste for puns and rhymes, a feature of Russian folk idiom which I have tried to reproduce in this scene.

p. 34, *The monks sing… passing my cell*: This song tells of how a young man who has been forced to become a monk invites a passing nun to come into his cell, take off his cassock and cap, and feel the beating of his heart; he then declares his intention to leave holy orders and marry her. A later line of the song is quoted in Varlaám's next speech. This ribald and worldly song is of course very much in character for Misaíl and Varlaám; but it is also appropriate in reminding us of the restless and adventure-hungry state in which Grigóry left his monastery. This whole passage, however, offended the censor, allergic as he was to suggestions of monastic misbehaviour, and Pushkin felt obliged to change the song.

For the published edition, therefore, Pushkin substituted a song beginning "One day, in the city of Kazán…" Interestingly there are two folk songs that begin with these words. One of these – presumably the one Pushkin had in mind – tells of a young man in Kazán who takes his vows as a monk, but then wishes he could still live it up. When he sees a group of pretty girls outside the monastery gates, he gives up trying to save his soul, says goodbye to his cell, throws off his monk's habit and decides it's time for a fine young man like himself to get married. (The line "A young monk took his vows…", which is allocated to Varlaám in the 1831 edition at the end of his fifth speech, is another line of the same song.) This song, though, hardly portrays monastic morality in a more favourable light than the original one. The second folk song beginning "One day, in the city of Kazán…" turns into a patriotic song about Iván IV's capture of Kazán from the Tatars. If Pushkin chose this ambiguous song title to confuse the censorious reader, he also confused Musorgsky, who incorporated the patriotic version into his opera.

The 1831 edition clearly allots the start of the song to Misaíl (who was indeed historically a chorister). The original version, however, gives the lead to Varlaám, though it makes it clear that both monks are to sing.

p. 34, *Why aren't you whining… wining with us*: Many modern editions assign this line to Varlaám, but the 1825 original apparently, and the 1831 edition clearly, give it to Misaíl.

p. 34, *Free will for those… for the saved*: Pushkin's text contains only the first seven words. His Russian readership would have recognized them as the opening words of the complete proverb, the end of which Varlaám goes on to misquote (much to the censor's disgust).

p. 35, *Where a fine young lad against his will*: This is a later line of the song 'Dear girl, you are passing my cell…' begun by Varlaám a few lines above – see earlier note.

p. 35, *he's smelt the filly*: "Smelling the filly" is said to have been a slang expression for being flogged as a criminal; so on one level Varlaám may be suggesting that Grigóry, for all his airs, could well be just a flogged criminal on the run. But here Varlaám is probably intending a more literal and coarser reference to Grigóry's imagined designs on the hostess, and no doubt this is why Pushkin felt it prudent to delete it from the 1831 edition.

p. 35, *Luyóv Hills*: The town of Luyóv (Loev, now in Belarus) is on the River Dnieper, nearly 200 kilometres north of Kiev.

p. 36, *That puts paid to your little bid for freedom, granny*: Literally: "There, granny, is your St George's Day!" St George's Day, the day in

November on or around which Russian peasants and servants were allowed to change their livelihood and residence, had become the symbol of the last vestige of freedom for the lower classes. For St George's Day see Appendix 1.

p. 38, *Bad, oh mine son, bad!*: In order to impress the police Varlaám makes a bungled attempt to introduce Church-Slavonic phraseology into this speech. I have accordingly introduced some deliberately clumsy biblical phraseology into the English translation.

p. 42, *He is small in stature*: The details here reflect a contemporary eyewitness description of the Pretender.

p. 42, *Scene 10*: This scene and Scene 11 are best imagined as happening in the spring of 1604, though the historical events mentioned as having taken place in the recent past were in fact spread over a period of eighteen months or so. Princess Xénia's husband-to-be (see Scene 11) died towards the end of October 1602; Grigóry Otrépyev's disclosure of himself as Dimítry took place in autumn 1603; and the Pretender did not have his audience with King Zygmunt till March 1604. News of the Pretender's appearance would in practice have reached Moscow piecemeal over a period of several months. For dramatic purposes Pushkin suggests a much brisker sequence of events.

p. 42, *Boy, read the prayer*: This prayer is Pushkin's shortened and simplified version of a prayer that Tsar Borís ordered to be read as a toast at meals on both official and domestic occasions. Much of its phraseology and imagery reflect the original prayer, as does the Church-Slavonic intonation of the language.

p. 43, *AFANÁSY MIKHÁYLOVICH PUSHKIN*: A.M. Pushkin was not quite a historical character. He is a conflation of various historical Pushkins of the time who were opposed to Borís Godunóv and supported the Románovs, especially Yevstáfy (Ostáfy) Mikháylovich Pushkin (not a direct ancestor of the poet), a nobleman, soldier and administrator, who was active during the reigns of Iván IV, Feódor I and Borís. Although Yevstáfy Pushkin had supported the election of Borís to the tsardom, he was informed on by his servants, disgraced, and exiled to Siberia in 1601, dying there two years later; he could not therefore have been in Moscow in 1603 at the time of the Pretender's appearance in Poland. He had a brother, Iván M. Pushkin, another prominent boyar, who remained in Moscow and was therefore in a position to have dealings with Shúysky during 1603. Alexander Pushkin evidently substituted the imaginary Afanásy so as not to do violence to the historical facts about Yevstáfy and other real Pushkins.

p. 44, *Cracow*: Cracow (Kraków) old capital of Poland.

p. 44, *Gavríla Pushkin*: Gavríla Grigóryevich Pushkin *was* a historical character, and a forebear of the poet. In a draft preface to *Boris Godunov* written in 1829 in the form of a letter Alexander Pushkin wrote: "I have portrayed Gavríla Pushkin – one of my ancestors – just as I found him in history and in my family papers. He was very gifted – as a soldier, as a courtier, and especially as a conspirator." Although Gavríla Pushkin did take an active part in the struggle against Borís on the side of the Pretender, the author has somewhat enhanced his role in the play; for instance, Gavríla Pushkin only joined the Pretender after the commencement of his campaign for the throne. A survivor both physically and politically, he participated in the election of the first Románov tsar in 1613 and died in 1638.

p. 45, *Wiśniowiecki's*: The Wiśniowieckis were an old princely family of Poland. In reality, it was Prince Adam Wiśniowiecki who first recognized his pageboy as "Dimítry"; he then made him known to his more influential cousin in Cracow, Prince Konstantin Wiśniowiecki (1564–1641), who in turn introduced him to his father-in-law Jerzy Mniszech. Pushkin has blended the two Wiśniowieckis, no doubt to avoid unnecessary complication.

p. 45, *of Wiśniowiecki's; one day on his sickbed*: The Russian version of this line (*u Vishnevétskogo, chto na odré bolézni*) has, uniquely, six feet (thirteen syllables), instead of the standard five (ten or eleven syllables) – presumably an uncharacteristic slip of Pushkin's.

p. 45, *King Zygmunt*: Sigismund Vasa (1566–1632) was born a Swedish prince. He was elected as King Zygmunt III of the Polish-Lithuanian Commonwealth in 1587. A zealous Roman Catholic, he would dearly have liked to bring his eastern neighbour Russia within the Roman Church, as well as to annex some Russian territory: hence his support for successive claimants to the Russian throne who offered to facilitate this. At this time Poland was formally at peace with Russia, and the Polish government as a whole did not favour war. But to promote his own agenda Zygmunt was prepared to let the Pretender Dimítry raise a private army on Polish soil with the help of his Polish backers such as the Mniszechs. His private audience with the Pretender took place in the spring of 1604.

p. 45, *So fierce a storm... keep the tsar's crown*: In his 1826 report to Nicholas I the censor recommended the deletion of the whole of this speech because of its harsh portrayal of tsarist autocracy and talk of peasant uprisings. Pushkin ignored the censor's objection in the 1831 edition, without apparently incurring Nicholas's displeasure.

p. 46, *the nightmarish reign of Tsar Iván*: The following five lines refer to actual punishments inflicted by Iván on his enemies during his campaign of terror.

p. 46, *the Románovs, Russia's hope and pride*: A diplomatic gesture by Pushkin to the dynasty still in power in his own day, perhaps in the hope of disarming the imperial censor.

p. 46, *resolved to end St George's Day*: See Appendix 1.

p. 47, *Scene 11*: This scene takes place the day after Scene 10.

p. 47, *The Crown Prince... the Princess*: For Borís's children see Appendix 1. By 1604 Xénia would, historically, have been about twenty-two and Feódor fifteen. Pushkin, however, portrays Xénia as a childlike figure, in stark contrast with the precocious Maryna Mniszech. Contemporaries remarked on her fine looks and on her qualities of gentleness, intelligence and good taste.

p. 47, *Why have your lips... I keep telling you, he did*: Xénia's opening lament and brief exchange with her brother were omitted from the 1831 edition. Pushkin's reasons for dropping the lines are obscure. The 1826 censor's report raised no objection to this passage. One effect of the 1831 cuts was to eliminate the two scenes, 6 and 13, that were written entirely in non-standard metres. So maybe Pushkin felt that the remaining passage that was neither in iambic pentameters nor in prose would stand out too much on its own. Moreover, now that the deletion of Scene 6 had upset the original parallelism that contrasted the Russian and the Polish girl in Scenes 11 and 15 (see Appendix 3), it was no longer necessary to give Xénia so much prominence. He may too have felt on reflection that the exchange was a little out of character for a princess in her early twenties and a brother seven years her junior.

p. 48, *tears are like the dew... dry the dew*: Pushkin took these words from a folk song, quoted by Karamzín, about a slain warrior: the song contrasts the tears of a mother and sister – "like rivers", which will never stop flowing – with the tears of a young wife, which "are like the dew that falls; the sun will rise and dry the dew".

p. 48, *A map of Muscovy*: Crown Prince Feódor was an intelligent and well-educated young man. He did indeed draw, or promote the drawing of, a map of Russia. After the fall of the Godunóvs and death of Feódor in 1605 the map was apparently smuggled out of the country by a young Dutchman who had been working in Moscow. It came into the hands of the eminent Dutch cartographer Hessel Gerritsz, who used it to produce in 1613–14 a famous map of Russia (the "Tabula Russiæ" dedicated to the first Románov tsar Mikhaíl), which was republished many times over the next half-century.

p. 48, *Nóvgorod... Ástrakhan... Perm*: Nóvgorod the Great was an important and powerful trading city in the west of Russia that was at one time a rival to Moscow, but was crushed and incorporated into Muscovy by Iván III in 1479; Perm, to the far east of European Russia, had been part of the Nóvgorod empire and was incorporated into Muscovy at the same time. Ástrakhan, on the Volga delta near the Caspian Sea, was the centre of a Tatar khanate conquered by Iván IV and annexed into Muscovy in 1556.

p. 48, *Siberia*: The Russian conquest and colonization of Siberia had commenced in the early 1580s under Tsar Iván IV and continued under Borís Godunóv.

p. 49, *Semyón Godunóv*: Semyón Nikítich Godunóv (named incorrectly in the 1825 version "Semyón *Ilyích*") was Borís's uncle, his "watchdog and executioner", in charge of his secret police. After the fall of the Godunóv family he was put to death on the orders of the Pretender in 1605.

p. 50, *the Miloslávskys... the Buturlíns*: The Miloslávskys and the Buturlíns were noble Russian families of the time. Mikhaíl Saltykóv served as a trusted official under Borís; after Borís's death he went over to the Pretender.

p. 50, *I can't abide this treacherous clan of Pushkins*: Pushkin was presumably smiling when he wrote this, exiled as he was himself by the reigning tsar, Alexander I.

p. 53, *Listen a moment, Prince Vasíly*: For the death of the real Crown Prince Dimítry in 1591 see Appendix 1.

p. 54, *the young face of the Crown Prince, though, was radiant*: According to Karamzín, when Shúysky's commission of inquiry came to Uglich to investigate Dimítry's death a few days after the event, the young Prince's features appeared impressively peaceful and angelic. Fifteen years later, in 1606, after the false Dimítry had been overthrown, Vasíly Shúysky, now tsar himself, claimed to have discovered that the boy's remains in Uglich were still miraculously undecayed and sweet-smelling. In a final attempt to give the lie to the false Dimítry's story and discourage further impostors he had the remains transferred to Moscow and buried, as those of a saint, among the graves of the tsars in the Archangel Cathedral (where they remain today). There were rumours, however, that the "miracle" had been contrived.

p. 55, *it's a heavy crown we tsars must wear*: Literally: "heavy are you, cap of Monomákh!" See second note to p. 15.

p. 55, *Scene 12*: This scene should be imagined as taking place in the spring of 1604, though it brings together encounters that probably happened at several different times and locations.

This is the first scene where Grigóry Otrépyev appears as pretender to the throne of Russia. In a draft preface to *Boris Godunov* written in 1829 in the form of a letter, Pushkin wrote of his character: "*Il y a beaucoup du Henri IV dans Dimitri. Il est comme lui brave, généreux et gascon, comme lui indifférent à la religion – tous deux abjurant leur foi pour cause politique, tous deux aimant les plaisirs et la guerre, tous deux donnant dans les projets chimériques – tous deux en butte aux conspirations...*" ("There is much of Henri IV [i.e. Henri of Navarre, King of France] in Dimítry. Like Henri, he is brave, generous and prone to extravagant promises; like Henri, he is indifferent to religion – both of them renouncing their faith for political advantage, both fond of pleasure and war, both with a penchant for unrealistic schemes – both the victim of conspiracies...")

p. 55, *Wiśniowiecki's*: See first note to p. 45.

p. 55, *Father Czernikowski*: A Polish Jesuit priest, who later accompanied the Pretender on his march on Moscow.

p. 55, *all the Eastern Church*: Some editions read here "all the *northern* Church", referring specifically to the Russian Church; but the 1831 edition, like the 1825 text, clearly reads "Eastern", thus having the Pretender undertake to bring *all* the Orthodox Churches of Eastern Europe and the Near East into allegiance to Rome. As the rest of the scene shows, it was characteristic of the Pretender to make extravagant promises to his prospective supporters. Karamzín confirms that the Pretender led the Jesuits of Cracow to believe that it was his earnest ambition to "bring into subordination to Rome all the vast lands of the East" (Karamzín, *History of the Russian State*, Vol. XI, Chapter 2). In fact the Pretender did not take any open steps to promote Roman Catholicism even in Russia during the single year of his reign.

p. 55, *will recognize the primacy of Rome*: Literally: "will acknowledge the authority of St Peter's deputy [i.e. the Pope]".

p. 55, *St Ignatius*: St Ignatius of Loyola, founder of the Jesuit order in 1540, one of the aims of which was to promote, by whatever means, the spread of Roman Catholicism worldwide.

p. 56, *Sambor*: A town on the upper Dniester river, now in western Ukraine, where the Mniszechs had their family seat.

p. 56, *Mniszech*: Jerzy Mniszech was a Polish nobleman who held the title of Palatine of Sandomierz, a Polish provincial centre on the Vistula between Cracow and Warsaw. He was known for his high living and no doubt saw his hazardous military and matrimonial support for the Pretender as means of recouping his fortunes.

p. 56, *Prince Kurbsky*: Imagined as the son of Prince Andréy Kurbsky – see Appendix 1. Andréy Kurbsky's first wife and child were put to death by Iván IV; he had another son Dimítry (b. 1581) by a later marriage contracted in Poland, but historically this son took no part in the Pretender's expedition. The Prince Kurbsky who appears here is one of the few fictional characters in the play.

p. 57, *Pskov*: Ancient city in the extreme west of Russia, often threatened by neighbouring Baltic Germans, Lithuanians, Poles and Swedes. Pushkin calls it here "Olga's city", after Olga (*c*.890–969), wife, mother and grandmother of successive rulers of Kiev, who was born at Pskov. Andréy Kurbsky took part in the Polish-Lithuanian attack on Pskov in 1581.

p. 57, *Volhynia*: Or Volynia, a region of western Ukraine, at that time part of Poland.

p. 57, *King Stefan Batory*: Stefan Batory (*Báthory István*) was a Hungarian-born nobleman and ruler of Transylvania, who was elected King of Poland, reigning from 1575 to 1586.

p. 58, *freeborn*: Sobański (or Pushkin) is making a guarded political point here: the Polish nobility (*szlachta*) were indeed free – in contrast to their Russian counterparts, who were regarded, at this time and long afterwards, as servants of the tsar, enjoying their privileges at the tsar's pleasure.

p. 58, *Yes, sire... ascend the throne of Russia*: Pushkin has allowed Khrushchóv to "spin" the historical facts somewhat here. Pyótr Lukich Khrushchóv (unlike other Muscovite refugees in Poland) had not himself been persecuted by Borís or driven from Moscow. He was a nobleman trusted by Tsar Borís and sent by him to the Cossacks of the Don in order to counter the Pretender's propaganda there. The Cossacks, however, stubbornly opposed as they were to Borís because of his attempts to control them, seized Khrushchóv and sent him as a prisoner to the Pretender in Poland. It was only then that Khrushchóv made common cause with the other Muscovite exiles and the Cossack rebels and went over to the Pretender's side.

p. 58, *then / Borís will have to settle up his debts*: These words are slightly amended and the following twenty-two lines omitted in the 1831 edition – see Appendix 2. The passage gives both the Pretender and the reader useful information about developments in Moscow, and it is not obvious why it was dropped. There is no evidence that the censor found it objectionable.

My own suggestion is based on the view, set out in the Extra Material, that Pushkin originally intended *Boris Godunov* to be read, in part, as a covert satire against Alexander I. Alexander, however, died unexpectedly less than two weeks after Pushkin had completed the play; though childless, he had not designated a successor, and the ensuing confusion precipitated the abortive Decembrist uprising. When Pushkin later reread lines 82–94 about Borís's growing reclusiveness, the hope for his early death and the uncertainty over his successor, he may well have feared that the passage might be interpreted not only as a prophecy of Alexander's early death and of a fraught succession, but even as a wish for those events, accompanied if necessary by violence and the overthrow of the dynasty. Such an interpretation, although no doubt going well beyond what was in Pushkin's mind when he wrote the words, would nonetheless, in the post-Decembrist political climate, have been acutely embarrassing and dangerous to Pushkin in his official relations with the regime and in his personal relations with the new emperor. (We know that Nicholas I feared that parts of the play might be read, however mistakenly, as alluding to the Decembrist uprising.) Hence Pushkin's decision – voluntary here, in my view – to suppress the whole passage despite its relevance to the plot.

p. 59, *some ailment's gnawing him*: Tsar Borís did indeed become unwell at this time and lived an increasingly reclusive life.

p. 59, *A Cossack from the Don… Cossacks of the Don*: Andréy Karéla was indeed a chieftain of the Don Cossacks sent by them to the Pretender in November 1603 to assist him in his preparations for war.

The Cossacks originated from a mixture of old soldiers, adventurers, runaway peasants and others who were allowed by the Russian and Polish authorities to settle on the southern and eastern fringes of their territory (notably on the middle and lower reaches of the Dnieper and Don rivers and in the Urals) as frontiersmen to guard against incursions by Turks and Tatars. Living under local chieftains (atamans or hetmen) they were allowed a good measure of autonomy, in return for which they were expected to give military service to the Russian and Polish governments in times of war. They were renowned for their bravado, their military skills, their horsemanship and their unruliness. The Pretender had spent some time among Cossacks learning "the mastery of horse and sabre" (Scene 15, ll. 103–4) before arriving in the Polish heartlands.

The line "indeed from all the Cossacks of the Don" – literally: "indeed from Cossacks upriver and downriver" – is supplied from the 1831 edition; it does not appear in the University of Wisconsin Press and Nóvoye Izdátelstvo editions of the full 1825 version.

p. 60, *the Latin Muse… Mount Parnassus*: In Greco-Roman mythology the Muses were goddesses of the arts – here the "Latin Muse" refers specifically to poetry in Latin. Mount Parnassus in Greece was sacred to the Muses.

p. 60, *Who's this… maybe "jester"*: This exchange between Khrushchóv and Gavríla Pushkin about poets, satirizing the lack of appreciation, or even awareness, of poetry among many Russians of the time, was omitted from the 1831 edition. We do not know why. Perhaps Pushkin concluded that the joke was too ostentatiously self-deprecating; or else someone – Pushkin himself or one of his friends

– felt that it might be read as casting a gratuitous slur on Russian culture, present as well as past. Pushkin seems to have included the lines in the 1825 version partly as a facetious counterbalance to the serious Russian poetry (in the mouth of a Pole!) at the end of the matching Scene 14. But this counterbalance was no longer required in the restructured play of 1831 – see Appendix 3.

p. 61, *Musa gloriam coronat, gloriaque Musam*: "The Muse crowns glory, and glory [crowns] the Muse" (Latin). In other words, "writers are good for celebrities; and celebrities are good for writers."

p. 61, *Scene 13*: This scene was omitted by Pushkin from the published edition of the play – a pity, as it gives an early insight into the character and outlook of Maryna Mniszech, and a delightful portrayal of her garrulous maid. It also helpfully bridges the gap in time between Scenes 12 and 14; and its ironic discussion of "Dimítry's" real identity enhances the dramatic effect of the encounter between him and Maryna in Scene 15.

There is no evidence that the censor objected to the scene. I suspect that Pushkin decided to drop it because, after the deletion of Scene 6, it interfered with his restructuring of the play; he may also have felt it obtruded as the only remaining scene not in iambic pentameters or prose.

The scene is indeed in a different metre from the rest of the play – in rhymed iambic lines of irregular length. In translating it I have kept the rhythm of the original, which fits perfectly with Róża's irrepressible chatter, but I have sacrificed the rhymes, which it would be impossible to reproduce in English without losing the naturalness and fluency of the language.

The scene should be imagined as taking place near the end of the Pretender's stay with the Mniszechs at Sambor, in late August 1604.

Musorgsky used a completely rewritten version of this scene at the start of the Polish section of his opera.

p. 64, *Scene 14*: The setting is later in the same evening as Scene 13.

The scene is constructed round a polonaise danced by the young people at the Mniszechs' castle and nicely framed by a contrasting conversation between two old men. The general ambience of this and the previous scene, with their femininity, fine dresses, music, dancing, gentle frivolity and Western sophistication, brings us as far as it is possible to come from the baleful male-dominated formality and severity of Muscovy.

p. 64, *Look, here he comes… ladyship!*: This line was omitted from the 1831 edition, presumably by oversight.

p. 66, *dig us up a vintage flask / of Magyar wine*: Some editors have amended Pushkin's *otryt* (dig up) to *otkryt* (open); but the 1831 edition clearly reads *otryt*. Good wine was buried in the earth to allow it slowly to mature at a stable temperature.

p. 66, *We old men now… Let's go then, friend*: The Western – and perhaps to Russian eyes decadent – sophistication of the scene is underlined by the versification of this speech. Pushkin, while retaining his iambic pentameters, has rhymed the lines in irregular pairs to create what is virtually a fourteen-line sonnet, with a fifteenth line divided between the two speakers that repeats the final rhyme. In the translation I have kept the alternate male rhymes, in an attempt to convey the heightened word music without distorting the sense.

p. 66, *Night-time, a Garden, a Fountain*: Pushkin sets the stage for a conventional love scene between the Pretender, now in his early twenties, and the precocious sixteen-year-old Maryna Mniszech; but it turns out very differently. In a draft preface to *Boris Godunov* written in 1829 in the form of a letter he wrote:

Une tragédie sans amour souriait à mon imagination. Mais outre que l'amour entrait beaucoup dans le caractère romanesque et passionné de mon aventurier, j'ai rendu Dimitri amoureux de Marina pour mieux faire ressortir l'étrange caractère de cette dernière… certes c'était une drôle de jolie femme. Elle n'a eu qu'une passion, et ce fut l'ambition, mais à un degré d'énergie, de rage, qu'on a peine à se figurer…

("A tragedy without love appealed to my imagination. It was not only that love was deeply embedded in the romantic and passionate nature of my adventurer, but I made Dimítry fall in love with Marina the better to bring out the strangeness of her personality… she certainly was odd for a pretty woman. She had one passion only, and that was ambition – but ambition as powerful and unbridled as one can scarcely imagine…")

The striking and original encounter between two contrasting characters turns into a stark analysis, albeit couched in fluent and realistic dialogue, of the political and personal factors that underlay the improbable success of "Dimítry's" seizure of the Russian throne. Framed at beginning and end by references to the Pretender's uncharacteristic sensation of fear, it reaches its climax in his defiant speech (l. 172*ff.*): "Know this: the ghost of Tsar Iván's proclaimed me Dimítry from the tomb...", a speech which Pushkin uniquely ascribes not to the "Pretender", but to "Dimítry". As some Russian commentators have observed, the scene, in its completeness and clarity of focus, almost constitutes a "Little Tragedy" in itself.

The action takes place the evening after Scene 14.

pp.72–73, *Know this: the ghost... you'll regret it*: This speech, as well as being uniquely assigned to "Dimítry" (see above), also stands out because Pushkin has rhymed the first four lines and two of the last four. Clearly Pushkin saw this as an important turning point in the drama – the moment when the fraudulent renegade monk at last took on the role and destiny of a future ruler of Russia.

p. 74, *Scene 16*: Pushkin's date for this scene was taken directly from Karamzín's *History*, Vol. XI, Chapter 2, where he gives 16th October as the date when the Pretender's army "entered Russia". However, later in the same chapter Karamzín states that the Pretender "set foot on Russian soil" on 18th October. The date is omitted in the 1831 edition. Either this was a printer's slip, or Pushkin deliberately left it out because he was unsure which of Karamzín's dates was correct. Modern historians believe the frontier crossing actually to have taken place on 13th October.

p. 74, *O Father... gladness!*: The 1831 edition changes both the tense of the first verb and the punctuation to read:

> O Father, now your soul
> has had its consolation in the grave.
> Your exiled bones can rest at last in gladness!

However, according to the 2008 Nóvoye Izdátelstvo edition this change in the Russian text was a printing error.

p. 75, *I'm showing / our foes the sacred road to our dear Moscow*: As Pushkin was aware, the Poles did indeed invade Russia in 1609; the following year a Polish force occupied Moscow and remained there for two years. But Pushkin will also have been thinking ruefully of Napoleon's invasion of Russia and capture of Moscow in 1812, when Pushkin, who had been born in Moscow and lived there till the previous year, was a boy of thirteen.

p. 75, *Scene 17*: For the course of the military campaign see Appendix 1. The scene should be imagined as taking place a week or two after Scene 16.

p. 75, *Chernígov*: In the north of modern Ukraine, about 150 kilometres north of Kiev. It fell to the Pretender on 26th October 1604.

p. 76, *we'll bring him in an iron cage to Moscow*: Pushkin is no doubt here recalling Marshal Ney's famous promise to Louis XVIII of France in 1815 to bring Napoleon to Paris in an iron cage – after which, like Basmánov, Ney defected to the other side.

p. 76, *Shchelkálov*: See second note to p. 17. Vasíly Shchelkálov had in fact left his post as Secretary to the Boyars' Council a few years earlier; but Pushkin ignored the change either out of ignorance or, more likely, to avoid unnecessary complication.

p. 78, *transfer the sacred relics / to the Archangel Cathedral*: Ironically, despite Shúysky's wariness of this course of action, this is precisely what he himself arranged when he became tsar in 1606 after the short reign of the false Dimítry. See note to p. 55.

p. 80, *Scene 18*: Pushkin changed the order of Scenes 18 and 19 in the 1831 edition to restore the parallelism between Scenes 8 and 18 that had been lost through the deletion of Scene 6. See Appendix 3.

The scene is imagined as taking place in midwinter 1604–05.

p. 80, *the holy man, the fool*: Although the scene is fictional in its context, it is clearly based on a passage from Karamzín's *History*, about "holy fools" (*yuródivye*). These *yuródivye* were idiots or madmen – or people who pretended to be such – who lived as vagrants and beggars, hair unkempt, often wearing chains or strange clothes or going naked even in winter. They were popularly regarded as especially godly men, and were credited with clairvoyant or miraculous powers. Because they were held in awe as saintly figures, they could criticize and insult the powerful with impunity.

Karamzín, after relating the death through illness of an infant son of the Regent Borís's in 1588, ten years before he became tsar, goes on:

There was in Moscow at that time a holy fool (*yuródivy*), held in awe for his sanctity, actual or supposed. With hair unkempt, roaming the streets naked in severe frosts, he used to foretell disasters and solemnly vilify Borís. But Borís kept his peace, and did not dare do him the least harm, whether for fear of the people or out of belief in the man's sanctity. Holy fools of this kind, or "blessed ones", often appeared in the capital: they used to wear shackles or chains; they could berate anyone, however high-ranking, to their face for wrongful living; and they could help themselves to anything they liked in the shops without payment – shopkeepers used to thank them for doing so, as if for a great favour. It is asserted that the Blessed Vasíly (who lived at the time of Iván the Terrible), like Nikóla of Pskov, did not shrink from criticizing the Tsar, but with astonishing pluck used to bewail his atrocities in the public squares.

(Karamzín, *History of the Russian State*, Vol. x, Chapter 4)

The Blessed Vasíly died in 1552 and was canonized in around 1580. He was buried near the cathedral in Red Square that now bears his name, St Basil's.

In a note Karamzín tells of another *yuródivy*, Iván, who died in Moscow in 1589. From youth he had disciplined himself with fasting and prayer, and he carried on his body crosses with iron chains, wore a heavy cap on his head, many copper rings and circlets on his fingers and carried wooden prayer beads in his hand. After his death his body was buried with great ceremony in St Basil's Cathedral

These links of famous *yuródivye* with St Basil's Cathedral on Red Square make it very likely that St Basil's is the cathedral where Pushkin imagined this scene taking place.

Nikóla (or Nikólka) of Pskov was another *yuródivy* who confronted Iván the Terrible and about whom Pushkin had information from Karamzín. Although the historical Nikólka died in 1576, Pushkin at first used the name for his own *yuródivy*. He suppressed the name for the 1831 edition, however, because the censor had objected to the conduct attributed to an Orthodox holy man and also probably out of respect for the name of the current Tsar Nicholas (Nikoláy) I – see Appendix 2.

Pushkin's use of the *yuródivy* to voice to the monarch harsh truths that no one else dared utter reflects Shakespeare's use of fools and jesters in *King Lear* and other plays.

p. 82, *Tsar Herod*: The holy fool is likening Borís to Herod the Great, King of Judaea, who just after the birth of Christ murdered the young boys of Bethlehem in order to eliminate a rival for his throne.

While Pushkin had still been working on the play, Karamzín had advised Pushkin, through Prince Pyótr Vyázemsky, a friend, to: "have in mind, when depicting the character of Borís, a savage mixture: piety and criminal passions. He constantly reread the Bible and sought in it justification for himself. That is a dramatic contradiction." Pushkin replied through the same friend in September 1825: "I thank you also for Karamzín's remark about the character of Borís. That was very helpful to me. I was looking at him from the political standpoint, not noticing his literary side. I shall sit him down behind the Gospels and make him read the story about Herod and suchlike."

p. 82, *Scene 19*: The historical battle near Nóvgorod-Séversky that forms the background to this scene took place on 21st December 1604.

Pushkin may have taken the idea of this multilingual battle scene from Shakespeare's *Henry V*, e.g. Act IV, Sc. 4.

p. 83, *Enter Captains Margeret and Walther Rosen*: Both are historical characters, commanders of units of foreign mercenaries in Borís's army. Walther von Rosen was a German nobleman from Livonia. Jacques Margeret was a Frenchman, who entered military service in Russia in 1600. After Borís's death he went on to serve the Pretender and Tsar Vasíly Shúysky. Later he returned to France and published memoirs of his experiences in Russia, which became an important source for the history of the Time of Troubles, used by both Karamzín and Pushkin.

p. 83, *Allons*: "Come on!" (French).

p. 83, *you damned heathen*: "Heathen" because Roman Catholic or Protestant, not Orthodox, like the fleeing Russians.

p. 83, *Quoi? Quoi?*: "What? What?" (French).

p. 83, *Qu'est-ce à dire "osodox"?... pour foutre le camp*: "What's it mean, 'orthodox'? Confounded riff-raff, damned scoundrels! Christ crucified, sir, it drives me crazy: you'd think they didn't have arms to strike with, just legs to bugger off on" (*1831 version:* "just legs to run away on") (French and German). Here and further on Pushkin had to tone down some of Margeret's barrack-room blasphemies and obscenities in order to meet the censor's (and Nicholas I's) sensitivities – see Appendix 2, item X.

p. 83, *Es ist Schande*: "It's a disgrace" (German).

p. 83, *Ventre-saint-gris!... Qu'en dites-vous, mein Herr?*: "The devil if I'm moving a step from here – when the wine's poured out, it needs to be drunk. What do you say, sir?" (French and German).

p. 83, *Sie haben Recht*: "You're right" (German).

p. 83, *Tudieu, il y fait chaud!... Qu'en pensez-vous, mein Herr?*: "God, it's hot here! This devil of a 'pri-tenn-der', as they call him, is a bugger with hair up his arse. What do you think of it, sir?" (French and German). The censor had this toned down in the 1831 edition – see item Y, Appendix 2, where the French may be translated roughly as follows: "The devil, it's hot here! This devil of a 'pri-tenn-der', as he calls himself, is a fine chap, with hair on his chest."

p. 84, *Ja*: "Yes" (German).

p. 84, *Hé! Voyez donc... qui aurait fait une sortie*: "Hey! Look now, look now! Fighting's broken out at the rear of the enemy. The excellent Basmánov must have made a sortie" (French).

p. 84, *Ich glaube das*: "I believe that" (German).

p. 84, *Ha, ha! Voici nos Allemands... chargeons!*: "Aha! Here are our Germans. Gentlemen!... So, tell them to form up, sir, and, goddammit, let's charge!" (French).

p. 84, *Sehr gut... Hilf Gott!*: "Very well. Halt!... Quick march!... God be with us!" (German).

p. 84, *An engagement*: This stage direction is absent from the 1825 text. I have included it from the 1831 edition as a helpful clarification by Pushkin.

p. 85, *Scene 20*: This scene should be imagined as taking place on or just before 20th January 1605.

p. 85, *Rozhnóv*: An imaginary character.

p. 89, *Scene 21*: The scene should be imagined as taking place late on 21st January 1605, just after the battle of Dobrýnichi.

p. 89, *FALSE DIMÍTRY*: At this point of defeat and failure for the Pretender, Pushkin for the first and only time calls him "False Dimítry". He seems to be signalling that the Pretender's ultimate (but temporary) triumph was not after all due to any merit on his own part (behind his engaging persona he was still a fraud), but to other forces, social or providential, that he neither actuated nor controlled.

p. 91, *Scene 22*: This scene takes place on 13th April 1605.

p. 91, *Registers of Rank*: See Appendix 1.

p. 92, *Iván the Great... his savage grandson's*: Iván III and Iván IV respectively.

p. 94, *But I've attained supreme power... for everything*: Compare the words of Shakespeare's Henry IV (who had, like Borís, once murdered the rightful occupant of the throne) to his son:

> God knows, my son,
> by what by-paths and indirect crook'd ways
> I met this crown; and I myself know well
> how troublesome it sat upon my head:
> to thee it shall descend with better quiet,
> better opinion, better confirmation;
> for all the soil of the achievement goes
> with me into the earth...
> (Shakespeare, *Henry IV Part 2*, Act IV, Sc. 5)

p. 96, *A monk's robe!*: Russian *skhima*. See second note to p. 25.

p. 96, *Scene 23*: This scene is best imagined as taking place at the beginning of May 1605, probably in the camp of Tsar Feódor's army besieging Kromy. Basmánov's conversation with Gavríla Pushkin is probably fictional. Basmánov's decision to join the conspiracy against the Godunóvs and defect to the Pretender seems to have been due to Tsar Feódor's government's decision, influenced by the traditionalists, to appoint a more senior boyar above him in the chain of command.

p. 99, *Summon the troops!*: Basmánov went over to the Pretender, with his troops, on 7th May 1605.

p. 99, *Place of a Skull*: In Russian *lóbnoye mesto*, the name of a raised stone platform or rostrum at the river end of Red Square in front of St Basil's Cathedral, used for reading out public proclamations and for performing certain religious ceremonies in which the tsar and patriarch participated.

The Russian word *lob* is normally translated *brow, crown of the head*, and *lóbnoye mesto* may originally have meant "place on a steep river bank". It is usually translated, however, "Place of a Skull", because it is the name given in the Church-Slavonic Bible (John 19:17) to the place called in Hebrew "Golgotha" and in Latin "Calvarium" (Calvary), where Christ was crucified. Despite the name's macabre connotations, executions did not normally take place there, but at another spot nearby.

Gavríla Pushkin did in fact enter Moscow on 1st June 1605 with a crowd of the Pretender's supporters from the suburbs and read out from here a proclamation on behalf of the Pretender that sparked off an uprising in the city. Pushkin has accurately summarized the gist of the proclamation.

p. 100, *sole heir to the long line of Russia's rulers*: Literally: "the grandson of Monomákh". For Monomákh see second note to p. 15.

p. 100, *Archbishop*: In the original "Metropolitan", the next-highest-ranking church official beneath the Patriarch. Patriarch Íov himself was a close ally of the Godunóvs and firm opponent of the Pretender. The Pretender had him arrested, deposed and banished to a distant monastery.

p. 101, *Scene 25*: The events of this scene took place on 10th June 1605.

p. 102, *Let's go up!... There's still a noise*: Karamzín records that the boyars and bodyguards strangled the Tsarítsa María immediately; but Feódor, a tough young man, put up a fierce struggle before being brutally overpowered and strangled in his turn.

In the 1831 edition the order of the populace's interjections is changed, to bring forward the reference to a woman screaming (see item EE in Appendix 2), and this may have been Pushkin's preferred text.

p. 103, *Long live Tsar Dimítry Ivánovich!*: This closing acclamation of "Dimítry" by a reluctant populace was replaced in the published version of 1831 by the famous stage direction "The people remain speechless".

The ending, in either of its versions, is (like Scene 3) strongly reminiscent of Shakespeare's *Richard III*, Act III, Sc. 7, where the Duke of Gloucester, soon to be King Richard III and to murder the boys who are the rightful heirs to the throne, is impatient to know the citizens' reaction to his own claim:

GLOUCESTER
How now, how now! What say the citizens?

BUCKINGHAM
Now, by the holy mother of our Lord,
the citizens are mum, say not a word[…]
And when mine oratory drew toward end
I bid them that did love their country's good
cry "God save Richard, England's royal King!"

GLOUCESTER
And did they so?

BUCKINGHAM
No, so God help me, they spake not a word;
but like dumb statues or breathing stones
star'd each on other and looked deadly pale.
Which when I saw, I reprehended them[…]
[…]some followers of mine own
at lower end of the hall hurl'd up their caps,
and some ten voices cried "God save King Richard".
And thus I took the vantage of those few –
"Thanks, gentle citizens and friends," quoth I.
"This general applause and cheerful shout
argues your wisdoms and your love to Richard."

Debate continues as to who initiated the change of ending (was it
made by Pushkin of his own volition? At the suggestion of friends?
Or under pressure from the authorities, even from Nicholas I
himself?) and over its aptness (does it improve the ending of the
play, or spoil it?). Much has been written, and I will only add the
following observations.

There is no evidence at all that the change was prompted by the
censorship or the Emperor.

Oddly, although at first sight the change diametrically reverses the
play's ending, it actually makes little difference. This is because it is
plain from what goes immediately before that the populace are at
this point disinclined to acclaim the Pretender as the new tsar. The

people have already refused to express their pleasure at the violent extinction of the Godunóv dynasty, and it is clear at the end that, even if they do acclaim the new tsar, they do so unwillingly and under duress. Whether they speak or remain silent, the message is the same.

It seems likely, however, that there is a connection between the deletion of the crowd's acclamation at the end of Scene 25 and the cutting of Scene 3. In the structure of the original play there is a symmetry between Scenes 3 and 25 (see Appendix 3). The people's forced acclamation of "Tsar Dimítry" at the end of Scene 25 in the original version balanced their contrived acclamation of Tsar Borís at the end of Scene 3. It may be that, once Pushkin had been induced to drop Scene 3 for the 1831 edition, he felt freer to make the people's defiance of authority more explicit at the end of Scene 25 through a silence that many feel is more telling.

The silent ending is fully in harmony with Karamzín's historical narrative, to which Pushkin generally adheres closely. It is true that Karamzín reports the crowd as hailing "Tsar Dimítry" on the occasion of the Pretender's proclamation on 1st June (as does Pushkin at the end of Scene 24), and again on his triumphal entry into the capital on 20th June (beyond the ending of the play). But on the occasion of the Godunóvs' murder, the subject of Scene 25, he reports the people's reaction differently, as follows:

It was explained to Moscow that Feódor and Maríya had taken their own lives by poison; but their corpses, brazenly exposed to dishonour, bore unmistakable marks of strangling. The people thronged to the pathetic biers where the two dynastic victims lay – wife and son of the power-hungry man who had adored them, and destroyed them, giving them a throne that brought them horror and a most cruel death... Many looked on simply out of curiosity, but many also with sympathy; they were sorry for Maríya, who... had devoted her life to good works... they felt still sorrier for Feódor, in whom there had been so much integrity and hope: he possessed, and promised, so much excellence for the good of Russia, had it pleased Providence!

(Karamzín, *History of the Russian State,* Vol. xi, Chapter 3)

Pushkin may well also have had in mind the widely reported remark made by Mirabeau after the storming of the Bastille in recommending that King Louis XVI be greeted in the Constituent Assembly with grim silence: "*Le silence des peuples est la leçon des rois.*" ("The people's silence has a message for monarchs.")

Thus, even though the silent ending of Scene 25 was not Pushkin's initial idea, I believe it to be probably his preferred ending once Scene 3 had been lost.

p. 103, *End of the comedy... AMEN*: In 1831 Pushkin omitted this provocative and ironic closure to the text and substituted the word "*KONÉTS*" ("The End"). This is discussed more fully in *Boris Godunov*: The Text in the Appendix.

Notes on Little Tragedies

The Mean-Spirited Knight

p. 109, *The Mean-Spirited Knight*: Pushkin apparently started work on *The Mean-Spirited Knight* in 1826 at Mikháylovskoye; the name occurs in a list of titles in rough draft from that year. The work was completed at Bóldino in 1830: the manuscript fair copy is dated 23rd October. It was printed anonymously by Pushkin in the first issue of his literary periodical *The Contemporary* in 1836.

The play was to have been performed on 1st February 1837 at the Alexandrinsky Theatre in St Petersburg, together with two insubstantial dramatic pieces by other authors, but the programme was deferred for a day because of Pushkin's death on 29th January. On the following day the programme was presented without *The Mean-Spirited Knight*, which was replaced by another play because the authorities feared a public demonstration of sympathy for Pushkin.

Pushkin has left the place and time of action vague. The place is in Western Europe, probably Flanders to judge by the reference in Scene 1 (l. 79). Such proper names as there are (e.g. Delorge, Thibault) point to a francophone environment. The timing of the action was clearly in the "age of chivalry" in the Middle Ages. Mention of Spanish coinage may point to a date as late as the early sixteenth century (see Scene 2, l. 41 and note), when jousting was still a popular sport. But Pushkin is focussing here on realism of characterization, not of historical background.

The title of the play – *Skupóy rytsar* in Russian – is usually translated "The Miserly Knight". But "miserly" is too narrow a translation of *skupóy*. "Covetous", the English adjective used by Pushkin in the subtitle, is better, but still too narrow, as well as now archaic. "Miserly" implies the possession of goods to hoard, and "covetous" focuses on the desire for more, whereas *skupóy* refers more broadly to the underlying attitude of mind, "meanness" or "mean-spiritedness": you can be *skupóy* whether you are rich or destitute, whether you crave more or are just ungenerous. Near the opening of the play Albert applies the noun *skupóst* to himself, not because he was broke, but to describe his own petulant conduct at the tournament. The translation "miserly knight" prevents us from appreciating the deliberate ambiguity of Pushkin's title, which he meant to be as apt to the son as to the father.

As well as being deliberately ambiguous, *Skupóy Rytsar*, "The Mean-Spirited Knight", is also a deliberate oxymoron. At the time of the play's action, the "age of chivalry", the essence of knighthood was understood to be courtesy, unselfishness and generosity (as personified in the Duke in Scene 3 of the play); meanness was the antithesis of knighthood, its very denial.

p. 109, *Scenes from… The Covetous Knight*: This subtitle is Pushkin's; He wrote the words "The Covetous Knight" in English. "Chenston" does not exist. It may be an incorrect Russian transliteration of "Shenstone" – referring to the minor English poet William Shenstone (1714–63). Shenstone wrote elegies, odes, songs and ballads, "moral pieces", and "levities", but no work that fits Pushkin's description. The explanation seems to be that this is an original work of Pushkin's, which (as in some other cases) he ascribed falsely to a little-known foreign writer in order to put the imperial censorship off its guard or (in this case at least) to disguise some autobiographical references that could otherwise have caused him embarrassment within his family (see Extra Material, pp. 267*ff.*).

p. 111, *Albert and Jan*: In Pushkin's Russian "Albert" is spelt without the final "t", indicating that Pushkin envisaged a French pronunciation of the name. Pushkin calls Albert's manservant "Iván", invoking for Russian readers an indigenous "man of the people"; I have accordingly used "Jan", the cognate Dutch-Flemish name with perhaps matching connotations for Western-European readers.

p. 111, *knocking him from his stirrups… he lay for days as dead*: Although jousting was a dangerous sport that sometimes resulted in death, the object was to knock an opponent from his horse, not to kill him.

p. 114, *guilders*: Russian "*chervóntsy*", a denomination of gold coins.

p. 119, *Scene 2*: The Baron's monologue is a wonderful piece of writing, one of the great passages of Russian literature. But the speech is also a grim one, portraying the Baron, as it does, as a man utterly corrupted by greed for money. Three features are perhaps especially noteworthy. Firstly, the Baron acknowledges that his hoards of money give him the same pleasures that another might gain from predatory sex, from gluttony, or even from murder: in those who are utterly corrupt all vices run together. Secondly, the Baron's miserliness has perverted all his human relationships: he can see no good in anyone, not in the people who owe him money, nor even in his own son. Finally, the Baron is obsessed by the power that money seems to put into his hands: the power to rule everyone and everything, the power to commission beautiful palaces and gardens, great works of art, great human achievements, even great deeds of evil; yet for the Baron this power is sterile: he can only exercise his power by spending the money, and spending it is what he's pathologically incapable of doing. So the money lies asleep, inactive, useless.

p. 119, *I'm sure that I've read… that rode at sea beyond*: The story may originate from an episode related by the Greek historian Herodotus (*c*.484–*c*.425 BC) concerning the Persian king Darius's invasion of southern Russia (then known as Scythia) near the beginning of the fifth century BC. As Darius was marching north to the Danube through what is now Bulgaria, "he indicated a certain spot where every man in the army was ordered to deposit a stone as he passed by. This was done, with the result that when Darius moved on he left great hills of stones behind him" (Herodotus, *Histories* IV). The story was later elaborated and adapted to other epochs and locations.

p. 120, *a Spanish gold coin*: Russian *dublón*, from the Spanish *doblón* (English "doubloon"), a Spanish gold coin. The presence of a Spanish coin in Flanders was unsurprising, as Flanders and Spain were both under Habsburg rule from the early sixteenth century.

p. 127, *he's thirsting for my death… My money*: This is not so far from the truth: Albert was desperately trying to borrow from the moneylender on the security of his supposedly healthy father's inheritance; and he said "Amen" to Solomon's prayer, "May God let you inherit soon!"

p. 129, *Grim times are these! And grim, too, human nature!*: The Duke's concluding remark is reminiscent of Cicero's famous lament over the moral degeneracy of his contemporary Rome: "*O tempora! O mores!*" (Cicero, *In Catilinam* I, 1).

Mozart and Salieri

p. 131, *Mozart and Salieri*: Pushkin conceived the idea of this play no later than the summer of 1826, the year after Salieri's death. There is evidence that he produced a first draft at that time. Certainly the thoughts about tyranny, revolution and deliverance from captivity that underlie the references to Beaumarchais and *Tarare* in Scene 2 (ll. 37–40) would fit better with Russia's and Pushkin's circumstances in mid-1826 than later. However that may be, the play only reached its final form four years later, during his autumn stay at Bóldino: the manuscript is dated 26th October 1830. It was first published during 1831.

Though Pushkin does not specify a time and place for the action of the play, it is clear from the subject matter that it is set in Vienna in late 1791. See the Extra Material, pp. 271*ff.*, for historical information on Salieri and Mozart.

p. 133, *My hard-won skill*: For Salieri's education, see paragraphs on his life in the Extra Material.

p. 134, *Gluck*: Christoph von Gluck (1714–87) was renowned across Europe as an innovative composer of operas. Born in Germany of a Bavarian family, he travelled widely, but spent most of his career in Vienna, with visits between 1773 and 1779 to Paris, where he produced several operas, two based on the story of the mythical Greek princess Iphigenia (*Iphigénie en Aulide*, 1774; and *Iphigénie en Tauride*, 1779).

p. 134, *I stepped out after Gluck*: In real life Salieri was one of the leading proponents of Gluck's operatic innovations.

p. 134, *Niccolò Piccini*: Opera composer (1728–1800), began his career in Naples but moved in 1776 to Paris, where an intense rivalry soon developed between his supporters and those of Gluck. In 1778 the directorate of the Paris Opéra arranged for each to compose an opera based on the classical myth of Iphigenia in Tauris (but with different libretti). Gluck's opera (produced the following year) gained the greater success.

p. 135, *Voi che sapete*: The first words of the famous aria sung by Cherubino in the second act of Mozart's opera *The Marriage of Figaro*.

p. 136, *I'm cheerful... or something similar*: Though Mozart (and Pushkin) are deliberately unspecific, it is possible that one of the musical passages they have in mind here is that in the last act of *Don Giovanni*, where the Don's dinner, in which he has been joined by Donna Elvira, is brutally interrupted by the appearance of the dead Commendatore's avenging statue.

p. 138, *What future's there for us, with Mozart living*: An early biographer of Mozart quotes an unnamed composer, possibly Salieri, as making the following comment on Mozart's death: "It's a shame that such a great genius has died, but a blessing for the rest of us; had he lived any longer, in truth the world would not have given us any more scraps of bread for our own compositions."

p. 138, *Haydn*: Josef Haydn (1732–1809), regarded as the leading composer of his day, a friend of both Mozart and Salieri.

p. 138, *loving cup*: It is implicit in this speech that what Salieri had in mind was not only the murder of his victim but his own simultaneous suicide by sharing the poisoned wine. Hence also his consternation in Scene 2 when Mozart empties the wine glass in one go.

p. 139, *Well, listen then*: In the following lines Pushkin draws on the true story of the commissioning of the *Requiem*, Mozart's last major work. In July 1791 Mozart really did receive a visit from a sombrely dressed man who, while refusing to reveal his identity, offered him a large sum of money for the composition of a requiem Mass. The truth of the matter – which Mozart never found out – was that the man was the steward of an Austrian nobleman and amateur musician who wanted a requiem Mass in memory of his recently deceased wife that he could pass off as his own work. Over the following months, Mozart received two or three further approaches from the mysterious agent enquiring about progress with the requiem. As his illness developed, Mozart became obsessed by this strange visitor and came to imagine him as a messenger from beyond the grave ordering him to write a requiem Mass for his own death. Mozart worked on the *Requiem*, as his strength allowed, up to the last days of his life. He left it unfinished, and immediately after his death his wife had pupils of his complete it so that she could claim the final instalment of the fee.

p. 140, *my young son*: Mozart had two surviving sons; the elder, Karl Thomas, would have been nearly seven at this time; the younger, Franz Xaver, was born on 26th July 1791, very close to the time of the mysterious stranger's first visit.

p. 140, *Beaumarchais*: Pierre-Augustin Caron de Beaumarchais (1732–99), among many other activities, was the author of the celebrated comedies *The Barber of Seville* (1775) and *The Marriage of Figaro* (1783), the second of which was the basis of Mozart's opera of the same name (1786). Shortly afterwards Beaumarchais wrote an opera libretto entitled *Tarare* (see next note), for which Salieri, who was at that time working for the Paris Opéra, wrote the music. Beaumarchais and Salieri collaborated closely on the composition and became friends. When the libretto was published, Beaumarchais prefaced it with a laudatory dedication to "*Monsieur Salieri, mon ami*".

p. 140, *Tarare*: The Beaumarchais-Salieri opera *Tarare* was first presented in Paris in 1787 and was widely acclaimed. The story tells of the conflict between the King Atar, a murderous tyrant, and Tarare, one of his soldiers, a man of humble origins, able, virtuous and loyal. Atar is insanely jealous of Tarare's military ability, popularity and contented disposition, and tries to have him killed. In the end, however, Atar, faced with a popular uprising, kills himself, and Tarare reluctantly accepts the kingship in his place.

There is some significance to Pushkin's putting a reference to *Tarare* in Mozart's mouth at this point. Firstly, Pushkin is suggesting a parallel between Atar's jealousy of Tarare and the highly placed Salieri's unreasoning jealousy of Mozart's musical ability, popularity and easy-going character. In Pushkin's play, however, "there is no justice up in heaven" (as Salieri himself remarks at the beginning) to bring about a happy denouement, so Salieri is condemned either to prolong his sterile domination of the Viennese music world, made ever more aware of his mediocrity by the masterworks of the humble Mozart, or to take matters into his own hands and destroy his rival.

The second point concerns the fact that *Tarare* is in fact primarily a manifesto for equality. Beaumarchais even chose the absurd name Tarare for his low-born hero to emphasize that he had no advantage in life beyond his character. In his introduction to the published libretto Beaumarchais explains that the work's meaning is summed up in its last three lines, addressed to mankind in general, which read: "*Homme! ta grandeur sur la terre / n'appartient point à ton état; / elle est toute à ton caractère.*" ("Man, your greatness on earth / is in no way due to your status, / but entirely to your character.")

Beaumarchais intended these lines (and the whole plot of *Tarare*) as a scornful comment on the incapacity and corruption of the French *ancien régime*, which was, like Atar, ferociously jealous of talented newcomers (like himself) and was attempting to cling on to its privileges, though faced with revolution. Pushkin here was ostensibly applying the thrust of Beaumarchais's drama to the professional relations between the two musicians; but he was probably also making a veiled political comment on contemporary Russia, where a harsh autocracy and a privileged aristocracy, ineffective and corrupt, were similarly trying jealously to defend their privileges against those who favoured a freer and more equal society that valued character and ability above status.

p. 141, *La la la la*: This is not an abstract musical reference, but a precise textual quotation. In a version of the opera from 1790 Beaumarchais added a final act portraying the coronation of Tarare and the triumph of law over tyranny. In the second scene of this act a deputation of black slaves arrives from Zanzibar to pay homage to Tarare. Tarare gives them their freedom; and the Africans, with less than fluent French, sing and dance a chorus of joy including the chant "la la la la..." By quoting this apparently meaningless chant Pushkin is perhaps covertly signalling, in a way unrecognizable to the censor, Mozart's (and his own) commitment to freedom and the supremacy of law. Perhaps there is another irony too: that to Mozart the most memorable piece of Salieri's music should be a nonsensical chant, while Salieri is compelled to characterize Mozart's music elsewhere in the play with words like "profundity", "ingenuity", "elegance", "ethereal" and "gorgeous".

p. 141, *Beaumarchais gave someone poison*: Beaumarchais's first two wives both died within a couple of years of his marrying them. His enemies, motivated by jealousy of his success in Parisian society despite his lowly origins, spread the false rumour that he had poisoned them in order to inherit their money. Again Pushkin's text needs to be read at several different levels. On the surface the reference to Beaumarchais is just a clever piece of dramatic irony, Salieri being disconcerted by Mozart's innocent mention of poisoning. It also serves to introduce the important theme of genius being incompatible with criminality, which is taken up again in Salieri's speech that closes the play. But at a deeper level still it gives another warning of the overpowering jealousy that may impel those who (like Salieri) rely on status to harm those who (like Mozart, and Beaumarchais himself) commend themselves by gifts and character alone.

p. 141, *he was far too fond of fun*: This comment was actually made about Beaumarchais by Voltaire in a letter of 1771: "*Ce Beaumarchais n'est point un empoisonneur, il est trop drôle.*" ("This Beaumarchais is no poisoner, he is too funny.")

p. 142, *Michelangelo… a killer?*: There was a widely repeated legend, without foundation in fact, that Michelangelo killed the man he was using as the model for a painting of the crucified Christ, so as to capture the appearance of death more realistically. The French poet Le Mierre, in recounting this legend in his poem *The Painting* (1769), adds the comment: "The moment of inspiration never coincides with crime. I cannot possibly believe that crime and genius can go together" – a very similar sentiment to that voiced by Mozart earlier in the scene and recalled just above by Salieri.

The Stone Guest

p. 143, *The Stone Guest*: The idea of this play was mentioned in a note of Pushkin's of 1826. However, the final version was only completed during Pushkin's stay at the family estate of Bóldino in the autumn of 1830. The autograph we have is dated 4th November that year. The play was not published during Pushkin's lifetime.

The play is set in and near Madrid. Pushkin is unspecific about the period: insofar as he had a precise time in mind, it is probably around the end of the sixteenth or early seventeenth century.

p. 144, *Don Juan*: The first problem encountered by anyone attempting a metrical translation of *The Stone Guest* into English is how to pronounce the hero's name: "Juan". The more usual Russian transliteration is "Zhuán", in imitation of the traditional French pronunciation, with the initial consonant resembling a normal French J. It would be pronounced with two syllables, with the stress on the A. The traditional English pronunciation gives the J its full English value and treats the name as having two syllables with the stress on the U. This is the pronunciation used by Byron in his *Don Juan*, a work known and admired by Pushkin. In the authentic Spanish pronunciation the J has the value of a strong H and the name sounds more like one syllable than two. Pushkin transliterates the name "Guán", using the Russian G in approximate imitation of the Spanish J, and he scans the name as two syllables, with the stress on the A.

I see no point in adopting a French form of the name in an English translation of a Russian play set in Spain. The semi-anglicized Byronic pronunciation now sounds aggressively insular and old-fashioned. I have therefore come down firmly in favour of the Spanish pronunciation, scanning it as one syllable: this is right for the Spanish background; it also comes closest to Pushkin's own intentions, since it is clear that he was rejecting the French and English versions of the name in favour of one imitative of the Spanish pronunciation.

I have also used the Spanish form of other names where they belong to Spaniards. Pushkin borrowed some of his characters from the libretto of the opera *Don Giovanni* – e.g. Donna Anna, and Don Juan's servant Leporello. I have therefore in the first instance adopted the Spanish spelling Doña Ana; in the second I have kept the traditional Italian spelling, since there was no ready Spanish equivalent and Don Juan must be assumed to have recruited his factotum during his Italian travels. Spanish diphthongs I have treated as one syllable, making Laura and Diego two-syllable words, not three as in Pushkin.

p. 145, *O statua gentilissima... Ah, Padrone!*: "Most gracious statue of the great Commendatore!... Ah, master!" (Italian). The words come from Lorenzo da Ponte's libretto to Mozart's opera *Don Giovanni*, thus providing a link with the preceding play. In the opera the words are spoken in Act II, Sc. 12, which parallels Scene 3 of Pushkin's play, being also set in a graveyard by the Commendatore's (Knight Commander's) tomb. In da Ponte's libretto Leporello utters the words at the point where he is browbeaten by the Don into starting to deliver his invitation to the statue, but turns away in terror to tell his master that he is too frightened to carry on.

Why has Pushkin made these particular words the epigraph to the whole play, when his own text – which otherwise follows da Ponte quite literally in this passage (Scene 3, l. 143*ff.*) – does not have Leporello mention his master explicitly at this point? Surely because, read out of context, da Ponte's version of Leporello's words take on a different meaning: Leporello starts to address the Knight Commander's statue and then cries out "Ah, master!", not turning away to someone else, but as though he is suddenly recognizing his master in the facial features of the statue. Pushkin is signalling to us that his Don Juan and Knight Commander are different manifestations of the same person, himself – see note to p. 163. Hence also the theme of disguise with which the play opens. See further the Extra Material, pp. 277ff.

p. 147, *my cloak wrapped... Nobody must know me*: The opening exchange between Don Juan and Leporello constitutes a challenge to the reader to recognize who is concealed behind the Don's disguise, the first clue to which has already been given in the epigraph – see note above.

p. 148, *He won't cut off my head*: Since Pushkin's idea for this play dates from 1826, when he was still living in exile at Mikháylovskoye and fantasizing, no doubt, about a return to the capital, he may well have composed these opening pages at that time. Whether or not this is so, he has given these lines of Don Juan a mischievous double meaning. During 1826 the reverberations of the abortive Decembrist uprising in St Petersburg the previous year were still fresh. The new emperor Nicholas I had had five of the conspirators executed and many others exiled to Siberia. Pushkin, though far away, at first feared guilt by association – many of the leading conspirators were his friends – but he seems to be reassuring himself here that, since he himself did not commit any "crime against the state", the worst that could happen to him was a further period of exile.

p. 148, *And what a country! Skies as grey as smoke*: Don Juan has apparently been spending his exile in Paris (see Scene 2, l. 73). However, by not giving a name here, Pushkin is perhaps inviting his readers to apply the comments in this speech on the northern weather and female society to St Petersburg (see *Eugene Onegin* I, 42; III, 22); and his praise of Andalusian lasses may reflect his preference for the girls he had met in the south (i.e. during his stays in the Crimea, Moldavia and Odessa).

p. 149, *Poor Iñez!... Oh my poor Iñez!*: In these lines Pushkin seems to be recalling an earlier love of his own. Amalia Riznić was the young wife of a Dalmatian businessman from Trieste, with whom he had had a passionate and stormy affair in Odessa during his sojourn there in 1823–24. Amalia suffered from a chronic chest complaint, and in May 1824 her husband sent her back to Trieste, ostensibly for health reasons. Pushkin, however, supposed that her husband had sent her away because of her affairs (she had had other lovers too), and suffered acute jealousy from the belief that she had betrayed him with a rival. In fact, Amalia's chest trouble grew worse, and she died of it in Trieste a year later. It was only in 1830 that Pushkin learnt through a friend connected with the Riznićes of suspicions that her husband had hastened her death in order to leave him free to make a better match. Pushkin, recalling the intensity of his feelings for Amalia, was overcome by the news, and his regret for her is reflected in other verses he wrote at this time.

p. 150, *Knight Commander*: This translates the Russian *komandór*, Pushkin's version of the Spanish title *comendador* (Italian *commendatore*). The cognate English title "commander" seemed to me to have by itself a too purely naval or military connotation in modern usage, whereas the Spanish title rather denotes the head of an order of chivalry. I have therefore usually translated the title as "knight commander" (occasionally "commander" for short) as conveying more accurately the chivalric flavour of the Spanish title.

p. 153, *I just observed the slenderest little heel… eyebrow or foot*: Another autobiographical touch – see *Eugene Onegin* I, 32:

> A girl's foot promises the gaze
> a reward beyond all price,
> and with its hints of beauty draws behind it
> a swarm of uncontrollable desires.

p. 158, *I hear the watchmen… 'Fine weather!'*: The night watchmen in Spanish towns would call out the weather for the information of citizens, and because the weather was usually fine they usually cried out "*sereno*" (clear sky); as a result *sereno* became a Spanish word for a night watchman.

p. 161, *in dreadful lodgings*: In the Russian (*za górodom, v proklyátoy vente. Ya Laúry*) Pushkin has inadvertently created a line of thirteen syllables here, when the metre requires only ten or eleven.

p. 162, *the Escorial*: El Escorial is the name of the extensive monastery and palace complex built by Philip II between 1563 and 1584 some forty kilometres north-west of Madrid. It became the summer residence of the Spanish court.

p. 163, *in life the man was short and puny... and determined*: Why this idiosyncratic characterization of the Knight Commander, required neither by Pushkin's sources nor by the rest of the play? It is hard not to see here a description of Pushkin himself, who was unusually short and lightly built, and self-confident, plucky and determined.

p. 171, *Scene 4*: Don Juan's wooing of the beautiful, but naive and unsophisticated, Doña Ana in this scene, with its progressive self-disclosure, can be read at one level as an account – albeit stylized and ironic – of Pushkin's courtship of the beautiful but naive and unsophisticated Natálya Goncharóva, culminating as it was about to do in the elimination of the wild and promiscuous bachelor by the staid husband, whose duty now would be to guard his home from other libertines. It was a transformation that Pushkin both dreaded and (because he loved Natálya) sincerely desired. Hence the mixture of pleasure and horror with which Don Juan finally greets the Stone Guest.

p. 172, *I'm tears... just like April*: There seems to be an echo here of one of Barry Cornwall's *Dramatic Scenes* – see Extra Material, p. 262. In his 'Ludovico Sforza' Isabella, addressing the lecherous Sforza who has murdered her husband and taken her as his reluctant wife, says:

> ...Even I, you see,
> although a widow, not divested of
> her sorrows quite, am here i' the midst of tears,
> to smile, like April, on you...

p. 172, *my mother made me marry... he was rich*: A reflection of Pushkin's own experience: his fiancée's family the Goncharóvs were impoverished and Natálya's mother (who took the lead) eventually decided that her daughter should accede to Pushkin's request for marriage in the belief (mistaken as it turned out) that his renown as a writer and his links with the court would lead to an improvement in the family's circumstances.

p. 175, *where is your dagger? Here's my heart*: Compare Shakespeare, *Richard III*, Act I, Sc. 2:

GLOUCESTER (*to the Lady Anne, mourning her dead husband*)
If thy revengeful heart cannot forgive,
lo here I lend thee this sharp-pointed sword;
which if thou please to hide in this true breast
and let the soul forth that adoreth thee,
I lay it naked to the deadly stroke,
and humbly beg the death upon my knee.

p. 177, *I've been described to you... keen student of depravity*: Confession and repentance of former dissipation were a feature of Pushkin's thinking and writing at this time, as he prepared for marriage.

p. 178, *Oh, who can know your mind*: Compare Lady Anne's words in Shakespeare's *Richard III*, Act I, Sc. 2: "I would I knew thy heart."

p. 178, *And you are anxious... heavenly soul?*: Between the two sentences of this speech Don Juan slips from the formal – and more proper – mode of address (*vy*) he has used hitherto to the familiar mode (*ty*) used by close friends, which he maintains for the rest of the scene. From line 128 Doña Ana reciprocates this familiarity.

A Feast during the Plague

p. 181, *A Feast during the Plague... John Wilson*: This play (unlike *The Mean-Spirited Knight*) really is a translation from English into Russian. What Pushkin has translated is part of one scene from a verse drama *The City of the Plague* by John Wilson (see Appendix 4). Pushkin will have found the work in the volume entitled *The Poetical Works of Milman, Bowles, Wilson and Barry Cornwall* that was published in Paris (in English) in 1829.

This is the only one of the *Little Tragedies* not to have been projected by Pushkin back in 1826. Pushkin completed the manuscript of the work at the family estate of Bóldino on 6th November 1830. It was first published in a Russian literary journal in 1832.

The reason this work of Wilson's took Pushkin's interest during the autumn of 1830 was no doubt that an epidemic of cholera was raging across Russia. The quarantine measures taken by the government to combat the epidemic were indeed the reason for Pushkin's confinement to Bóldino at that time. Plague, therefore, and the sudden and indiscriminate death it brought, were occupying Pushkin's mind.

Though not explicit in Pushkin, it is clear from Wilson's original work that the action is set in London during the great plague in the summer of 1665.

p. 183, *Jackson*: Wilson calls the man "Harry Wentworth". But Russian has no precise equivalent to "w" or "th", and Pushkin's purpose in changing the name is evidently to make it easier for a Russian to pronounce.

p. 184, *so that we then can go back... then wakes*: Pushkin's text reads literally: "...so that we then can go back to our pleasures more madly, like the one who has been transported from the world by some vision." The last clause lacks Pushkin's usual clarity, perhaps because he didn't fully understand Wilson's text. I have given Pushkin the benefit of the doubt and have clarified Pushkin's simile by reference to Wilson, whose original words were: "[that] we may address ourselves to revelry, / more passionate from the calm, as men leap up / to this world's business from some heavenly dream."

p. 185, *Time was... in the world beyond*: Mary's song in Wilson's scene consists of sixteen four-line stanzas, all describing in some detail the unnamed narrator's homecoming one July to his native village in Scotland (called Denholm) and finding it empty, depopulated by some unspecified disaster (perhaps, but only by implication, the plague). It is written (unlike Mary's speeches in the rest of the play) in Scottish dialect. Pushkin has rewritten Wilson's song completely: it is much shorter than Wilson's song; it is in a different metre to Wilson's and in an unaffected Russian that does not attempt to reproduce any regional dialect. The subject matter of Wilson's song is covered in a much condensed form in Pushkin's first three stanzas. Pushkin's stanzas four and five, introducing two names (Jenny, the narrator, and Edmund, her husband or betrothed) are entirely his own, and introduce a counterpoint to the actual situation of Walsingham. In Mary's song Jenny begs Edmund, if she contracts the plague, to go away, and to come back later in remembrance and loyalty; Walsingham, however, having lost his wife Matilda in the plague, has not prudently left the plague-ridden place of her death to return later in loyal homage, but has stayed on in despair and tried to forget his wife in a life of reckless dissipation.

My translation reproduces Pushkin's metre and rhyme scheme, except that, to avoid undue distortion of the sense, I have not followed Pushkin in rhyming the odd-numbered lines.

p. 187, *rest yourself on my breast*: In Wilson Mary continues for another line and a half: "Sick must be your heart / after a fainting fit so like to death."

p. 187, *jabbering... dreadful sounds*: Pushkin clearly understands the corpses to be jabbering; but Wilson, though not free from ambiguity, seems to have envisaged the sound coming from the Negro: "he beckoned on me to ascend a cart / filled with dead bodies, muttering all the while / an unknown language of most dreadful sounds."

p. 187, *So listen now... the song*: For these one and a half lines of Pushkin Wilson has: "But you shall have it [i.e. the song], though my vile cracked voice / won't mend the matter much."

p. 188, PRESIDENT *(sings)*: As with Mary's song, Walsingham's is virtually a fresh composition of Pushkin's. In Wilson, Walsingham's song is much longer, consisting of five sixteen-line stanzas (eight pairs of rhyming couplets) each followed by a four-line chorus:

> Then, leaning on this snow-white breast,
> I sing the praises of the Pest!
> If me thou wouldst this night destroy,
> come, smite me in the arms of Joy.

This chorus, which finds a dim reflection in the last stanza of Pushkin's version, is really the only point of contact between the two songs.

My translation of Walsingham's song follows the metre and rhyme scheme of Pushkin's song (except that Pushkin rhymes the third and fifth lines too).

The two songs, Mary's and Walsingham's, present alternative human responses to the plague and its threat of imminent death. Mary's song is one of unselfish resignation in the Christian tradition; Walsingham's is a pagan, or even godless, hymn of individual defiance and bravado.

p. 190, *The way he talks of Hell... mind your business!*: In Wilson the two lines addressed to the priest read: "How well he talks of Hell! Go on, old boy! / The devil pays his tithes – yet he abuses him."

Pushkin does not attempt to translate the rather abstruse jibe in the second line.

p. 190, *Is that you, Walsingham?... on her grave*: Pushkin has scaled down the melodrama of Wilson's six lines to four. See Appendix 4.

p. 190, *Do you imagine... Why is it you have come / to trouble me?*: Here Pushkin first changes Wilson's meaning and then cuts out fifteen and a half lines. For Wilson's version, see Appendix 4. Wilson's words serve to expose the rising tension between Walsingham and the Young Man, which later results in their duel; but this is beyond the scope of Pushkin's excerpt.

p. 191, *cursed be any that goes with you!*: In Wilson it is not others that Walsingham is threatening with his curse, but himself: "But curst be these feet if they do follow thee."

p. 191, PRESIDENT *(standing up)*: Wilson's stage direction reads: "*starting distractedly from his seat*".

p. 191, *Swear to me... not mention it again!*: In Wilson, Walsingham accuses the priest of already having sworn not to mention Matilda's name to him again.

p. 191, *dead and buried*: Pushkin has shortened Wilson's text here by about five lines – see Appendix 4.

p. 192, *He goes off... deep in contemplation*: This closing stage direction is Pushkin's. Wilson's direction at this point simply reads: "*The Priest walks mournfully away*"; and he continues the scene for nearly ninety more lines. In this final section of Wilson's text the young man (whom Wilson names Fitzgerald) speaks flippantly about Walsingham and Mary, then derisively about the old priest. His remarks incense Walsingham to the point where a fight breaks out between them. The fight is broken up by the intervention of two of the main characters of the play (who do not appear at all in Pushkin's excerpt); and Fitzgerald and Walsingham agree to meet for a duel later that night. In the meantime Walsingham has declared his continuing love for Mary. By his change of the final direction Pushkin refocuses the scene as a reflection on the implications of imminent death, leaving it to readers to work out what conclusion Walsingham, and they themselves, should draw.

Extra Material

on

Alexander Pushkin's

Boris Godunov

and

Little Tragedies

Alexander Pushkin's Life

Alexander Pushkin was born in Moscow in 1799. He came *Family, Birth and*
of an ancient, but largely undistinguished, aristocratic line. *Childhood*
Some members of his father's family took a part in the events
of the reign of Tsar Borís Godunóv (r. 1598–1605) and appear
in Pushkin's historical drama about that Tsar. Perhaps his
most famous ancestor – and the one of whom Pushkin was
most proud – was his mother's grandfather, Abrám Petróvich
Gannibál (or Annibál) (c.1693–1781), who was an African,
most probably from Ethiopia or Cameroon. According to
family tradition he was abducted from home at the age of
seven by slave traders and taken to Istanbul. There in 1704
he was purchased by order of the Russian foreign minister
and sent to Moscow, where the minister made a gift of him
to Tsar Peter the Great. Peter took a liking to the boy and
in 1707 stood godfather to him at his christening (hence his
patronymic Petróvich, "son of Peter"). Later he adopted the
surname "Gannibál", a Russian transliteration of Hannibal,
the famous African general of Roman times. Peter sent him
abroad as a young man to study fortification and military
mining. After seven years in France he was recalled to Russia,
where he followed a career as a military engineer. Peter's
daughter, the Empress Elizabeth, made him a general, and he
eventually died in retirement well into his eighties on one of
the estates granted him by the crown.

Pushkin had an older sister, Olga, and a younger brother,
Lev. His parents did not show him much affection as a child,
and he was left to the care of his grandmother and servants,
including a nurse of whom he became very fond. As was usual
in those days, his early schooling was received at home, mostly
from French tutors and in the French language.

School   In 1811 at the age of twelve Pushkin was sent by his parents to St Petersburg to be educated at the new Lyceum (Lycée, or high school) that the Emperor Alexander I had just established in a wing of his summer palace at Tsárskoye Seló to prepare the sons of noblemen for careers in the government service. Pushkin spent six happy years there, studying (his curriculum included Russian, French, Latin, German, state economy and finance, scripture, logic, moral philosophy, law, history, geography, statistics and mathematics), socializing with teachers and fellow students, and relaxing in the palace park. To the end of his life he remained deeply attached to his memories and friends from those years. In 1817 he graduated with the rank of collegial secretary, the tenth rank in the civil service, and was attached to the Ministry of Foreign Affairs, with duties that he was allowed to interpret as minimal. While still at the Lyceum Pushkin had already started writing poetry, some of which had attracted the admiration of leading Russian literary figures of the time.

St Petersburg 1817–20   Pushkin spent the next three years in St Petersburg living a life of pleasure and dissipation. He loved the company of friends, drinking parties, cards, the theatre and particularly women. He took an interest in radical politics. And he continued to write poetry – mostly lyric verses and epigrams on personal, amatory or political subjects – often light and ribald, but always crisply, lucidly and euphoniously expressed. Some of these verses, even unpublished, gained wide currency in St Petersburg and attracted the unfavourable notice of the Emperor.

Pushkin's major work of this period was *Ruslan and Lyudmila*, a mock epic in six cantos, completed in 1820 and enthusiastically received by the public. Before it could be published, however, the Emperor finally lost patience with the subversiveness of some of Pushkin's shorter verses and determined to remove him from the capital. He first considered exiling Pushkin to Siberia or the White Sea, but at the intercession of high-placed admirers of Pushkin's the proposed sentence was commuted to a posting to the south of Russia. Even so, some supposed friends hurt and infuriated Pushkin by spreading exaggerated rumours about his disgrace.

Travels in the South   Pushkin was detailed to report to Lieutenant-General Iván Inzóv (1768–1845), who was at the time Commissioner for the Protection for Foreign Colonists in Southern Russia based at

Yekaterinosláv (now Dnepropetróvsk) on the lower Dnieper. Inzóv gave him a friendly welcome, but little work to do, and before long Pushkin caught a fever from bathing in the river and was confined to bed in his poor lodgings. He was rescued by General Nikoláy Rayévsky, a soldier who had distinguished himself in the war of 1812 against Napoleon. Rayévsky, who from 1817 to 1824 commanded the Fourth Infantry Corps in Kiev, was travelling through Yekaterinosláv with his younger son (also called Nikoláy), his two youngest daughters María and Sófya, a personal physician and other attendants; they were on their way to join the elder son Alexándr, who was taking a cure at the mineral springs in the Caucasus. General Rayévsky generously invited Pushkin to join them, and Inzóv gave his leave.

The party arrived in Pyatigórsk, in the northern foothills of the Caucasus, in June. Pushkin, along with his hosts, benefited from the waters and was soon well again. He accompanied the Rayévskys on long trips into the surrounding country, where he enjoyed the mountain scenery and observed the way of life of the local Circassian and Chechen tribes. In early August they set off westwards to join the rest of the Rayévsky family (the General's wife and two older daughters) in the Crimea. On the way they passed through the Cossack-patrolled lands on the northern bank of the Kubán river and learnt more about the warlike Circassians of the mountains to the south.

General Rayévsky and his party including Pushkin met up with the rest of the family at Gurzúf on the Crimean coast, where they had the use of a villa near the shore. Pushkin enjoyed his time in the Crimea, particularly the majestic coastal scenery, the southern climate, and the new experience of living in the midst of a harmonious, hospitable and intelligent family. He also fell in love with Yekaterína, the General's oldest daughter, a love that was not reciprocated. Before leaving the Crimea Pushkin travelled with the Rayévskys through the coastal mountains and inland to Bahchisaráy, an oriental town which had till forty years before been the capital of the Tatar khans of the Crimea and where the khans' palace still stood (and stands).

After a month in the Crimea it was time for the party to return to the mainland. During the summer General Inzóv had been transferred from Yekaterinosláv to be governor of Bessarabia (the northern slice of Moldavia, which Russia had annexed from Turkey only eight years previously). His new headquarters was in Kishinyóv (*Chişinău*), the chief town of Bessarabia. So it was to Kishinyóv that Pushkin went back to duty in September 1820. Pushkin remained there (with spells of local leave) till 1823.

Bessarabia 1820–23 Kishinyóv was still, apart from recently arrived Russian officials and soldiers, a raw near-eastern town, with few buildings of stone or brick, populated by Moldavians and other Balkan nationalities. Despite the contrast with St Petersburg, Pushkin still passed a lot of his time in a similar lifestyle of camaraderie, drinking, gambling, womanizing and quarrelling, with little official work. But he wrote too. And he also, as in the Caucasus and Crimea, took a close interest in the indigenous cultures, visiting local fairs and living for a few days with a band of Moldavian gypsies, an experience on which he later drew in his narrative poem *Gypsies*.

In the winter of 1820–21 Pushkin finished the first of his "southern" narrative poems, *A Prisoner in the Caucasus*, which he had already begun in the Crimea. (The epilogue he added in May 1821.) This poem reflects the experiences of his Caucasus visit. The work was published in August 1822. It had considerable public success, not so much for the plot and characterization, which were criticized even by Pushkin himself, but rather, as Pushkin acknowledged, for its "truthful, though only lightly sketched, descriptions of the Caucasus and the customs of its mountain peoples".

Having completed *A Prisoner in the Caucasus*, Pushkin went on to write a narrative poem reflecting his impressions of the Crimea, *The Fountain of Bahchisaráy*. This was started in 1821, finished in 1823 and published in March 1824. It was also a great popular success, though again Pushkin dismissed it as "rubbish". Both poems, as Pushkin admitted, show the influence of Lord Byron, a poet whom, particularly at this period, Pushkin admired.

Just before his departure from Kishinyóv in 1823, Pushkin composed the first few stanzas of Chapter One of his greatest work, the novel-in-verse *Eugene Onegin*. It took him eight years to complete. Each chapter was published separately (except Chapters Four and Five, which came out together) between the years 1825 and 1832; the work was first published as a whole in 1833.

Odessa 1823–24 In the summer of 1823, through the influence of his friends in St Petersburg, Pushkin was posted to work for Count

Mikhaíl Vorontsóv, who had just been appointed Governor General of the newly-Russianized region south of the Ukraine. Vorontsóv's headquarters were to be in Odessa, the port city on the Black Sea founded by Catherine the Great thirty years previously. Despite its newness Odessa was a far more lively, cosmopolitan and cultured place than Kishinyóv, and Pushkin was pleased with the change. But he only remained there a year.

Pushkin did not get on well with his new chief, partly because of temperamental differences, partly because Pushkin objected to the work Count Vorontsóv expected him to do, and partly because Pushkin had an affair with the Countess. Vorontsóv tried hard to get Pushkin transferred elsewhere, and Pushkin for his part became so unhappy with his position on the Count's staff that he tried to resign and even contemplated escaping overseas. But before matters came to a head the police intercepted a letter from Pushkin to a friend in which he spoke approvingly of the atheistic views of an Englishman he had met in the city. The authorities in St Petersburg now finally lost patience with Pushkin: he was dismissed from the service and sent to indefinite banishment on his mother's country estate of Mikháylovskoye in the west of Russia. He left Odessa for Mikháylovskoye on 1st August 1824; he had by now written two and a half chapters of *Eugene Onegin*, and had begun *Gypsies*.

Pushkin spent more than two years under police surveillance *Exile at Mikháylovskoye* at Mikháylovskoye. The enforced leisure gave him a lot of time for writing. Within a couple of months he had completed *Gypsies*, which was first published in full in 1827. *Gypsies* is a terser, starker, more thoughtful, and more dramatic work than *A Prisoner in the Caucasus* or *The Fountain of Bahchisaráy*; along with *Eugene Onegin* it marks a transition from the discursive romanticism of Pushkin's earliest years to the compressed realism of his mature style. At Mikháylovskoye Pushkin progressively completed Chapters Three to Six of *Eugene Onegin*, many passages of which reflect Pushkin's observation of country life and love of the countryside. He also wrote his historical drama *Boris Godunov* at this period and his entertaining verse tale *Count Nulin*.

In November 1825 Alexander I died. He left no legitimate *The Decembrist Revolt* children, and there was initially confusion over the succession. *1825* In December some liberally-minded members of the army and the intelligentsia (subsequently known as the "Decembrists") seized the opportunity to attempt a coup d'état. This was put down by the new Emperor, Nicholas I, a younger brother of Alexander's. Among the conspirators were several old friends of Pushkin, and he might well have joined them had he been at liberty. As it was, the leading conspirators were executed, and many of the rest were sent to Siberia for long spells of hard labour and exile. Pushkin feared that he too might be punished.

Rehabilitation 1826–31   The following autumn Pushkin was summoned unexpectedly to Moscow to see the new Emperor. Nicholas surprised Pushkin by offering him his freedom, and Pushkin assured Nicholas of his future good conduct. Pushkin complained that he had difficulty in making money from his writing because of the censorship, and Nicholas undertook to oversee Pushkin's work personally. In practice, however, the Emperor delegated the task to the Chief of the Secret Police, and, despite occasional interventions from Nicholas, Pushkin continued to have difficulty with the censors.

After a few months in Moscow Pushkin returned to St Petersburg, where he spent most of his time in the coming years, though he continued periodically to visit Moscow, call at the family's estates, and stay with friends in the country. In 1829 he made his only visit abroad, following the Russian army on a campaign into north-eastern Turkey. During the late 1820s he made several attempts to find a wife, with a view to settling down. In 1829 he met Natálya Goncharóva, whom he married early in 1831.

It was during the four years between his return from exile and his marriage that he wrote Chapter Seven (1827–28) and most of Chapter Eight (1829–31) of *Eugene Onegin*. In 1828 he also wrote *Poltáva* (published in 1829), a kind of historical novella-in-verse. This seems to have been the first attempt in Russian at a work of this kind based on the study of historical material. In its application of the imagination to real historical events, it prefigured Pushkin's later historical novel in prose *The Captain's Daughter* and helped to set a pattern for subsequent historical novels in Russia. It is also notable for the terse realism of its descriptions and for the pace and drama of its narratives and dialogues.

In the autumn of 1830 a cholera epidemic caused Pushkin to be marooned for a couple of months on another family estate, Bóldino, some 600 kilometres east of Moscow. He took advantage of the enforced leisure to write. This was when he virtually completed Chapter Eight of *Eugene Onegin*. He also composed at this time his collection of short stories in prose *Belkin's Stories*, another verse tale, *The Little House in Kolómna*, and his set of four one-act dramas known together as *The Little Tragedies*.

The 1830s were not on the whole happy years for Pushkin. His marriage, it is true, was more successful than might have been expected. Natálya was thirteen years his junior; her remarkable beauty and susceptibility to admiration constantly exposed her to the attentions of other men; she showed more liking for society and its entertainments than for intellectual or artistic pursuits or for household management; her fashionable tastes and social aspirations incurred outlays that the pair could ill afford; and she took little interest in her husband's writing. Nonetheless, despite all this they seem to have remained a loyal and loving couple; Natálya bore him four children in their less than six years of marriage, and she showed real anguish at his untimely death.

But there were other difficulties. Pushkin, though short of money himself and with a costly family of his own to maintain, was often called upon to help out his parents, his brother and sister and his in-laws, and so fell ever deeper into debt. Both his wife and the Emperor demanded his presence in the capital so that he would be available to attend social and court functions, while he would much have preferred to be in the country, writing. Though Nicholas gave him intermittent support socially and financially, many at court and in the government, wounded by his jibes or shocked by his supposed political and sexual liberalism, disliked or despised him. And a new generation of writers and readers were beginning to look on him as a man of the past.

In 1831 Pushkin at length completed *Eugene Onegin*. The final chapter was published at the beginning of 1832, the first complete edition of the work coming out in 1833. But overall in these years Pushkin wrote less, and when he did write he turned increasingly to prose. In 1833 he spent another productive autumn at the Bóldino estate, producing his most famous prose novella, *The Queen of Spades*, and one of his finest narrative poems, *The Bronze Horseman*. He also developed in these years his interest in history, already evident

The Final Years 1831–37

249

in *Boris Godunov* and *Poltáva*: Nicholas I commissioned him to write a history of Peter the Great, but alas he only left copious notes for this at his death. He did, however, complete in 1833 a history of the eighteenth-century peasant uprising known as the Pugachóv rebellion, and he built on his research into this episode to write his longest work of prose fiction, *The Captain's Daughter* (1836). Over these years too he produced his five metrical fairy stories; these are mostly based on Russian folk tales, but one, *The Golden Cockerel* (1834), is an adaptation of one of Washington Irving's *Tales of the Alhambra*.

Writings   From his school days till his death Pushkin also composed well over 600 shorter verses, comprising many lyrics of love and friendship, brief narratives, protests, invectives, epigrams, epitaphs, dedications and others. He left numerous letters from his adult years that give us an invaluable insight into his thoughts and activities and those of his contemporaries. And, as a man of keen intelligence and interest in literature, he produced throughout his career many articles and shorter notes – some published in his lifetime, others not – containing a wide variety of literary criticism and comment.

It is indeed hard to name a literary genre that Pushkin did not use in his lifetime, or it would be truer to say that he wrote across the genres, ignoring traditional categories with his characteristic independence and originality. All his writing is marked by an extraordinary polish, succinctness and clarity, an extraordinary sense for the beauty of sounds and rhythms, an extraordinary human sympathy and insight, an extraordinary feel for what is appropriate to the occasion, and an extraordinary directness and naturalness of diction that is never pompous, insincere or carelessly obscure.

Death   Early in 1837 Pushkin's career was cut tragically short. Following a series of improper advances to his wife and insults to himself, he felt obliged to fight a duel with a young Frenchman who was serving as an officer in the Imperial Horse Guards in St Petersburg. Pushkin was fatally wounded in the stomach and died at his home in St Petersburg two days later. The authorities denied him a public funeral in the capital for fear of demonstrations, and he was buried privately at the Svyatýe Góry monastery near Mikháylovskoye, where his memorial has remained a place of popular pilgrimage.

Boris Godunov

Pushkin completed *Boris Godunov* on 7th November 1825, *Composition* having worked on it for about a year. During the whole of this time he was living under detention and police surveillance on his family's country estate at Mikháylovskoye.

The play is a historical drama about a man who reigned *Subject Matter* as tsar of Russia between 1598 and 1605. It is based on the premise, questioned by some later historians but accepted by Pushkin and his sources, that Borís came to the throne only because seven years earlier he had murdered the boy who was the last rightful heir of the previous dynasty. As Borís's peaceable and well-intentioned policies founder on natural disaster, social upheaval and the opposition of vested interests, his regime becomes increasingly repressive and unpopular. Then his rule is challenged by a foreign-backed pretender claiming to be the prince he murdered. (The full story is set out in Appendix 1.) These successive setbacks inflame Borís's conscience; and his reign is more and more shadowed by his sense of guilt for the murder, with consequences that finally engulf both him and his family.

In a draft preface to the play written in 1829–30, Pushkin *Genesis of the Play* describes the genesis of *Boris Godunov* as follows:

> It was the study of Shakespeare, Karamzín and our ancient chronicles that gave me the idea of clothing in dramatic forms one of the most dramatic epochs of modern history. Undistracted by any other influence, I imitated Shakespeare in his free and broad portrayal of characters and in the casual and simple arrangement of scenarios; I followed Karamzín in his lucid exposition of events; and in the chronicles I tried to understand the mental outlook and language of that time. Rich sources! I do not know whether I proved capable of making use of them – at least my efforts were wholehearted and conscientious.

This points to two of the stimuli that led Pushkin to write this work – artistic and historical; I believe that there was also a third, subsidiary but important, stimulus – political – which it would not have been possible for him to acknowledge in public. I deal with the three in turn.

Artistic Stimulus   First and foremost Pushkin had artistic reasons for composing this play. When still in St Petersburg Pushkin had been an avid theatregoer; but he had become impatient with the prevailing taste for French classical drama and its insipid Russian imitations. Subsequently he had encountered Shakespeare (whom he read initially in French translation).

Debt to Shakespeare   Pushkin was impressed by Shakespeare's freedom from the constricting conventions of classical drama (unities of time, place, action and style); by his variety of metre, diction and setting; by his mingling of the serious and the comic; by his versatile and penetrating treatment of history; and by the range, depth and realism of his characterization. Pushkin determined to write a historical drama of his own in the manner of the Shakespearean history plays, to demonstrate to the Russian public an alternative theatrical style more powerful in its effect and richer in its potential, more lifelike in its situations and dialogue. He wrote to a friend, N.N. Rayévsky, while he was at work on the play: "*La vraisemblance des situations et la vérité du dialogue – voilà la véritable règle de la tragédie... Quel homme que ce Schakespeare! Je n'en reviens pas.*" ("Plausibility of situations and authenticity of dialogue – that's the true yardstick of serious drama... Shakespeare – what a man! I'm astounded.") And *Boris Godunov* shows a strong Shakespearean influence in all the areas mentioned above. Pushkin ignores the classical unities. He writes in the Shakespearean unrhymed iambic pentameter, intermixed with passages of prose, varying the diction according to the speaker and context. He includes realistic scenes and characters from every level of society, mixing tragedy and comedy, and seeing the vulnerable human being even in the dynast. And he shares Shakespeare's interest in and insight into history, like him often viewing characters and events from the standpoint of ordinary folk, not just of the ruling classes.

Historical Stimulus   Pushkin, like Shakespeare, was fascinated by history – by the psychology of rulers, the limitations of power and the cyclical forces that seemed to give events a momentum beyond human control. During the previous decade the Russian literary public had been enthralled by the publication of successive volumes of a magisterial *History of the Russian State* by the writer Nikoláy Karamzín. Volumes X and XI of this work, dealing with the period of Borís Godunóv, had appeared in 1824, and Pushkin had spent the early months of his exile in an enthusiastic reading of them. His interest in the personal traits and impersonal forces that actuated historical events inspired him to set to work on a play that would transpose Karamzín's crowded and absorbing narrative into a theatrical experience.

Pushkin based himself closely on Karamzín, broadly following *Influence of Karamzín* his narrative of events, drawing on him for many minor incidents and references, and often echoing his language. While he was still working on the play, he wrote to a friend, Prince Pyótr Vyázemsky, in September 1825: "You want a scenario? Take the end of volume x and the whole of volume xi, there's your scenario." But Pushkin was not a slave of Karamzín: to deepen his understanding of the times, Pushkin also consulted other sources, including his own family papers, the memoirs of contemporary travellers and the assiduous records of monastic chroniclers typified by Pimen in the play. And he did not share Karamzín's political or moral standpoint. Although Karamzín was a fine writer and in many ways an excellent historian – thorough, conscientious, systematic – he was not impartial: he was a committed supporter of autocracy in Russia and of the Orthodox Church, and he took a strong, if simplistic, moral view of history, regularly condemning both Borís and the Pretender, for example, for their supposed crimes.

Pushkin, on the other hand, though hardly a democrat, *Pushkin's View of* was more open to the reform and moderation of autocracy; *Historical Characters* he was more sceptical, at least up to the time of writing the *and Events* play, in religious matters; and, though he by no means lacked moral sense, he took a less polarized view of his characters than Karamzín: he wrote in a draft article on popular drama and on the play *Martha the Governor's Wife* in 1830: "It is not [the dramatic poet's] business to justify, blame or prompt. His business is to bring a past age back to life in all its truth".

There are no heroes or villains in *Boris Godunov*: Borís and the Pretender are both ready to murder in order to gain the throne; but they also possess good, even endearing qualities. Borís aspires to be a reforming ruler; he cares for his people; he loves his family. The Pretender is often generous, humane and anxious to please, and he shows himself a courageous leader. Earlier commentators, especially in the Communist era, sometimes suggested the populace as the true hero of the play; but in Pushkin the common people too show contradictory characteristics of cheerfulness and cynicism, compassion and cruelty, pliability and stubbornness. They chiefly react to the initiatives of others, initiating nothing of themselves. So the populace too are neither heroes nor villains. Pushkin emulates his own portrait of the impassive chronicler:

> Just like a clerk, grey-haired with years in court,
> he views good men and bad without emotion,
> listening impassively to right and wrong,
> immune alike to pity and to anger.
> (Scene 5, ll. 43–46)

Moreover, Pushkin saw the working out of morality in history less in the punishment of individuals by a "Providence" that often seemed arbitrary and cruel than in the inexorable and self-perpetuating cycle of power and the crime and retribution it engenders within society – a cycle of ambition, lust for power, its seizure and retention by violence and murder, prompting in others a desire to punish and to overthrow, thus generating fresh ambition, fresh lust for power, and so on. Pushkin saw this cycle in the careers first of Borís Godunóv and then of the false Dimítry, reflecting it in the structure of the play; and, had he achieved his original plan of developing *Boris Godunov* into a historical trilogy spanning the rest of the Time of Troubles, he would no doubt have traced further repetitions of the cycle through the rest of the period. He also believed he saw it in the politics of his own day.

Political Stimulus   There was indeed a third stimulus behind Pushkin's interest in Borís Godunóv, a political one. Although Pushkin was trying to present a historical situation without bias, he found certain inescapable parallels with the personalities and events of his own day. Pushkin had been a victim of the increasingly repressive policies of the Emperor Alexander I. It was the Emperor's irritation with Pushkin's libertarian poetry, undisciplined conduct and supposedly radical and irreligious views that had led him, by fiat and not by any process of law, first to banish Pushkin from St Petersburg and then to place him under detention at Mikháylovskoye, thus excluding him from metropolitan society for over six years. Pushkin's personal resentment at Alexander's high-handed treatment and his distaste for the Emperor's latter-day reactionary policies at home and abroad were reinforced by his outrage at the wrongful and dishonourable way Alexander had come to the throne twenty-four years earlier. In 1801 Alexander's

254

father, the Emperor Paul, had been assassinated by disaffected army officers, and Pushkin had been led to understand that Alexander, as well as benefiting from the crime, had also abetted it.

So Alexander, like both Borís and the false Dimítry, had *Alexander I and Borís* come to the throne through the murder (by agents) of its *Godunóv* rightful occupant. But Pushkin saw further parallels too. Like Borís, Alexander had begun his reign as a well-meaning, if indecisive, reformer; but subsequently external circumstances, a deepening religious preoccupation (attributed by some to guilt) and his own disposition made him ever more autocratic and remote. When writing the play during 1825, Pushkin was aware that many army officers and intellectuals (among them some of his friends), disillusioned by Alexander's growing authoritarianism and influenced by liberal ideas from Western Europe, were plotting revolution: proposals included the overthrow and even assassination of Alexander and the setting up of a constitutional monarchy or republic.

So Pushkin in *Boris Godunov*, without falsifying the history as he understood it, seems to have been noting a suggestive parallel with the politics of his own day: a ruler whose legitimacy was called into question by a murder; whose early promise had been belied by events and by psychological deterioration; whose growing unpopularity was fomenting conspiracy and revolution; and whom dissidents planned to depose in favour of a regime influenced by Western values. Pushkin wanted to use the story of Borís Godunóv to examine the psychology of a man whose humane and enlightened instincts (for these were present in both Borís and Alexander) were perverted by guilt for the self-interested murder of a legitimate ruler.

The parallel did not give Pushkin cause for optimism. As Pushkin knew, the populist Pretender's invasion from Poland to overthrow Borís brought only chaos and misery till Russian autocracy was re-established. Perhaps Pushkin already sensed that the Western-inspired revolutionaries of his own day would also fail and give way to renewed autocracy.

In November 1825 Pushkin completed his drama. Although *Events Following* he was extremely pleased with it, he was under no illusion *Completion of the Play* that it would be acceptable to the authorities. He wrote to his friend Pyótr Vyázemsky in November 1825:

I greet you, my dear friend, with a romantic tragedy,
in which the principal character is Borís Godunóv! My
tragedy's finished; I read it through aloud, by myself, and
clapped my hands, and cried, hurrah, Pushkin, hurrah, you
son of a bitch! – My holy fool is a highly amusing chap;
Maryna will give you thrills – as she's Polish and more than
a treat to look at... The others are very nice too – apart
from Captain Margeret, who's always shouting obscenities;
the censor won't let him through. Zhukóvsky says that the
Tsar will pardon me because of the tragedy – hardly, my
dear fellow. Although it's written in a really good spirit,
there was no way I could hide all my ears beneath a fool's
cap. They stick out!

Before the end of that month Alexander I died unexpectedly
while visiting a remote part of Russia. The imperial couple
had no children, and initially the succession was in doubt. In
the confusion of that December the conspirators (later known
as the Decembrists) decided to act. They instigated uprisings
in St Petersburg and elsewhere; but these were ill-prepared
and quickly quashed. The new emperor, Alexander's brother
Nicholas, proceeded to establish an even more rigid autocracy
than before.

A faltering regime; a challenge from Western ideas that did
not prevail; autocracy renewed. A cycle that recurs...

Pushkin and the New Emperor

Pushkin believed at first that the political climate of the
new reign would be as unsympathetic to him as the previous
one. Nicholas I had the Decembrists punished severely, and
the poet feared that he too would be charged. In September
1826 Nicholas unexpectedly gave him his freedom; in
return Pushkin promised his good conduct. When Pushkin
complained about the censorship, Nicholas undertook to be
his personal censor. Pushkin's animosity towards the reigning
monarch was replaced by a sense of gratitude and (sometimes
reluctant) respect.

Initial Reception of the Play

In Moscow during the ensuing weeks Pushkin gave private
readings of his play; it was ecstatically received. However, the
new censorship regime did not work out as he had hoped.
When the play reached the Emperor's desk it was under cover
of a report from the regular censorship, whose views Nicholas
had sought. The censor remarked on the disjointedness of the
play and on its closeness to Karamzín's *History*. More seriously,

his report identified six passages that "must certainly be cut". These passages were (in the censor's order):

1. Margeret's fifth speech in Scene 19, for its indecent language;
2. the holy fool's words at the end of Scene 18 about not praying for Tsar Herod, apparently on the grounds that such language was not appropriate to an Orthodox Christian (as the historical Nikólka was presumed to have been);
3. the passage in Scene 22, ll. 27–33, as containing "unpleasant" sentiments that should not be published without refutation;
4. ll. 18–26 of Scene 3, for its flippant portrayal of popular feeling about the choice of a new tsar;
5. Scene 9, from the stage direction in Misaíl's second speech to his fifth speech, on the grounds of unseemly behaviour and language, especially on the part of those with a "monastic vocation";
6. Afanásy Pushkin's monologue in Scene 10, ll. 67–94, because of its grim portrayal of tsarist autocracy and its suggestion that anyone promising freedom to the serfs would set off a peasant uprising.

Despite these criticisms Nicholas reportedly read the play "with great pleasure"; he commented, however: "I consider that Mr Pushkin's aim would be achieved if, with the necessary expurgations, he were to change his comedy into a historical narrative or novel in the manner of Walter Scott." For the moment Nicholas withheld permission for publication of the play as a whole. Neither could Pushkin get permission for a theatrical performance: in his report the censor had written: "It goes without saying that [the play] cannot and should not be performed, for Patriarch and monks are never represented on our stage." During the next few years extracts from the play appeared in journals, to public acclaim, but the stalemate over publication of the whole work continued.

It is striking that the censor's objections focus on issues *Publication* of propriety rather than politics. His main concerns seem to have been coarseness and flippancy of language and the inappropriate portrayal of Orthodox monks and holy men. Only the third and sixth items of his list reflect primarily political considerations. Pushkin, who had been informed of the passages to which the censor objected but not of his reasons, worked on amendments that would accommodate some at least of his supposed objections. At length in 1830 Nicholas, who evidently still admired Pushkin's play, gave authority for Pushkin to publish it "on his own responsibility".

The published edition, dated 1831, was a somewhat mutilated version of the original play. Interestingly, although Pushkin went to some lengths to meet the censor's criticisms of the passages at items one, two, four and five, it is precisely the political criticisms that he decided to ignore. This may indicate Pushkin's awareness that the Emperor's concerns too were mainly ones of propriety. Nicholas reportedly derived "especial pleasure" from reading in 1831 the amended version of the play when it came out; but when after Pushkin's death a few years later Vasíly Zhukóvsky, as Pushkin's literary executor, was preparing a posthumous edition of Pushkin's works, Nicholas directed him once more to cut out "everything indecent" from the play.

Pushkin himself was relieved not to have lost more of the play on publication. He wrote to a friend, Prince Pyótr Vyázemsky, at the beginning of January, 1831: "A pity about one thing – in my *Boris* the people's scenes have been left out, as have the obscenities in French and in our ancestral tongue; but for the rest, it's extraordinary to read the much that has been printed."

An Authentic Text   Appendix 2 analyses the changes Pushkin made to the play for the 1831 edition and the reasons for these. It is clear both from the preceding paragraphs and from that analysis that nearly all the substantial amendments were designed, directly or indirectly, to meet the censor's objections as Pushkin understood them. This being so it seems truer to Pushkin's conception and purpose as author to use his original text of 1825, rather than the "bowdlerized" version of 1831, as the basis of the present edition.

Two More Questions   The 1825 text presents two puzzling but important features that merit further consideration. The first is the designation of the play as a "comedy", and the second is the play's unusual and enigmatic structure.

Comedy or Tragedy?   Pushkin originally subtitled the play: "A comedy concerning Tsar Borís and Grishka Otrépyev". And at the end he wrote: "End of the comedy, in which the main character is Tsar Borís

Godunóv. Glory be to the Father and to the Son and to the Holy
Ghost. AMEN." The conception of *Boris Godunov* as a comedy
has been discussed in depth elsewhere, notably by Dunning,
Emerson and Fomichev in the essays prefacing the University
of Wisconsin edition of 2006. I will not go over the same
ground here. It is sufficient to point out that, in his choice of
the word "comedy" and of the wordy style of the title, Pushkin
was imitating early Russian playwrights of the seventeenth
and eighteenth centuries, whose works predated the influence
of French classical drama. The word "comedy", moreover,
has over the centuries been used in many different ways, not
just to designate works that have, in modern terminology, a
markedly "comic" component. In a draft article on popular
drama and on the play *Martha the Governor's Wife* from 1830,
Pushkin himself commented: "high comedy is not based solely
on laughter, but on the development of characters, and... it
frequently comes near to tragedy." Moreover, as Emerson points
out in the University of Wisconsin edition, Pushkin throughout
his creative career delighted in mixing the genres – *Eugene
Onegin*: verse narrative or novel? *Poltava*: history or romance?
So with *Boris Godunov*: tragedy or comedy?

However, it is clear that in *Boris Godunov* Pushkin's
designation of the play as a "comedy" was, more even than
usual for him, an exercise in provocative irony. From the start
Pushkin spoke of the play privately using the more obvious
term "tragedy": this was the word he used several times in his
letter to Vyázemsky of November 1825 quoted above.

Why, then, did he use the provocative word "comedy" *Why "Comedy"?*
both at the start and the end of his play? Perhaps it was in
part because he wanted to mark *Boris Godunov* off from the
stilted tragedies of the classical French tradition and draw
attention to its Shakespearian blend of the comic and the
serious. He may also have meant it as a sardonic comment
on the capriciousness of Providence in visiting the crimes of
Borís on his innocent children while favouring the fraudulent
imposter with undeserved success; the final tongue-in-cheek
invocation of the Holy Trinity, mimicking the way a monastic
chronicler would sign off his chronicle, would then be an
ironic expression of scepticism over divine intervention in
human politics. Perhaps. But I believe that Pushkin may have
meant the word "comedy" also to signal that (as suggested on
p. 253) the play was designed as a pasquinade (albeit carefully

guarded) against Alexander I, the final invocation of the
Trinity then being a stab at Alexander's well-known religiosity.
In any event, for the published edition he dropped the word
"comedy", along with the invocation of the Trinity, and
substituted at the beginning the neutral term "composition"
(*sochinéniye*). Maybe he felt that the joke in the original title
had grown stale; with Alexander's death the satirical element
in the play had lost both its impulse and its target; and it
was in neither his interests nor his wishes to offend the new
Emperor's susceptibilities, familial or religious.

Structure of the Play   One would have expected a play of this nature and length,
by analogy whether with French classical drama or with
Shakespeare, to have been divided into five acts. Indeed a five-
act structure is not hard to discern (Act I: Scenes 1–4; Act II:
Scenes 5–11; Act III: Scenes 12–15; Act IV: Scenes 16–21; and
Act V: Scenes 22–25).

But Pushkin did not group the play's twenty-five scenes into
acts; they follow on one from another in an unbroken series.
He did not even number the scenes. As a result, despite the
brilliance of individual speeches and episodes, many readers,
from Pushkin's contemporaries onwards, have found the play
as a whole puzzling and disappointing because they have
been unable to see it as more than just a loose succession of
disjointed historical tableaux. No doubt it is partly a similar
puzzlement and disappointment that have discouraged theatre
directors, outside Russia at least, from staging the play.
However, the apparent lack of structure in *Boris Godunov* is
deceptive. Pushkin rejected the five-act model for a reason: a
conventional division into acts and numbered scenes would
have distorted and damaged the subtler and more innovative
architecture he had in mind for the play.

Pushkin's Dramatic   In fact the original play is made up of scenes, or groups
Architecture   of scenes, that rise and fall symmetrically, like an arch. *Boris
Godunov*: Architecture of the Play in the Appendix analyses
this architecture in detail; it explains how the cuts forced on
Pushkin by the censor's comments seriously damaged this
architecture and how Pushkin attempted to repair this damage
in the 1831 edition. The analysis reveals Pushkin's fondness,
traceable in other works too, for discerning suggestive motifs
and correspondences in apparently random and unconnected
circumstances. He did this both for artistic reasons (he liked
symmetry and matching contrast for their own sake) and for

reasons of his own psychology (he was a superstitious man, alert to hidden meanings in events). So the subtle and complex architecture that he incorporated into *Boris Godunov* was partly an expression of his desire, as a poet, to produce something balanced, patterned, aesthetically pleasing; but it was also his attempt, as a thoughtful historian, to make sense of history by identifying the impersonal forces and personal characteristics that made events, as it seemed to him, repeat themselves in successive cycles.

Boris Godunov was never staged during Pushkin's lifetime. *Boris Godunov on Stage* The first stage production in Russia, in a cut version, did not take place until 1870. Since then the play has been performed from time to time in Russia, but seldom abroad

Criticisms of *Boris Godunov*'s stageability have centred on three main areas: practicality (swift scene changes, crowds and battles, mounted horsemen and dying horses on stage, etc.); coherence and comprehensibility (abrupt scene changes, disjointedness between one scene and the next, difficulty for the audience to discern progression of the action, need for familiarity with historical background, etc. – even Nicholas I's censor commented that, although the subject of the play would be of great interest to Russians, it would be lost on foreigners); and character (audiences would be put off by lack of a hero and of any love interest).

As Lídya Lotman remarks, however, in the Russian edition of the play of 2008, the first objection underestimates the resources and resourcefulness of impresarios of Pushkin's day, let alone our own; and the other two objections could also, to a large degree, be levelled against the historical plays of Shakespeare, Schiller and others, though it must be admitted that Pushkin's trademark brevity somewhat aggravates the comprehensibility problem for a newcomer to the subject matter. It is significant, however, that these objections have not proved a barrier to the popularity of Mussorgsky's opera.

The only *Boris Godunov* familiar to theatregoers outside *Mussorgsky's Opera* Russia is the musical adaptation of Pushkin's play by Modést Mussorgsky, first performed in St Petersburg in 1874. The opera is closer to Pushkin in its settings than in its text. The outline of the plot is similar, but Mussorgsky has left out almost half of Pushkin's scenes and has combined others. The only Pushkin scenes to have been included in the opera virtually unaltered are 5 and 9.

261

In general Mussorgsky's libretto considerably writes up the role of the Russian people, emphasizing their poverty, oppression and forebodings for the future; understandably for a musical presentation, it contains a much greater folk-song element; and in the opera's Polish and Kromy scenes it greatly exaggerates the baleful influence of the Jesuits on the Pretender and his cause – a topic that Pushkin limits virtually to the exchange between the Pretender and Father Czernikowski at the beginning of Scene 12. Needless to say, the subtleties of Pushkin's structure identified in Appendix 3 are lost in Mussorgsky's version.

Little Tragedies

Composition Pushkin jotted down a list of titles that included three of the *Little Tragedies* (but not *A Feast during the Plague*) as early as 1826. We do not know how much, if any, of the composition dates from that time. Certainly the four plays did not reach their final form until the autumn of 1830 that Pushkin spent at Bóldino, one of the family's country estates, where he worked on them in October and early November.

Publication Although it is clear from Pushkin's notes that he envisaged the four plays as a cycle (along with a verse introduction which never seems to have been written), they were not published together until after his death. Three of the plays were published separately between 1831 and 1836.

Title Before settling on the name *Little Tragedies*, Pushkin referred to the plays by a number of different names – "*Dramatic Scenes*", "*Dramatic Sketches*", "*Dramatic Studies*", "*An Experiment in Dramatic Studies*". The title "*Dramatic Scenes*" recalls the *Dramatic Scenes* of the English writer Barry Cornwall, a work which seems to have had some influence over Pushkin's cycle of plays, at least at the final stage of its formation.

Barry Cornwall Pushkin had apparently obtained a copy of *The Poetical Works of Milman, Bowles, Wilson and Barry Cornwall*, a volume of English poetry that had been published in Paris (in English) in 1829. This volume contained Wilson's play *The City of the Plague*, one scene of which Pushkin translated as *A Feast during the Plague*, one of the *Little Tragedies*. It also contained short poems, a few of which Pushkin also adapted into Russian in the same year. Among Barry Cornwall's works contained in this volume were his *Dramatic Scenes*.

"Barry Cornwall" was a pseudonym for Bryan Waller Proctor (1787–1874). His *Dramatic Scenes* were first published in 1819. They are a collection of short verse plays on semi-historical, mythical or fictitious subjects, some based on stories by Boccaccio. Pushkin was evidently struck by the style and scale of Cornwall's *Dramatic Scenes* and took them as something of a model for his own short plays. Cornwall had written of his *Scenes*:

> One object that I had in view, when I wrote these *Scenes*, was to try the effect of a more natural style than that which has for a long time prevailed in our dramatic literature.
>
> I have endeavoured to mingle poetic imagery with expressions of natural emotion: but it has been my wish, where the one seemed to jar with the other, that the former should give place to the latter. In this spirit I have ventured to let several passages, little interesting perhaps otherwise than as a representation of human dialogue, remain.
>
> It may be observed, that several parts touching upon description are merely poetical, and such as men, in the general course of life, might never use. Let it be recollected, however, that the persons on whom these passages have been imposed, existed in ages more chivalrous than the present; and when men were apt to indulge in all the extravagances of romance...

Despite these protestations of "a more natural style", Cornwall's *Scenes* read today with a literary and archaic timbre, even if less so than most other examples of English dramatic verse of the eighteenth and early nineteenth centuries.

Pushkin took Cornwall's manifesto more literally and has *Pushkin's Style* produced Russian verse dialogue that reads generally with a marked contemporary naturalness, with some heightening of the language for passages of poetic description or of emotional intensity (whether real or feigned).

Except for the two songs in *A Feast during the Plague*, *Metre* Pushkin wrote the *Little Tragedies* in unrhymed iambic pentameters (lines of ten or eleven syllables with the stress on the even syllables), the same blank-verse metre as he had used for his full-length historical drama *Boris Godunov* a few years earlier. This is the same metre as that used by many English dramatists, including Shakespeare in his plays, Barry

Cornwall in his *Dramatic Scenes*, and John Wilson in *The City of the Plague*.

Description Though all the *Little Tragedies* are short, one-act plays, they range from one to four scenes and from 232 to 542 lines in length. Because of their brevity the words have an unusual intensity of meaning; and the action deals less with the development of situations than with their climaxes. Pushkin entitled the plays "tragedies", but there is a Pushkinian irony in this description – just as there was in his entitling *Boris Godunov* a "comedy". True, the subject matter of the *Little Tragedies* is full of destructive obsession and death (see below), but they are also written in a lively, entertaining, perceptive and often humorous style that belies the word "tragedy". They are remarkable too for their concision, their pace, their lucidity, their fluent dialogues, their psychological insights, and their irruptions of arresting poetry.

Settings Unlike most of Pushkin's works of the imagination, all the *Little Tragedies* have a Western-European background. Geographically the settings range between Flanders (*The Mean-Spirited Knight*), Vienna (*Mozart and Salieri*), Madrid (*The Stone Guest*) and London (*A Feast during the Plague*), and in period from the late Middle Ages (*The Mean-Spirited Knight*), through the seventeenth century (*The Stone Guest* and *A Feast during the Plague*), to just eight years before Pushkin's birth (*Mozart and Salieri*). Pushkin never visited Western Europe at all, but it is remarkable how much local atmosphere – in an unobtrusive way – the plays have, a result of the breadth of Pushkin's reading and the impressionability and retentiveness of his mind. In a speech made in June 1880 at a meeting of the Society for Russian Literature, Dostoevsky wrote of this aspect of Pushkin's achievement:

Of all the world's poets Pushkin alone possessed the property of identifying himself fully with a foreign culture. Take... *The Mean-Spirited Knight*... Reread [*The Stone Guest*] and if Pushkin's name was not attached to it, you would never know that it had not been written by a Spaniard. What profound and evocative images there are in the poem *A Feast during the Plague*! But in those evocative images the genius of Britain can be heard; that wonderful song about the plague that the hero sings, that

song of Mary... they are British songs, with the melancholy
of the British genius, its tears, its agonizing presentiment of
the future...

Despite their variety of atmosphere, the *Little Tragedies* have a *Subject Matter*
number of common themes and characteristics.

In the first place, they all concentrate on a driving obsession *Obsession*
on the part of the leading character and its destructive effects.
In each case the obsession is one of which Pushkin had himself
had close experience.

In *The Mean-Spirited Knight* the obsession is that of greed
for money and the power it confers; it traces the effect of that
obsession on the "mean-spirited" knight himself (and the
ideals of knightly generosity that he should have stood for),
on the knight's son, and beyond. Pushkin was drawing here
on his own painful relations with his tight-fisted, yet status-
conscious father.

In the second play, *Mozart and Salieri*, the obsession is
the craving for recognition and status felt by industrious
mediocrity and that mediocrity's overpowering jealousy of
apparently effortless genius. Again, Pushkin – the facility and
felicity of whose art has often been compared to Mozart's
– had had plenty of experience of the jealousy and malice of
his less talented contemporaries.

The focus of the third play, *The Stone Guest*, is on Don
Juan's obsession with sexual gratification, whatever the cost
in emotional upheaval or physical violence. Here Pushkin's
autobiographical reference is more ambivalent, because
Pushkin had sometimes seen himself as a Russian Don Juan
– and this is one reason why his portrait of Don Juan is a more
sympathetic and engaging one than its literary and operatic
predecessors.

The fourth play, *A Feast during the Plague*, deals with the
hero's obsession with risk. Walsingham, instead of retiring
to the safety of the countryside after the deaths of his wife
and mother, has thrown himself recklessly into the devil-may-
care society that has stayed behind in the doomed capital,
determined to live what is left of life to the full; and this
obsession with risk is so strong as to overwhelm all other claims
on him of common sense, family, community and religion.
Pushkin too, in his eventful life, had himself experienced this
same obsession, living recklessly in the way he talked, the

way he wrote, the way he loved, the way he gambled, and the way he hazarded his life in duels. The "thrill in... treading a dark chasm's door" was a thrill Pushkin himself had often courted.

The Mirage of   Pushkin's experience of these powerful and destructive
Happiness obsessions, in himself and others, had led him to doubt the possibility of happiness. In a letter written to Praskóvya Ósipova in November 1830, when he was writing the plays, he described himself as "*l'athée de bonheur*" ("the one who could not believe in happiness"). His personal circumstances at the time reinforced this doubt. After a long search for a wife he had recently become engaged following a difficult courtship; now impatient for marriage he found himself cut off in his estate at Bóldino for an indefinite period by emergency travel restrictions imposed by the government because of a serious cholera outbreak in much of Russia. He was unable to communicate with his fiancée in Moscow, unsure of her frame of mind, uncertain of the effect of their separation on his wedding plans, and apprehensive even of her well-being and that of other friends. Little wonder that he lost faith in happiness.

Death   Another theme running through all these plays – a theme accentuated by his personal predicament – is that of sudden death. In *The Mean-Spirited Knight* the father is haunted by fear of death, and the son comes close to willing his father's death and even in the end occasions it. *Mozart and Salieri* is straightforwardly the story of a murder, as well as an examination of the qualities of mind and character that are capable of committing it. Despite *The Stone Guest*'s light-hearted tone, death is a recurring feature of the play: Don Juan courts the death penalty by even coming to Madrid; we are told about the deaths of Doña Iñez and the Knight Commander; we witness at first hand the deaths of Don Carlos and Don Juan. *A Feast during the Plague* is set in the midst of those facing death in an epidemic and deals throughout with various characters' responses to this prospect.

Open-endedness   Despite each play's preoccupation with moral and existential issues, however, they are by no means moralizing essays. Pushkin wrote in some notes on popular drama in late 1830: "What is necessary to a dramatist? A philosophy, impartiality, the political acumen of an historian, insight, a lively imagination. No prejudices or preconceived ideas. Freedom." This philosophy of drama is what Pushkin applied to the *Little Tragedies*, which he was writing at that time. Each of the tragedies examines the issues it raises with impartiality, without prejudices or preconceived ideas; and each ends not with answers, but with a puzzle, a question, a dilemma. At the end of *The Mean-Spirited Knight* we, like the Duke, are aghast at the corruption that has manifested itself in the conduct of the Baron and his son; but we are invited to see the pair not as guilty perpetrators but as victims, less to condemn the deadly outcome than to ask ourselves how and why. *Mozart and Salieri* ends not with a condemnation of Salieri, but with a question about what kind of man could have committed his crime and why. *The Stone Guest* is far less condemnatory of Don Juan than other versions of the tale, inviting us to reflect on the characters rather than to judge them. And *A Feast during the Plague* closes with Walsingham pondering on how he should react to his predicament, not with a justification for any particular option. The essence of the *Little Tragedies* is to present us with the issues in all their baffling complexity and to encourage us to think them through for ourselves.

The *Little Tragedies* are seldom performed as plays. Only *Mozart and Salieri* was performed during Pushkin's lifetime, in 1832, but without conspicuous success. The plays are often dismissed as more suitable for the study than the stage. It is true that the compactness of Pushkin's writing and thought stands in the way of too hurried or casual a delivery; and the one-act format is not a popular one in the major commercial theatres. But I see no reason why, under a resourceful director, the first three plays at least should not be successfully staged, especially in a chamber setting. *Staging*

All the plays have been set to music as operas by Russian composers: *The Mean-Spirited Knight* by Rachmaninov (1904); *Mozart and Salieri* by Rimsky-Korsakov (1897); *The Stone Guest* by Dargomýzhsky (1869); and *A Feast during the Plague* by César Cui (1900). But stage performances of the operas are rare outside Russia.

The Mean-Spirited Knight

Literary portrayals of "the miser" that may have influenced Pushkin occur in works of the Roman dramatist Plautus (*Aulularia*), Shakespeare (*Merchant of Venice*), Molière *Origins*

267

ALEXANDER PUSHKIN • BORIS GODUNOV AND LITTLE TRAGEDIES

(*L'Avare*), Goldoni (*L'avaro*), Hoffmann (*Majorat*), and Scott (*The Fair Maid of Perth*). In an illuminating essay on the play in *Little Tragedies: The Poetics of Brevity* Vladímir Golstein has also pointed out Pushkin's debt to Dante and to Montaigne in his portrayal of the deadly effects of the Baron's meanness on himself and on his relationships with his son and others.

The tension between father and son also reflects Pushkin's experience of relations with his own father, who was notoriously mean; and the quarrel that erupts in the last pages of the play seems to echo an unpleasant incident that took place within the Pushkin family at the end of 1824. Pushkin, then twenty-five, had that summer been banished to the family estate at Mikháylovskoye, where he grew increasingly irritated by his father's tetchiness, by the derogatory remarks his father made about him in front of his brother and sister, and by his father's consenting to vet his son's correspondence on behalf of the government. By the autumn relations had become so bad that one day (as Pushkin wrote in a letter to Zhukóvsky of October 1824):

> ...my head began to boil. I went to Father, found him with Mother, and blurted out everything I'd been holding back for three whole months. I ended by saying that I was speaking to him for the last time. My father, taking advantage of the absence of witnesses, rushed out and declared to the entire household that I'd "beaten him", "meant to beat him", "raised my arm against him", "could have thrashed him"...

It was probably these echoes of conflict with his own mean-spirited father that led Pushkin to present his play, diplomatically, as a translation of a non-existent English original and to have it published, when the time came, anonymously.

Who Is the "Mean-Spirited Knight"? As we read this play, it is worth asking ourselves whom Pushkin identified as "the mean-spirited knight" (*skupóy rytsar*). Ostensibly, of course, Pushkin was applying the title to the Baron, whose hideous miserliness lies at the heart of the work both literally – in the middle-scene monologue – and figuratively – as the mainspring of the action. But the title stretches wider than that. The word (in its noun form *skupost*) only occurs twice in the text of the play; and, significantly, it is Albert who uses the term first, of himself. After describing

268

the extraordinary bravado he had shown in the tournament,
he explains:

> It was the damaged helmet that enraged me.
> What was the cause of those heroics? – Meanness (*skupost*),
> yes! It's not hard to catch that illness here,
> living beneath the same roof as my father.
> (Scene 1, ll. 35–38)

Albert likens his father's mean-spiritedness (*skupost*) to a
disease that has also infected him and has begun to make him,
like his father, the opposite of what a noble and generous
knight should be. The contagion of his father's *skupost*
is shown not only by his recklessly petulant conduct at the
tournament, but also in his treatment of the moneylender –
overbearing in itself and dishonourable in refusing to pay back
old debts, yet attempting to extort more money that he had no
early prospect of repaying. His falling short of knightly ideals
appears, too, in his lack of self-control when he confronts his
father at the end of Scene 3.

Pushkin also traces a link from *skupost* to violence,
murder and death. Again this is apparent from events at the
tournament (when Albert risked killing his opponent in what
was supposed to be a friendly sport), from the course of
Albert's conversation with Solomon (when his apparent wish
for his father's early death leads the moneylender to suggest
murder), and from Albert's readiness to fight his father at the
end. Indeed it is Albert's behaviour in disobeying the Duke
that finally precipitates the Baron's death.

And the deadly contagion of *skupost* spreads more widely
still. Solomon the moneylender is clearly infected by it to the
extent of taking his degrading servility to the point of offering
to abet a murder. Then, in the Scene 2 monologue, the Baron
credits Thibault with having mugged (or worse) to repay his
debt; he speaks of the "tears and blood and sweat" shed for his
precious treasures; and in perhaps the most chilling passage of
all he confesses:

> The medics tell us that some folk there are
> who get a kick from murder. And when I
> insert the key into the lock, I feel
> the same sensation as they must when they

bury the dagger in their victim: pleasant,
but at the same time dreadful.
(Scene 2, ll. 65–70)

Pushkin seems to be pointing out that *skupost* – miserliness, meanness, ungenerosity – spreads all too easily from one person to another, generating much of the world's violence and misery: "so many human worries, tears and lies!..." (Scene 2, l. 39).

At the denouement the Duke, who stands for the ideal of knightly courtesy and generosity, expresses outrage at the attitudes of both father and son. For the Duke (and for Pushkin) the "mean-spirited knight" is not just the Baron but Albert too; and he goes further, pointing to a human malaise that extends far beyond the protagonists in the play: "Grim times are these! And grim, too, human nature!" (Scene 3, l. 104).

Structure　The structure of *The Mean-Spirited Knight* shows once again Pushkin's use of symmetry both to create a pleasing aesthetic effect and to convey his full meaning. Most obviously, there is a symmetry in the arrangement of scenes – a monologue between two dialogues. Scene 2, the monologue, is crucial in laying bare the frightening intensity of the Baron's mean-spiritedness – his selfishness and avarice. Of the two flanking dialogues, Scene 1 ends with Albert's decision to appeal to the Duke, and Scene 3 begins with the final words of Albert's appeal. The first scene opens with an account of Albert's impulsive violence towards his jousting opponent, provoked, as he admits, by his own unknightly meanness contracted from his father. The last scene ends with Albert's impulsive violence towards his father, again provoked by a meanness of spirit contracted from his father.

The middle section of each outer scene is taken up with two lengthy conversations: Scene 1's conversation between Albert and the moneylender is matched in Scene 3 by the conversation between the Duke and the Baron. In each case Albert and the Duke are pressing a shifty social inferior to comply with a request. But the manner each adopts is sharply contrasted. The Duke's approach to the Baron, though firm, is a model of knightly friendliness and courtesy; Albert's approach to the moneylender, on the other hand, though equally determined, is characterized by an offensive and hectoring tone and a conspicuous absence of knightly qualities. On this reading, the

Jewish moneylender is less an example of *skupost* than its victim. Each scene, too, contains a couple of hints of how much better a man each of the protagonists might have been but for their contagious meanness: the Baron was evidently once on terms of cordial familiarity with the Duke's grandfather and played affectionately with his grandson; Albert, for his part, is still able to feel compassion for the lowlier creatures indispensable to his profession as a knight – his horse and his blacksmith.

An awareness of these symmetries in Pushkin's play is essential to a full understanding of the characters and their motivations.

Mozart and Salieri

Salieri was born in northern Italy in 1750 and came to *Antonio Salieri* Vienna at the age of sixteen. In Italy he had already learnt the harpsichord, violin, singing and harmony. In Vienna he continued to learn the violin and harmony and also studied counterpoint, Latin, German, French and the art of Italian poetry.

Salieri soon established himself in Vienna as a successful musician and opera composer. While still in his teens he met the illustrious Gluck, who was to become his patron and lifelong friend. Early on he attracted the notice of the Emperor Joseph II, and at the age of only twenty-four he gained appointment as court composer and conductor of the Italian Opera – one of the most important musical positions in Europe. The next year, 1775, he married Theresia Helferstorfer, by whom he had eight children.

In the late 1770s Salieri was given leave to spend some time travelling and working in Italy; and between 1784 and 1787 he also made visits to Paris to fulfil a commission for the composition and presentation of operas that Gluck was too ill to undertake. But otherwise he remained in Vienna for the rest of his life. There his prestigious post (he also became Kapellmeister in 1788), the Emperor's continuing favour, his other connections in high places, and his adeptness at political manoeuvre made him a powerful figure in the musical world and his influence was felt in every area.

Mozart, six years Salieri's junior, arrived in Vienna in the early 1780s as a newcomer and outsider. He could have benefited from Salieri's help and support. Salieri did not,

271

however, give it, but rather intrigued against him and kept him at bay, whether through personal distaste or fear of him as a rival. A contemporary characterized him as "a clever, shrewd man possessed of... 'crooked wisdom'". However, after some years of distance, if not hostility, between the two men, by the early 1790s relations seem to have improved: in October 1791 Salieri attended *The Magic Flute* as Mozart's guest and praised it enthusiastically.

From the 1790s onwards Salieri composed less; he wrote no operas after 1804. However, he remained a respected figure of the Viennese musical establishment for many more years. He was known as a good administrator, a supporter and organizer of musical charities, and as an encourager and teacher of the younger generation of musicians. Among his many pupils were Beethoven and Schubert and even Mozart's younger son.

In the early 1820s, when Salieri was already in his seventies, his mental health deteriorated and in 1823 he made an attempt on his own life. He died at the age of seventy-four in 1825. His funeral was impressive and well attended.

Mozart and Salieri   This is the only one of Pushkin's four *Little Tragedies* to portray historical characters. Many details mentioned in the text are based on fact; in particular, there is contemporary evidence of rivalry and friction between Mozart and Salieri when they were both working in Vienna in the 1780s. However, there is widespread doubt over the historicity of the culminating event of the play, the poisoning of Mozart by Salieri. Even at the time of its first publication critics questioned the veracity of this version of Mozart's death. This provoked Pushkin to record among his notes in 1832 (although only published in 1855) the grounds for his own belief in the story. The text of this note is as follows:

At the first performance of *Don Giovanni*, when the whole theatre, full of astonished music-lovers, was silently feasting their senses on Mozart's music, someone let out a hiss. Everyone looked round in indignation, and the celebrated Salieri left the auditorium in a frenzy, consumed with jealousy.

Salieri died eight years ago. Some German magazines reported that on his deathbed he had confessed to a dreadful crime – to the poisoning of the great Mozart.

A man who was jealous enough to hiss *Don Giovanni* was capable of poisoning its creator.

The source of Pushkin's *Don Giovanni* story, however, is unclear, and scholars today discount it on the grounds that Salieri could not have been present for the first performance of the opera in Prague on 29th October 1787. If the story refers to the Vienna premiere in May 1788, the audience on that occasion was less enthusiastic than the story implies; and there is no known contemporary account of the incident. As for the alleged confession, it is true that during the last year or two of Salieri's life there were circulating in Vienna persistent reports (as well as denials) that he had admitted to poisoning Mozart. But in any case Salieri was then old and suffering from dementia; so the reports, even if accepted, do not count for much.

The malaise that caused Mozart's death in December 1791 in his thirty-sixth year is now believed to have been either a recurrence of the rheumatic fever from which he had suffered before or chronic renal failure with complications. At the time, however, the symptoms mystified Mozart and his family. On occasions, weighed down by pain, weakness and depression, Mozart confided to his wife that he thought he had been poisoned, though without naming a culprit. Rumours of poisoning resurfaced soon after his death, and recurred periodically in the ensuing years, but Salieri was not mentioned as a suspect until the reports of his own confession began to circulate late in 1823, just after his attempted suicide.

The historical verdict on Salieri as Mozart's poisoner must therefore be "not guilty". Nonetheless, some commentators have found Salieri guilty of a contributory part in bringing about Mozart's premature death. Echoing a remark of Mozart's younger son many years later, they claim that, though Salieri did not murder Mozart, he had "truly poisoned his life with his intrigues", and that it was perhaps this burden on Salieri's conscience that led to his deranged confession at the end of his life. The irony of Salieri's career is that his name lives on only by reason of his association with Mozart. His works died with him. As W.H. Auden wrote in his 'Metalogue to The Magic Flute':

We should,
As Mozart, were he living, surely would,
Remember kindly Salieri's shade,
Accused of murder and his works unplayed.

Fiction and Truth So does the unhistoricity of the poisoning story discredit Pushkin's "little tragedy"? No. *Mozart and Salieri*, even if unhistorical, draws its authority, as does any good work of creative art, from the inherent truth of its portrayal of life and character, as validated by the experience of author and audience. Pushkin has often been likened to Mozart for perfection of technique, for felicity of artistry, and for lightness and spontaneity of personality. Pushkin too suffered from the covert jealousy and hatred of some of his professed friends and fellow artists. The play remains a fascinating and persuasive study of a craving for status, of professional jealousy and of the nature of artistic inspiration, drawing on Pushkin's own experience.

Peter Shaffer's Amadeus The similarity of subject matter between Pushkin's *Mozart and Salieri* and Peter Shaffer's play *Amadeus* (which received its premiere in London in 1979 and was later made into a celebrated film) is striking. It provokes the question: was Shaffer aware of Pushkin's play and was he influenced by it?

Shaffer is said to have denied prior knowledge of Pushkin's play. But in his edition of *Amadeus* Richard Adams writes:

> Shaffer's sources must certainly have included Pushkin's "little tragedy"... A number of narrative details have found their way into *Amadeus* unmodified: Salieri's burning ambition to achieve great ness as a composer, for instance; his envy of the careless ease with which Mozart can write music of unarguable genius; finally, his decision – while pretending to be the younger man's friend – to engineer his destruction.

Other parallels include Salieri's shouting of the name "Mozart" at the climax of Shaffer's "overture" (just as Pushkin has Salieri culminating his opening speech with a shout of "Mozart!"); Salieri's comparing Mozart the musician to a god, while recoiling from Mozart the man as "an obscene child" (in Pushkin "an idiot, an idle good-for-nothing"); Salieri's defiant soliloquy of jealousy at the end of the first act of both plays;

in the second act of both, Salieri's false friendship for Mozart; and towards the end Mozart's obsession with the visitor in black. In general, however, the similarities between the two plays are of form and outline rather than of detail, and some at least of the parallels could have arisen independently from the common subject matter rather than through borrowing by Shaffer from Pushkin.

The Stone Guest

The legend of Don Juan – arrogant, unprincipled nobleman, *Origins* combative adventurer, serial seducer, who is eventually dragged down to hell by the stone statue of a relation of one of his female victims – was a recurrent theme of European literature from the seventeenth century – partly no doubt because of the opportunity the storyline offers for a popular combination of sex, violence, comedy and stern morality, and partly because of the scope Don Juan's multiplicity of adventures gives the author for infinite variation of incident within the standard framework of murder and retribution. Its first manifestation seems to have been in a play by Tirso de Molina (a pseudonym for the Spanish monk Fray Gabriel Téllez), published in 1630. The play, called *El burlador de Sevilla o El convidado de piedra*, tells of the amorous adventures of a nobleman from Seville, Don Juan Tenorio, in both Italy and Spain. Back in Seville after his travels Don Juan attempts the rape of Doña Ana, daughter of the *comendador* Don Gonzalo, who comes to the help of his daughter. Don Juan kills the father and escapes. After further adventures, he comes across the tomb of the *comendador* in a Seville graveyard, insults it and mockingly invites it to dinner with him. The statue accepts, and offers in return to show Don Juan the family sepulchre. Don Juan in his turn recklessly accepts the invitation, shakes hands with the statue, and is dragged by it into hell.

The French playwright Molière came to know of Tirso de Molina's play in Paris, probably through adaptations by travelling French and Italian players. Molière produced his own play on the same theme – *Don Juan ou le festin de pierre* (1665) – though he moved the setting to Sicily, increased the comic element, and changed many of the characters and incidents (Doña Ana, for instance, does not appear).

During the later seventeenth century and the eighteenth century there were many further adaptations of the story in Western-European literature, including latterly several Italian opera libretti, most famously that by Lorenzo da Ponte for Mozart's opera *Don Giovanni* (1787). Again, the libretto brings out the comedy, though within a frame of melodrama: the action opens with Don Giovanni's attempted rape of Donna Anna and murder of her father and ends (as usual) with his enforced descent to hell at the hands of the dead man's statue.

In 1812 Ernst Theodor Amadeus Hoffmann wrote a short story about the legend, or rather about Mozart's opera *Don Giovanni*; but Pushkin's play shows no sign of influence from that quarter. Lord Byron wrote his long and unfinished narrative poem *Don Juan* (1818–23) on the same theme; but he uses the traditional legend largely as a vehicle for a satirical and autobiographical commentary on his own times and contemporaries. Pushkin knew and admired Byron, and his *Don Juan* in particular, but he did not follow the Byronic version of the legend in his play, except in his use of it as a vehicle for autobiography.

One important source that he did use was Mozart's opera, as is evidenced, for example, by the epigraph, which is a direct quotation from the da Ponte libretto, and by the naming of Don Juan's servant Leporello (he has different names in Tirso de Molina and in Molière); the link with Mozart is also suggested by his placing *The Stone Guest* immediately after *Mozart and Salieri* in the cycle of *Little Tragedies*. Although Pushkin presumably knew Molière's play too, it is interesting that he made little use of that, preferring to go back to the original Spanish setting by Tirso de Molina, to which is due Don Juan's exile and unauthorized return, the closeness of the noble hero to the king, his temporary stay in a monastery near the capital, and a series of other details.

Pushkin also drew, however, on other works outside the Don Juan tradition. For example he may owe the wooing of Doña Ana by her husband's tomb to the *Satyricon*, the long novel by the Latin author Petronius (d. 65 AD), which includes the story of the widow of Ephesus, who, while mourning in her husband's funeral vault, is approached and seduced by a Roman soldier. He seems to have been influenced too by Shakespeare's *Richard III*, where the courtship scene between

Gloucester and the Lady Anne (who is both widow and daughter-in-law of men whom Gloucester is supposed to have killed) presents several parallels with the encounters between Don Juan and Doña Ana in Scenes 3 and 4. And there is an echo or two of Barry Cornwall's *Dramatic Scenes*.

These extraneous references, together with Pushkin's own contributions, make *The Stone Guest* a largely original work within the Don Juan tradition. Pushkin is the first writer to make Doña Ana the Knight Commander's widow, rather than his daughter; he is the first to have the stone guest invited, not to supper, but to abet the seduction of his widow as doorkeeper; and he is the first to place the punishment of Don Juan at the end of the love scene with Doña Ana and to have him die with her name on his lips and without any overt moral judgements. Pushkin's Don Juan also shows some appreciation of the personalities of others, both men and women, and is capable of speaking with a poetic intensity of feeling, however transitory those feelings may be. These features, the characterization of Don Juan as more feckless than intrinsically evil, and the consistent liveliness of the dialogue make for a tighter, more realistic and more compelling drama, in which the human and comic elements outshine the grimness of the main storyline.

As in *The Mean-Spirited Knight* and *Boris Godunov* there is *Structure* an external symmetry in the construction of *The Stone Guest*. This is best shown in tabular form:

Scene 1	Scene 3
Outdoors, by a cemetery; Leporello, Don Juan in disguise, monk, Doña Ana	Outdoors, in the cemetery; Leporello, Don Juan disguised as monk, Doña Ana

Scene 2	Scene 4
In a girlfriend's room; Don Juan, girlfriend, rival who dies; after a struggle Don Juan lives on	In a girlfriend's room; Don Juan, girlfriend, rival who comes back from the dead; after a struggle Don Juan goes to hell.

Once more Pushkin's love of balance and matching contrasts is evident.

277

The Stone Guest as Autobiography

What gives *The Stone Guest* much of its originality and interest is Pushkin's use of it as a vehicle for reflection on his own life, past and future. Anna Akhmatova commented on this in an essay reprinted in *Little Tragedies: The Poetics of Brevity*. Although some of the parallels between the play and Pushkin's experience are obvious, he included some subtler clues to confirm the autobiographical significance of the play. The note on the epigraph on p. 230 shows how Pushkin saw Don Juan and the Knight Commander as different aspects of the same person. It is worth considering too that Pushkin himself was an inveterate lover of women, with a catalogue of conquests that rivalled Don Juan's, to whom indeed in his bachelor days he sometimes likened himself, and (as pointed out in the note to p. 161) the features of the Knight Commander's statue are in fact Pushkin's own.

This concept of *The Stone Guest* as, to an important extent, autobiographical makes sense of some other ostensibly gratuitous features: the jocular discussion between Don Juan and Leporello in the opening lines about the effectiveness of the Don's disguise; the distinctive and touching sketch in Scene 1, l. 46*ff.* of Doña Iñez, a character of no relevance to the rest of the play (see note to p. 147); transference of the action of the play to Madrid, the capital city, instead of Seville; Don Juan's reputed atheism ("godlessness"), mentioned several times in the play, as noted by Anna Akhmatova; Pushkin's unique presentation of Doña Ana as the Knight Commander's wife, not his daughter; the reference in Scene 2, l. 22 to Don Juan as a poet; and lastly the unusual portrayal of Don Juan himself in the play, despite his violence and rakishness as a markedly cheerful and engaging character.

This strongly personal and autobiographical nature of *The Stone Guest* may also explain why Pushkin never published it, alone of the *Little Tragedies*, during his lifetime.

Pushkin wrote *The Stone Guest* at a turning point in his life. By autumn 1830, now thirty-one years old, after a disorganized and turbulent career, he was at last engaged and would shortly be settling down to married life. As well as seeing his past self as a Don Juan, prepared if necessary to fight duels over a woman claimed by another man, he was beginning to see his future self as the protective husband of a vulnerable young wife, destined to stand stiffly on guard while younger men tried to seduce her. As David Bethea has written, in *Little Tragedies: The Poetics of Brevity*: "the Pushkin of *The Stone Guest* is *both* the Juan hoping to be reborn *and* the husband (his new role) protecting what is his by right."

Just as the vital and irrepressible Don Juan is consigned to perdition by the stone statue of the Knight Commander, in the same way the hot-blooded and profligate young Pushkin of the past is about to be supplanted by a supposedly cold and staid middle-aged Pushkin of the future. Read in this way, *The Stone Guest*, unlike its antecedents, is not a far-fetched moral tale about retribution, but a realistic observation, half-rueful, half-ironic, about a man's transition from bachelorhood to married life, from youth to middle age.

A Feast during the Plague

John Wilson (1785–1854) was a Scottish poet, journalist *John Wilson* and essayist, who under his pseudonym of Christopher North took a leading part in directing and contributing to *Blackwood's Magazine*. He was born in Paisley, the son of a wealthy manufacturer, and educated first locally, then at Glasgow University and Magdalen College, Oxford. With his inherited wealth he bought the small estate of Elleray in the Lake District, and became a friend of Wordsworth and Coleridge. He published *The City of the Plague* in 1816. Having lost much of his remaining fortune through the failure of a commercial enterprise in which it was invested, he secured election in 1820 to the post of Professor of Moral Philosophy in the University of Edinburgh, a post that he held till 1852, when a paralytic seizure compelled him to resign his chair.

Wilson's lengthy drama *The City of the Plague*, written *The City of the Plague* like Pushkin's translation in blank verse, consists of thirteen scenes grouped into three acts. The main action describes numerous deaths in plague-ridden London, and the reaction of the surviving characters to those deaths. The general effect, though sometimes moving, tends to pietism, morbidity and sentimentality.

The excerpt chosen by Pushkin covers only about three quarters of one scene (Act I, Sc. 4) of the play. This scene is not an integral part of the plot: apart from the priest, only

Walsingham and the Young Man (Fitzgerald) reappear at all, and then only once in Act II, Sc. 5, when Walsingham and Fitzgerald meet in a churchyard for their duel and Fitzgerald impales himself on Walsingham's sword. All the main characters of the play (except the priest) are absent from Pushkin's excerpt.

Pushkin's translation is for the most part close. The main exceptions are the songs of Mary and Walsingham (see notes), which are largely Pushkin's original composition. Other significant respects in which Pushkin diverges from Wilson are mentioned in the notes.

Wilson's language is fluent, though somewhat literary and archaic. Pushkin transposes it into the much more direct and contemporary idiom that he uses for his other *Little Tragedies*, and it is this idiom that I have tried to reproduce in my translation.

The text of the relevant part of Wilson's play is reproduced in Appendix 4.

Translator's Note

Language While Pushkin was working on *Boris Godunov* in May 1825 a friend of his, N.N. Rayévsky, prophesied: "*Vous achèverez de faire descendre la poésie de ses échasses.*" ("You will succeed in bringing poetry down off its stilts.") This was indeed one of Pushkin's achievements. The aim of these translations is accordingly to offer Pushkin's plays to the English-speaking public in a version that is equally unstilted – faithful, of course, to the original, but expressed in English that is as clear and modern as was Pushkin's Russian. Like Pushkin, I have introduced archaic expressions only where the context demands; and where he varies the register between the straightforward, the formal, the poetic, the ecclesiastical, the colloquial, the ironic, etc, I have tried to do likewise. My intention has also been to produce a rendering that is 'speakable' as well as readable, in the hope that someone may be encouraged to present these great works in English as dramas.

Metre In *Boris Godunov* Pushkin has followed Shakespeare in writing mainly in blank verse (i.e. in unrhymed pentameters – lines of ten or eleven syllables, with an iambic rhythm), though (like Shakespeare) he has rhymed the pentameters in a

few short passages for special effect. I have followed Pushkin
in this. Some scenes or parts of scenes are in prose, and I
have rendered them into prose accordingly. Two scenes are in
quite different metres: Scene 6 is in largely unrhymed trochaic
octameters, which I have reproduced unrhymed; Scene 13 is
in rhymed iambic lines of varied length, where again I have
kept the rhythm, but without the rhymes, as explained in the
commentary (p. 212).

Pushkin's pentameters in *Boris Godunov* include a caesura
(a break between words) after the fourth syllable. Pushkin
commented on this in a draft preface written in 1829:

> The metre I have used (the iambic pentameter) has been
> adopted as normal by the English and Germans… I have
> retained the caesura in the second foot from the French
> pentameter – and I believe that I was mistaken in this
> because I wilfully deprived my line of its inherent variety.

In view of Pushkin's second thoughts I have not included a
regular caesura in my pentameter translations.

The *Little Tragedies* are composed in unrhymed pentameters (without regular caesura) throughout, apart from the
two songs in *A Feast during the Plague*. I have again followed
Pushkin, even to the extent of producing a rhymed version
of the songs.

I have found in translating Pushkin's dramas that the
number of syllables required to produce an adequate
English translation happens, approximately and on average,
to equate to the number of syllables in Pushkin's original.
Consequently the number of lines in my translation
corresponds to the number of lines in Pushkin's Russian.
Matching my English version, sentence by sentence, to
Pushkin's lines has been a good discipline for me and should
be helpful to students.

Russian names of people and places have been *Names in Boris*
transliterated phonetically from the Cyrillic script. In view *Godunov*
of the importance, and unpredictability, of stress in Russian,
I have indicated the correct pronunciation by adding an
accent over the stressed vowel of polysyllabic names (except
where disyllables – like "Pushkin" – are accented on the first
syllable). It should be noted, in particular, that in Russian,
and in this translation, "Iván" and "Borís" are both stressed

on the second syllable, not on the first as they often are in English.

Polish names I have transliterated from Cyrillic into their Polish spelling, to give, to the reader at least, a useful visual effect of foreignness and authenticity. To help the uninitiated I have given a phonetic transliteration of the more difficult Polish names in the list of characters. All Polish names should be stressed on the last syllable but one. (The accents over Polish names – often over consonants – are a feature of Polish spelling and have nothing to do with stress.)

Poland and Lithuania Pushkin usually refers to Russia's western neighbour as "Lithuania" and uses the adjective "Lithuanian", though he does also employ the Russian equivalent of "Poland", "Polish", and "Pole". At the time in which the play is set Poland and Lithuania formed a unified state. In view of this, and because Pushkin used the two names interchangeably, I have for the sake of simplicity used the name Poland and its cognates exclusively.

Other Translations Translations from Russian, French and other languages in the supporting material are mine unless otherwise stated.

– Roger Clarke
January 2017

Select Bibliography

Standard Edition:
Texts of *Boris Godunov* and the *Little Tragedies* are available in numerous collections of Pushkin's works, published in the Soviet Union and in Russia during the last half-century and more, for example: vol. IV, *Sobranie Sochineniy Pushkina* (Moscow: Gosudarstvennoye Izdatelstvo Hudozestvennoy Literatury, 1959–62).

Other Critical Editions:
Dunning, Chester; Emerson, Caryl; Fomichev, Sergey; Lotman, Lidiia and Wood, Antony, eds., *The Uncensored Boris Godunov – The Case for Pushkin's Original Comedy* (Madison, WI: University of Wisconsin Press, 2006)
Fomichev, Sergey; Virolainen, Maria; Dolinin, Alexander et al, eds., *Pushkin: Boris Godunov, Text and Commentary* (Moscow, Nóvoye Izdátelstvo, 2008)

Anderson, Nancy K., ed., *The Little Tragedies – Translation with Critical Essays* (New Haven, CT: Yale University Press, 2000)

Evdokimova, Svetlana, ed., *Little Tragedies: The Poetics of Brevity* (Madison, WI: University of Wisconsin Press, 2003)

Biographies:

Binyon, *T.J., Pushkin: A Biography* (London: HarperCollins, 2002)

Arinshtein, Leonid M., Pushkin: *Neprichosannaya biografiya* (Moscow: Rossiysky Fond Kultury, 2007)

Additional Recommended Background Material:

Karamzin, N.M., *Istoriya Gosudarstva Rossiyskovo* (St Petersburg, 1842)

Perrie, Maureen, *Pretenders and Popular Monarchism in Early Modern Russia* (Cambridge: Cambridge University Press, 1995)

Wolff, Tatiana, *Pushkin on Literature* (London: The Athlone Press, 1986)

On the Web:
www.rvb.ru/pushkin

Appendices

Appendix 1

Boris Godunov: *Historical Background*

The history of the Russian state traditionally starts with *Russian Origins* Ryúrik, a legendary Scandinavian chieftain invited to become *– Ryúrik* ruler of Nóvgorod in the ninth century. All the princely families of later Russia traced their ancestry back to Ryúrik.

Ryúrik's immediate heirs established Kiev as their centre *Kiev* of power; and from the tenth century the rulers of Kiev, and through them the Slavs of all the Russian lands, were converted to Eastern (Orthodox) Christianity under the influence of the Byzantine Empire in Constantinople. For a couple of centuries Kiev flourished as a centre of Slav power and culture.

In the twelfth century the leadership of Kiev waned and the *Tatar Rule and the Rise* Russian lands broke up into rival regional and city states each *of Muscovy* under its own prince. In the thirteenth century most of the Russian lands, including Kiev, were overrun by the Muslim Tatars from the east. Insofar as the Russians retained power of their own it was as local princes under Tatar suzerainty. With time the princes of Muscovy emerged as the strongest, extending their authority over other Russian principalities and gradually increasing their independence from the Tatar khan. This process reached a climax under the Muscovite Grand Prince Iván III "the Great" (r. 1462–1505), who threw off the last vestige of Tatar control, established himself as the ruler of most of north and central Russia, and by marrying the niece of the last Emperor of Constantinople presented Muscovy as the successor to the extinguished Byzantine Empire and new centre of Christian Orthodoxy.

The social order in Muscovy in the sixteenth century was *Russian Society in the* already firmly stratified. At the top level (below the grand *Sixteenth Century* prince or tsar) were the nobles, or boyars, numbering perhaps 300 at the end of the century; about a half of them held the title of prince (*"knyáz"*), tracing their ancestry back to Ryúrik. Formerly these princes had been local rulers under the authority – more nominal at some times than at others

– of the grand prince and (since the thirteenth century) of the Tatar khan. As the power of the grand princes of Muscovy grew, the local princes were expected to demonstrate their loyalty by giving the ruler of Moscow the service he required of them, whether in the civil administration or in the army or in other ways. In the eyes of the grand prince, a boyar's continued enjoyment of his privileges and his lands was conditional on his continuing to provide this loyal service to the state. The boyars saw it differently: they regarded their privileges and their lands as their right; the grand prince was only entitled to their service and support to the extent that he respected their rights and played the game of government to their rules. This difference of view underlay much of the tension between boyars and tsar in the sixteenth century. Below the boyars, titled and untitled, there were other strata of lesser nobles, landowners, merchants, and so on, down to the peasants.

Main Organs of Government The tsar was assisted in the task of ruling the country by a council of leading boyars, from whom high officials and military leaders were usually chosen. In times of crisis a more widely representative body was summoned to express its views. This was the Assembly of the Land, attended by representatives not only of the boyars, but of the clergy, the lower ranks of nobles and landowners, merchants, and delegates from other cities in Muscovy.

Registers of Rank One of the rules that the boyars expected the tsar to observe was that all appointments in the civil service and the army should be made according to order of heredity and as recorded in special registers. It was therefore very hard for men from the lower strata of society to rise to the top; and when they did so they faced resentment and hostility.

Lower Orders The bulk of the population were peasants and slaves. The boyars took the view that as landowners by right, they were free to move peasants on or off their lands as he chose. Peasants too enjoyed a traditional right to change their employment and residence during the two weeks around St George's Day (celebrated in Russia on 26th November, the traditional end of the season for farm work). The tsars' contention, on the other hand, that the boyars (and other landowners) held their lands at the sovereign's pleasure inclined them to the view that the peasants belonged with the lands. They regarded it as their duty to prevent landowners

288

both from arbitrarily evicting peasants and from seizing them from each other; they also wished to ensure that peasants remained available to work the land, and to curb the growth of a landless and rootless peasantry. For such not entirely unworthy motives the sixteenth century tsars made it more and more difficult to separate peasants from the land where they lived, a process culminating in Borís Godunóv's suspension of the St George's Day right of transfer and producing, almost inadvertently, the conditions of serfdom that persisted in Russia till 1861.

Iván the Great's grandson Iván IV came to the throne in *Iván IV (r. 1533–84)* 1533 at the age of three. The early years of his reign were characterized by fierce struggles among the boyars for dominance among themselves and over himself as ruler. The young Iván made it his purpose to break the power of the boyars, centralize the state and strengthen his own position as autocrat.

Iván was the first of the Grand Princes of Muscovy to assume officially the title of "tsar" (derived from the Roman imperial title "Caesar"), again reflecting Muscovy's ambition to be regarded as the "Third Rome", the true successor to Constantinople.

Iván conducted a series of aggressive foreign wars. In the *Iván IV's Campaigns* east he besieged and captured (1552) the city of Kazán, centre of a powerful Tatar khanate; he also subsequently annexed the Tatar khanates of Ástrakhan (1556) and western Siberia (1582). In the west Iván fought a long and fruitless war against Sweden and the Union of Poland and Lithuania, at one point in which Prince Iván Petróvich Shúysky, father of the Vasíly Shúysky who figures in the play, defended Pskov against a Polish onslaught (1581). One of the heroes of Iván's Kazán campaign was Prince Andréy Kurbsky (1528–83), who later fell out with Iván and fled to Poland in 1563, where he fought on the Polish side against Russia and lived out the rest of his life.

To further his aim of centralizing and consolidating his *Iván IV and the Boyars* power, Iván carried on a constant struggle against the boyars. He created for this purpose a special corps of men (known as the *opríchnina*) largely from the lower ranks of nobility: in return for their services as police and executioners he gave them landholdings from lands he had seized for himself; and with the help of these "*opríchniki*" he conducted a campaign of terror against his opponents by extremely cruel and bloodthirsty means, thus earning for himself the nickname "Iván the Terrible".

Iván IV's Character　Despite his early promise Iván developed later in life into a man of erratic and unstable character. He was capable of charm, energy and far-sightedness. But he also indulged in bouts of extravagant debauchery, violence and cruelty, which were often followed by phases of abject penitence and temporary withdrawal into monastic life, in which he obliged his leading henchmen to accompany him. In 1581, in one of his fits of violent temper he struck and killed his eldest and favourite son, leaving as his heir his second son Feódor, a deeply religious but weak-minded and sickly young man unsuited to a position of power.

Rise of Borís Godunóv　After the death of Iván's eldest son, Borís Godunóv came into prominence as an increasingly influential figure under the Tsar. Godunóv, born around 1551, did not come from one of the princely families: he was from an untitled boyar family from the town of Kostromá, which was allegedly descended from a Tatar prince who early in the fourteenth century had joined the service of Iván I of Muscovy and had adopted Christianity. Borís had not been one of Iván's *opríchniki*; but he married Maríya, the daughter of Grigóry "Malyúta" Skurátov-Belsky, who had been a notoriously ferocious *opríchnik* leader and a favourite of the Tsar. Borís was a clever, energetic and ambitious man, and his closeness to Iván and Feódor paved the way for the marriage of his sister Irína to the Crown Prince. Just before s... h Ivi... ppc ned C... un... as Feódor's gu..dian.

Tsar Feód[or] I (r. 1584-?)　Tsar Iván died in 1584. ...e ... suc..e..ed by Feódor w... Godunóv as regent, initial wi.. (the)s..l...er...l..d. Coun... was the de facto ruler of R..si..irtua..h..t..roug out...eodo...s reign. Feódor himself devo..d ...ime t... ors ii, fa..ing a ... prayer.

Russian Pa[triarch]e　In 1588 Godunóv took ...v...ge of t..e v si..to ...Mos..o... of the Ec...nical Patri...h, emi...f C..c.sta..inop..., to obtain auth..rity for t...e..lish..r..ir..Mosc.w.of.. "Patriarchate of all Russia" as head of the Orthodox Church in Russia. Godunóv had one of his supporters chosen as the first patriarch. Patriarch Íov (Job) continued in office from 1589 to 1605. This step was not only in consonance with Tsar Feódor's religious leanings; it was also a further demonstration of Moscow's position as the Third Rome and as the only centre of the Orthodox Church not under Islamic domination.

Initially the heir to the throne after Feódor was his half-brother Dimítry, son of Iván by his last wife María Nagáya, aged less than two at the time of his father's death. Godunóv used his influence to have Dimítry and his mother exiled to the town of Uglich on the Volga (about 140 kilometres north of Moscow), which his father Tsar Iván had assigned to him as his personal fiefdom. In Uglich on 15th May 1591 Dimítry, still only eight, met a violent death in enigmatic circumstances. *Crown Prince Dimítry (1582–91)*

Rumour had it that the boy had been murdered by assassins sent by Godunóv, with the complicity of one of his nurses. It was said that Godunóv had tried unsuccessfully to bribe an eminent soldier, N.P. Chepchugóv, to kill Dimítry. Suspicion also surrounded the appointment of an official Mikháylo Bityagóvsky by Borís to have oversight of the Tsarítsa Maríya's household in Uglich; Bityagóvsky, his son Danílo, his nephew N.D. Kachálov and Osip Volókhov, son of the suspect nurse Vasilísa Volókhova, were lynched by a mob in Uglich after Dimítry's death in the belief that they were his murderers.

A boyar, Prince Vasíly Ivánovich Shúysky (1552–1612), was sent in the name of Tsar Feódor to conduct an investigation into the Prince's death. Shúysky was a cunning and two-faced man, who played a significant part in the history of this period. Shúysky's commission of inquiry reported that the young Dimítry had stabbed himself with a knife during an epileptic fit. But the suspicions of murder lingered on. Even now it is uncertain where the truth lies. Pushkin followed the tradition that Godunóv had indeed instigated the Crown Prince's murder; and his play is based on this assumption. *Investigation of Prince Dimítry's Death*

Whatever the truth about Dimítry's death, on the night of 6th January 1598 Tsar Feódor died childless; within a week the heir presumptive, his wife Irína, retired to the Novodévichy convent on the outskirts of Moscow. There was no other survivor from the old dynasty to occupy the throne, and in the interregnum the Boyar Council took control of government. It is at this point that Pushkin's play commences. *Death of Tsar Feódor*

In the absence of anyone from the dead Tsar's family, the most obvious candidate to succeed to the tsardom was Borís Godunóv: he was Feódor's brother-in-law; and he had in fact ruled the country for the past thirteen years. But Irína and Borís both refused to agree to Borís's accession, and he took *Tsar Borís (r. 1598–1605) – Accession* refuge with her in the convent. Those who wanted him as tsar, including the Patriarch Íov and senior state officials, summoned an Assembly of the Land (the "Grand Assembly" mentioned in Scene 1) for 17th February 1598, which proceeded to appoint Borís as tsar; but he maintained his refusal. Whether this was evidence of a genuine desire to retire from public life, or a political ruse to maximize popular support and sort out his enemies from his friends, the powers of Church and State united to campaign for his acceptance of the tsardom and to mobilize public demonstrations to this end. It was only after further organized demonstrations and a threat from the Patriarch of excommunication and the suspension of all religious services that he gave way. He was crowned later in the year.

Borís's Administration   As both regent and tsar, Borís showed himself an able and conscientious administrator. He strengthened Russian commerce and contacts with the West. He conducted a largely peaceable foreign policy, seeking to consolidate the gains made by Iván IV rather than embark on further military ventures. He continued Iván IV's policy of trying to limit the power of the highest nobility, the princely boyars, of whom there were about 130 at this time. By "abolishing St George's Day" (see above) he aimed to reinforce Iván's attempts to curb evictions of peasants from the land.

Borís's Children   Borís had two children, whose interests he seems to have had at heart. He tried to give his son Feódor (b. 1589) a good education; and Feódor took part in the production of a map of the Russian lands, which was the best map of Russia to have been drawn up to that time. Bor planned to marry his daughter Xénia (b. 1582) to Prince Jo n of D ark 15 3–16 2, brother of the Danish King Ch an IV d c Ar ie. consorted King James VI of Scotland; u the y g n , ill c y nine een, fell ill and died sho ly a te his at l i u ia in O :tob r 1602.

Mounting Pro lei   Borís encountered other setb cks, v ch le o h re gn be n ; counted as the beginning of the ' ne o cou es , a per od of civil strife, foreign inv ion d th ar les ct or th t laste d until 1613. His meas es, b g n und he ge cy to restrict the mobility of peasants were unpopular with the large landowners and with the peasants alike. Additionally the boyars had always resented the appointment as tsar of someone whom they regarded as a social inferior and an upstart. There were plots against him, and in 1601 Borís had many members of leading boyar families – among them the Sitskys, Shestunóvs and Románovs – shut up in monasteries, murdered or exiled. From 1601 to 1603 there were three successive years of crop failures, leading to severe famine and epidemics, and provoking – despite Borís's attempts to provide relief – serious popular unrest in the country. In 1603 there was a peasant uprising, and the insurgents reached Moscow before being driven back with difficulty. Borís's insecurity made him increasingly reliant on informers, among them the servants of prominent boyars, and on the ruthless persecution of his opponents.

The disaffected parties found a focus for their common dissatisfaction when in 1603 an unknown young man appeared in Poland claiming that he was the Crown Prince Dimítry, son of Iván IV, who had after all escaped Godunóv's assassins eleven years before. Tsar Borís's administration declared that the young man was in fact a runaway monk, by name Grigóry Otrépyev. But the Pretender obtained the support of king and church in Poland by promising to cede substantial Russian territories to Poland and to make Roman Catholicism Russia's official religion (he secretly became a Roman Catholic himself); and Russian exiles in Poland were attracted to him by the prospect of being able to return home in safety. He was helped to gather an armed force by the powerful Wiśniowiecki family, in the house of one member of which the Pretender had first declared himself, and by Jerzy Mniszech, the Governor of Sandomierz, whose daughter Maryna (1588–1614) the Pretender proposed to marry and make his tsarítsa. He was also joined by bands of Cossacks who had come over to him and by serfs on the run from their owners. *Appearance of the False Dimítry*

In October 1604 the Pretender crossed into Russia. At first the Russian armies were commanded by Pyótr Basmánov, an ambitious man from the lower ranks of the nobility. Basmánov was an able general. He and Prince Andréy Trubetskóy originally set out to defend Chernígov, but hearing that the town had already been lost they shut themselves up in Nóvgorod-Séversky, about 160 kilometres to the north-east. From here they made a successful sortie and temporarily repulsed the Pretender. Meanwhile Prince Fyódor Mstislávsky, who had been sent to relieve Basmánov with 50,000 troops, engaged with the Pretender with his 15,000 men near the town on 21st December 1604, but Mstislávsky *The Pretender's Campaign*

was wounded and badly defeated (an episode from this battle
is depicted in Scene 19). Borís sent Vasíly Shúysky out to
deputize for Mstislávsky. The Cossack Andréy Karéla fighting
for the Pretender captured the fortress of Krómy, and held it
against Borís until Borís's death. Putívl was surrendered to
the Pretender by Prince Mosálsky, who became one of the
Pretender's closest associates.

Despite these early successes, the Pretender abandoned
his blocade of Nóvgorod-Séversky at the end of December,
allowing Basmánov to return to Moscow, where he was
hailed as a victor and made a boyar. After the fighting around
Nóvgorod-Séversky the Pretender's Polish troops became
restive from the discomforts of the winter campaign and from
arrears of pay, and many left him. With the help of Cossack
reinforcements, however, the Pretender took Sevsk and tried
to reach Karéla in Kromy, but Shúysky intercepted him and
forced him to give battle at Dobrýnichi, just north of Sevsk,
on 21st January 1605, where, once again greatly outnumbered
and deserted by some of his Cossacks and remaining Poles,
he was thoroughly beaten, with the loss of nearly half his
army. (This is the background to Scene 21.) The Pretender
then fell back through forested country to Rylsk, and thence
to Putívl. But Shúysky, instead of pursuing him, stopped
to besiege Rylsk. Mstislávsky, who had recovered from his
wound, then returned to the front and decided to lay siege to
Karéla in Kromy. The delay allowed the Pretender to gather

The Pretender's Appeal strengthen and demoralized the government's force.
espite the reverses there by the Pretender in January
atisfaction with Borís's government made many willing
believe that the young heir the previous dynasty had not
appeared; and the same that Borís was a illegitimate
usurper, deprived him of the prospective ratification that let us would
therwise have enjoyed among the common people. This too
led the Pretender attract popular support.

Borís's Death and the Then, unexpectedly, in April 1605 Borís died, probably of
Pretender's Victory brain hemorrhage and stroke. His sixteen-year-old son
Fyodor was proclaimed tsar in his place. He immediately
appointed Basmánov to a senior command position in the army.
But in view of the now deep unpopularity of the Godunóv
family and the extent of popular unrest, the military leaders
(including Basmánov and Prince Golítsyn) sent a deputation
in early May to the Pretender in Putívl to offer him their

allegiance. The Pretender then advanced on Moscow, sending ahead a nobleman-supporter Gavríla Pushkin and another envoy to read out a proclamation addressed to the populace at all levels offering them an amnesty if they accepted him as tsar. The proclamation, read out on 1st June, ignited a popular uprising in the city, which induced the Moscow nobility, too, to go over to the side of the Pretender. Feódor and his mother were arrested and removed from the tsar's palace to Borís's old house in the Kremlin. Some days later, in anticipation of the Pretender's arrival, they were murdered there by several of the turncoat boyars, including Golítsyn and Mosálsky. Borís's daughter Xénia was forced to take the veil and banished to a convent. (Here Pushkin's play ends.) On 20th June the Pretender entered Moscow in triumph to general acclamation and was in due course crowned tsar as Iván's son Dimítry.

Maryna Mniszech came to Moscow the following year with a large Polish retinue and was ostentatiously married to the False Dimítry in May. Only a week later the False Dimítry was deposed and killed in an anti-Polish uprising instigated by Vasíly Shúysky. Basmánov was killed at the same time. Shúysky had himself chosen by the boyars as the new tsar; but this choice was not accepted by the Cossacks and rebellious peasants, who feared boyar oppression and joined in a rising in southern Russia which spread north towards the capital. Although this rising was put down, Shúysky had the real Dimítry's remains transferred from Uglich to the Moscow Kremlin, in the hope of forestalling future claims that the young Crown Prince had survived. Despite this, in 1608 the Polish nobles intervened again in support of a second False Dimítry and besieged Moscow. Shúysky called on Sweden for help. The siege was lifted, and the new "Dimítry" eventually killed; but in the meantime, in defence of Polish interests King Zygmunt had invaded Russia with the Polish army. Faced with this threat the boyars ousted Shúysky in 1610 and made peace with the Poles on the understanding that they would accept the Polish prince Władisław, Zygmunt's son, as tsar. Shúysky was made to enter a monastery and later taken to Poland, where he died two years later.

Epilogue: Subsequent Events

Meanwhile Maryna Mniszech, ever ambitious, made vain attempts to regain the Russian throne, allying herself first to the Second Pretender, by whom she had a son, and later to a Cossack chieftain Zarútsky. When it was clear that Polish

The End of Maryna Mniszech

intervention had failed she fled east with Zarútsky and her son in the autumn of 1613. The next year, the three of them were captured by government forces near the Urál river. Taken to Moscow, Zarútsky and the boy were executed, and Maryna died in captivity soon afterwards.

A New Dynasty   After the fall of Vasíly Shúysky in 1610 Polish troops occupied the Moscow Kremlin on behalf of the King and his son. A period of anarchy followed, until 1612 when a nationalist army organized by Kuzmá Minin and Prince Dimítry Pozhársky recaptured Moscow and drove the Poles out. In the following year an Assembly of the Land chose a young member of the Románov family, Mikhaíl, as the new tsar, thus ending the Time of Troubles and establishing the dynasty that ruled Russia till 1917.

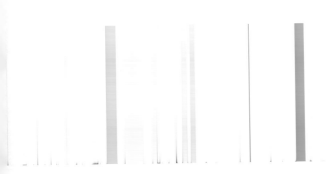

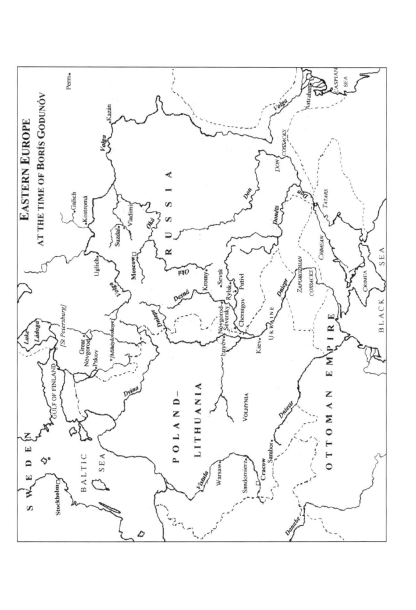

EASTERN EUROPE
AT THE TIME OF BORÍS GODUNÓV

Family Tree

showing members of the Ryúrik dynasty of Russian rulers
and members of Tsar Borís's immediate family mentioned in
Borís Godunóv

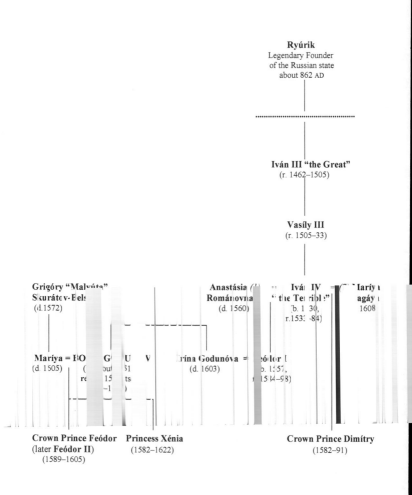

Appendix 2

Boris Godunov: *The Text*

Up till recently there has been confusion over an authoritative text of *Boris Godunov*. Surprisingly, until a few years ago there were no editions available giving the exact text of the play either as written by Pushkin in 1825 or as published by him in 1831 (the only text published under his name during his lifetime). From immediately after Pushkin's death successive editors have published versions of the play that restore *some* of the 1831 cuts; but they have done so subjectively and arbitrarily. For instance, all editions reverse the main changes to Scenes 9 and 19; most editions reinstate Scene 3; some restore Scene 13; but few put back Scene 6. Consequently, till recently the canonical text of *Boris Godunov* has been one that lacked the author's own imprimatur. Moreover, there has been no comprehensive analysis of the nature and rationale of the cuts and other changes made by Pushkin between 1825 and 1831, whether of his own accord or to meet the requirements (as he understood them) of the censorship.

The University of Wisconsin Press have done scholarship a great service by publishing in 2004, in Russian and in English, the text of the play as Pushkin originally wrote it. But even they sometimes overlook or misstate the differences between the original version and the 1831 edition. (They ignore, for instance, the significant rebranding of the "vagrant monks" of Scene 9 to "vagrants disguised as monks", and the suppression of the fool's name "Nikólka" in Scene 18. They also state that "Pushkin's reference to the 'Eastern Church' [in Scene 12, l. 7] was changed to 'Northern Church' in the 1831 edition…" when in fact the 1831 edition keeps the reference to the "Eastern Church".) More recently a valuable new Russian edition of the play has come out under the auspices of the Russian Academy of Sciences and the University of Wisconsin, containing both the 1825 text and a facsimile of the 1831 edition, with extensive commentary. The present volume is, however, I believe, the first English edition, based on a study of the 1831 text itself, to list and comment on all the significant differences between it and the original version.

The following table lists the changes Pushkin made to his original text of 1825 for the edition of 1831. The likely reasons for the changes are discussed further in the paragraphs that follow the table and, in particular cases, in the commentary.

Item	Changes made to original 1825 version for published 1831 edition	Likely reason
A	Dedication to Nikoláy Karamzín: added in 1831	acknowledge debt to deceased historian on publication of play
B	Heading and footing: Replacement of heading with the words "Boris Godunov, a composition (*sochinéniye*) of Alexander Pushkin. St Petersburg. 1831"; and replacement of final date and footing with "THE END" (*KONÉTS*).	death of Alexander I, and changed political and personal circumstances rendering provocative title obsolete
C	Scene 3: Deletion of whole scene	eliminate flippant portrayal of populace and choice of tsar
D	Scene 6: Deletion of whole scene	avoid portrayal of disreputable monk; standardize metres
E	Scene 9: Change of list of characters to read: Misaíl and Varlaám, vagrants disguised as monks;...	avoid portrayal of disreputable monks
F	Sce ne ` M sa íl's th` l speech rea`  ` h yo u da lir God b ess y`   (*He sings.*)   ` D da in th e`  of Kazán.  V 'h  re 't you w `ing with u . Th re no e plic t ntion of si ng in Var a s t i d spe but h is fif speech enc :	repla e so to obvi usly u disre utab ne c

...and now *he* turns the cold shoulder. *(Drinks and sings.)*

"A young monk took his vows…"

G   Scene 9: Varlaám's fifth speech: deletion of: eliminate coarseness and obscenity

        p'rhaps he's smelt the filly...

H   Scene 9: The monk's interventions between Grigóry's seventh and eighth speeches are omitted, and Grigóry's speeches are run together as follows: eliminate coarseness and obscenity

        GRIGÓRY *(to himself)*
            That puts paid to your little bid for freedom, granny! *(aloud)* But who on earth are they after? Who's on the run from Moscow?

I   Scene 9: In Varlaám's tenth speech, instead of "you sons of a whore":   eliminate coarseness and obscenity

        you scoundrels

J   Scene 11: Deletion of Xénia's lament and her first exchange with her brother   uncertain; perhaps consequential to loss of Scene 6 and resultant restructuring

K   Scene 11: "Semyón Nikítich" is Pushkin's 1831 correction of the original "Semyón Ilyích".   correction of factual error

L   Scene 12: ll. 72–95 replaced by: eliminate risky contemporary reference

                ...then,
        Boris will have to pay his debts in full.
        And who are you?

M   Scene 12: l. 97, supplied from 1831 edition; absent from the recently published 1825 texts   accidental omission in recently published texts?

N   Scene 12: Everything from the end of l. 116 to the end of l. 119 (including stage directions) deleted   eliminate facetious comment no longer required by structure

O	Scene 13: Deletion of whole scene	adjust structure in view of deletion of Scene 6; standardize metres
P	Scene 14: Omission of l. 12	printing error?
Q	Scene 14: l. 25 changed to read:	remove anachronism
	we're not attracted by the music's din	
R	Scene 15: In ll. 11 and 12 omission of the words:	printing error?
	So what is it I fear? / I don't myself know.	
S	Scene 16: Omission of date in heading	doubt over correct date? or printing error?
T	Scene 16: l. 6 – tense of verb and punctuation changed, to read:	printing error

> ...now your soul
> has had its consolation in the grave.
> Your exiled bones.

U	Scenes 18 and 19: Order of scenes reversed in 1831 edition	adjust structure in view of deletion of Scene 6
V	Scene 18: All seven occurrences of the name Nikólka are eliminated in the 1831 edition, with the following things:	avoid inappropriate portrayal of named Orthodox holy man; avoid disrespectful use of the name of the reigning tsar

URCHINS
Iron numbskull! Iron numbskull!... Tr-r-r-r...

OLD WOMAN
Let him alone, you little fiends. – Say a prayer for
me, holy man; I'm such a sinner...

AN URCHIN
Hullo, fool; why don't you take your cap off?…

HOLY FOOL *(crying)*
They've taken my poor kopeck; they're being cruel to God's fool!…

HOLY FOOL
Borís! Borís! The brats are being cruel to God's fool.

TSAR
Give him money. What's he crying about?

HOLY FOOL
The brats are being cruel to me…

W — Scene 18: The nonsensical fourth line of Nikólka's ditty is omitted in the 1831 edition — minor drafting

X — Scene 19: In the second deserter's speech, "Foreign crow" replaced by "Foreign frog" — drafting

Y — Scene 19: The last phrase of Margeret's third speech replaced by: — eliminate coarseness and obscenity

…*ça n'a que des jambes pour fuir*

Z — Scene 19: Margeret's fifth speech amended to read: — eliminate coarseness and obscenity

Diable, il y fait chaud! Ce diable de "Pri-tenn-der", comme il s'appelle, est un brave à trois poils.

AA — Scene 19: In the stage direction before the last two speeches, the words "*An engagement.*" added in 1831. — clarification

BB — Scene 21: In the fourth line "My poor old comrade" is replaced with: — minor drafting

My poor old charger.

CC Scene 21: In l. 38 "as a placid child" is   drafting
    replaced with:

    as a foolish child

DD Scene 24: In the third line, "Let's listen to him!"   drafting
    is replaced with:

    This way! This way!

EE Scene 25: In the penultimate speech of the   drafting
    populace the order of phrases is changed,
    as follows:

    Do you hear? Shrieking! That's a woman's voice…
    Let's go up! – The doors are locked – the shouts
    have died down. – There's still a noise.

FF Scene 25: The populace's final acclamation is   clarify the ending and
    replaced with the stage direction: bring it more into line
        with Karamzín,
    (The people remain speechless.)   following the cut of
        Scene 3

GG Date and footing: See item B above.

The differences between the 1831 text and Pushkin's 1825 manuscript can be considered under different categories, as follows.

The first category are changes attributable directly to the censorship. Most of the big changes made for the 1831 edition (C, D, E–I, and Y–Z above) plainly represent Pushkin's attempts to remove the "improprieties", linguistic and religious, highlighted by the censor. It may be that Pushkin was not greatly troubled by the loss of the linguistic 'improprieties'. In writing about the play in 1829 he said: *…quand aux grossièrtes indécences, n'y faites pas attention: cela a été écrit au courant de la plume et disparaîtra à la première copie…*" ("…as for the worst obscenities don't worry about them: the pen ran away with me as I was writing, they'll disappear with the first print run.") Nonetheless, these changes represent alterations to the original text of the play imposed on Pushkin from outside and should not, in principle, be accepted in a canonical text.

A second category of revisions in the 1831 edition (O, U, FF and possibly J) are indirectly attributable to the censorship. They were evidently due to Pushkin's attempts to make good the damage to the play's structure caused by the loss of Scenes 3 and 6 (see Appendix 3). These too, then, will be changes that Pushkin would have avoided were it not for the censorship's interference.

A third category of changes (B, L and GG, and perhaps N) represent Pushkin's adaptation of the play to changed personal and dynastic circumstances, such as are described in the Extra Material, p. 258.

A fourth group of amendments are mostly very small and seem to represent minor corrections (K and Q), clarifications (AA and EE) and drafting changes (W, X, BB, CC and DD) made by Pushkin of his own volition.

A few differences (M, P, R, S and T) are probably due to printing errors.

The authentic text of *Boris Godunov* should be the one that represents most faithfully Pushkin's unconstrained intentions. This points to the reversal of all the changes that Pushkin made in response, directly or indirectly, to the censor's comments (i.e. those in the first two categories above). There is more room for debate about the changes in the third and fourth categories, in that here Pushkin's "unconstrained intentions" may have changed between 1825 and 1831. However, in nearly all cases Pushkin's reasons for changing his original text are matters of (more or less) informed conjecture rather than of certain knowledge; and in the absence of certain knowledge of Pushkin's motives for particular changes I have decided to follow his original text. Only in one case (K), where Pushkin was undoubtedly correcting a factual error, and in another (AA), where he added a clarificatory stage direction, have I preferred the 1831 wording. This edition, then, I believe, comes as close as it is possible to come to the authentic *Boris Godunov* – the play as Pushkin, in the freedom of his own will, would have had it published, read and performed.

Appendix 3

Boris Godunov: *Architecture of the Play*

One of the remarkable and distinctive aspects of *Boris Godunov* is its architecture. As several Russian scholars, notably Dmitry Blagóy and Irena Ronen, have previously noted, the play has a markedly symmetrical structure. But their analysis has been flawed because it has been based (like nearly all discussion of the play hitherto) neither on Pushkin's original version of 1825 nor on the cut version he reluctantly approved for publication in 1831, but on a hybrid.

Design of the 1825 Play

It is most helpful to imagine the play as a series of scenes arranged in the shape of an arch. The two pillars rest on the murders (offstage) of a rightful heir to the throne of Russia – Dimítry Ivánovich at the beginning and Feódor Borísovich at the end, in both cases at the hands of agents of the usurper. As has been observed before, the first three scenes of *Boris Godunov* match the last three scenes (23–25). The first three scenes can be seen as a kind of prologue in which neither of the protagonists – neither Borís nor the Pretender – appears on stage. Similarly the last three scenes form a kind of epilogue in which, again, neither of the protagonists appears on stage. There are a number of other parallels and contrasts between Scenes 1–3 and Scenes 23–25 of the original play, as shown in the following table.

Scene 1	Scene 23
in Moscow, time of peace; seditious conversation between two noblemen, about replacing the Ryúrik dynasty with the Godunóvs	in the field, time of war; seditious conversation between two noblemen, about replacing the Godunóvs with (supposedly) the Ryúrik dynasty
Scene 2	Scene 24
in Red Square; calm, ordered assembly; begins with conversation among people, leading to solemn and formal	in Red Square; excited, riotous assembly; begins with emotional and rabble-rousing proclamation urging

307

proclamation announcing deputation of church and state to wait on Borís; ends with prayer that Godunóvs will accept throne

deputation of church and state to wait on "Dimítry", leading to conversation among people; ends with call to depose Godunóvs from throne

Scene 3
verse; in Moscow; viewed from crowd; main action is within building housing prospective tsar and nun-sister, entered by boyars; watching crowd manipulated by boyars to acclaim the new tsar; inauguration of Godunóv dynasty

Scene 25
prose; in Moscow; viewed from crowd; main action is within building housing deposed tsar and nun-sister, entered by boyars; watching crowd manipulated by boyars to acclaim the new tsar; termination of Godunóv dynasty

These two units may be seen as forming the bases of the two columns of the arch. As we move further into the play from either end, correspondences are discernible between other scenes, as shown in arch-like form in following diagram:

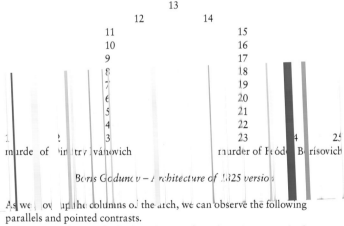

Boris Godunov – Architecture of 1825 version

As we move up the columns of the arch, we can observe the following parallels and pointed contrasts.

Scenes 4 and 22 are both set in the Kremlin Palace. Scene 4 is the first scene in which Borís appears: he is beginning his reign as tsar after leaving the Novodévichy Convent. The scene begins with Borís addressing the Patriarch and boyars; the boyars reaffirm their oath of allegiance to the new tsar. The scene ends with a private dialogue: a boyar (Shúysky), who has previously seemed disloyal, now expresses loyalty. Scene 22 begins with a private dialogue, in which a boyar (Basmánov), who later proves disloyal, expresses loyalty. The scene ends with Borís relinquishing the tsarship to become a monk; he addresses the Patriarch and boyars; the boyars give their oath of allegiance to the new tsar. Scene 22 is the last scene in which Borís appears.

Scenes 5 and 21 are both about Grigóry/the Pretender. He appears for the first time at the beginning of Scene 5, awakening from sleep, apparently a nonentity without prospects, longing to take part in victorious battles; in Scene 21 he appears for the last time, finally falling back to sleep, apparently now a failure without prospects, having been defeated in battle. Each scene is taken up with a dialogue between Grigóry/the Pretender and a mentor.

Scenes 6 and 20 are also about Grigóry/the Pretender. In Scene 6 Grigóry is encouraged to act in pursuit of his claim to the throne; although known to be a fraud he proclaims himself as "Dimítry" and is acknowledged as heir to the throne. In Scene 20 the Pretender is now acting in pursuit of this claim; although known to be a fraud, he is acknowledged as heir to the throne. In Scene 6 Grigóry longs to defend Russia from a Polish invasion; in Scene 20 the Pretender relies on Polish help to invade Russia.

Scenes 7 and 19 are again about Grigóry/the Pretender. Both scenes are in prose and are comic in tone. In Scene 7 Grigóry is said to be "possessed of the devil"; in Scene 19 the Pretender is referred to as a "devil". In Scene 7 Grigóry is accused of saying "I will be tsar"; in Scene 19 the Pretender is hailed as tsar.

Scenes 8 and 18 are both about Borís, and both are set in Moscow; the first is in verse, the second in prose. Both scenes open with a conversation between bystanders. In Scene 8 Borís, in his bedchamber, is said to be seeking supernatural aid in his misfortunes; in Scene 18 Borís, in the cathedral, is again said to be seeking supernatural aid in his misfortunes. In Scene 8 Borís emerges from his bedchamber weighed down with guilt, his kindnesses to the people repaid with blame; he talks of seeing "young boys streaming with blood". In Scene 18 Borís emerges from the cathedral weighed down with guilt; his kindness to the holy fool is repaid with blame; he is urged to have the urchins' throats cut and is compared to King Herod.

Scenes 9 and 17 both deal with the measures taken by Borís's government to capture Grigóry/the Pretender and counter the threat from him; the first is in prose, the second in verse. Scene 9 is a comic scene featuring dissolute monks who feign piety; at the end of the scene Grigóry is about to cross the frontier into Poland. At the beginning of Scene 17 the Pretender has just crossed the frontier back into Russia; it is a serious scene featuring the story of a devout old man who is genuinely pious.

Scene 10 is a cynical and seditious dialogue between two members of the Russian ruling class; Grigóry has just appeared in Poland. Scene 16 is an idealistic and patriotic dialogue between two outcasts from Russia; the Pretender is about to cross back from Poland into Russia.

Scene 11 begins by featuring an innocent, inexperienced Muscovite princess, who was betrothed to a true prince whom she never saw but adored; they never married. Scene 15 features a precocious, power-hungry Polish noblewoman, who is betrothed to a false prince whom she has met, yet despises; they will marry. Both scenes expose the tension between personal affection and political power; both consist largely of a dialogue between two people who come to distrust and despise each other but use each other for their own ends; and both raise the issue: "Can a pretender known to be false succeed?"

Scenes 12 and 14 are both set against a Western-European background; both relate to the Pretender. In Scene 12 Wiśniowecki and Mniszech are present but silent; most of the talking is done by the Pretender; in Scene 14 the Pretender is present but silent; most of the talking is done by Wiśniowecki and Mniszech. The opening of both scenes reveals attempts by Polish interests to use the Pretender for their own ends; the close of both scenes deals with poetry: Scene 12 puts facetious remarks into Russian mouths suggesting a lack of understanding of poetry in Russia and suggests the stilted nature of formal Western-European verse; Scene 14 ends with an elegant and spontaneous Russian sonnet, in the mouth of a Pole. In between, in both scenes, there are a series of brief dialogues in a semi-formal setting that disclose something of the personality, and personableness, of the Pretender.

In Scene 13 neither Borís nor the Pretender appear. In its position in the play, in its characters, in the unique lightness of its metre and dialogue, and in its atmosphere of Western-European affluence and sophistication the scene is as far removed as possible from the world of Muscovy. Insubstantial in itself, it constitutes the "appogee" of the play beyond which the forces released in the first half come onto the rebound and against Borís and the Godunóv dynasty.

Not all of these linkages are incontestable; but they are so numerous and in most cases so striking as to prove that this arch-shaped structure, with its pronounced symmetries, lying right out the central forces at work, was an integral and important element of Pushkin's plan for the play.

Feeble seaming 31

Consider however, the imputation that his intricate architecture of the guts I undoubtedly felt obliged to make for the 1831 edition to meet the censor's objections – particularly the deletion of Scenes 3 and 6. The loss of Scene 3 left Scene 25 without a counterpart. Pushkin apparently adjusted to this by regarding the orphaned Scene 25 as a self-standing coda or postscript, and it was arguably this that enabled him to dispense with the reluctant acclamation of "Tsar Dimítry" at the end of the play, which balanced the similarly unspontaneous acclamation of Tsar Borís at the end of Scene 3, and substitute the people's silence, which many have considered a more powerful ending. Scenes 1 and 2 and Scenes 23 and 24 could still retain their function of matching prologue and epilogue, albeit curtailed. The correspondences between Scenes 4 and 22 and Scenes 5 and 21 also remained in place.

But with the loss of Scene 6 the rest of the structure tottered. Two consequences were particularly serious. First, Pushkin was left with an even number of scenes to make up the rest of the arch, which robbed him of his single Polish "apogee"; it was presumably this that led him to drop Scene 13, with its unique metre, which could no longer form the apex of the arch; he could then treat the Polish Scenes 12 and 15 as the last matching pair and use Scene 14, with its lightness of tone, its Western-European dancing and wine-sipping, its emancipated women and its rhyming sonnet in substitution for Scene 13 as the new apex, the new Polish "apogee" to Muscovy. (This rearrangement may even explain why in Scene 12 Pushkin cut out so many of Khrushchóv's lines, thus leaving the scene with a more dominantly Polish flavour to match the entirely Polish Scene 15; and why he omitted the comments on Russian poetry, no longer required to balance the actual Russian poem at the end of Scene 14, and abbreviated Xenia's part at the beginning of Scene 11, where the structure no longer called for her as a foil for Marina Mniszech in Scene 15.)

Secondly, Pushkin had lost the parallels of subject matter noted above between Scenes 4–8 (Borís, 3 x Pretender, Borís) and 18–22 (Borís, 3 x Pretender, Borís), including the striking match between Scenes 8 and 18, which he evidently considered important. He then deftly recreated a similar structure, again with matching Borís scenes (including 8 and 18), but with two matching Pretender scenes instead of three, by switching the order of Scenes 18 and 19, a change in the 1831 edition that has previously seemed particularly hard to understand.

Pushkin's modified architecture for the 1831 edition can be summarized in the following diagram (in which the scenes keep the numbers given them for the 1825 version):

```
                              14
                 12                   15
             11                           16
             10                           17
              9                           19
              8                           18
              7                           20
              5                           21
              4                           22
  1           2                           23         24
  murder of Dimítry                       murder of Feódor
  Ivánovich                               Borísovich (25)
```

Boris Godunov – Architecture of 1831 version

Pushkin was presumably prepared to acquiesce in the mismatch between the other new pairs: 7 and 20, 9 and 19, 10 and 17, and 11 and 16. As it happened, Scenes 9 and 19 had in common that they were both comic scenes in prose; Shúysky's duplicity and cunning play an important part in both Scenes 10 and 17; and the Polish frontier figures prominently both in Scene 11 (Borís has it sealed) and Scene 16 (the Pretender crosses it). So no doubt Pushkin felt that enough of his original structure had been salvaged to allow him to publish the play in good conscience, even in its mutilated form.

Appendix 4

A Feast during the Plague:
Extract from John Wilson's The City of the Plague

THE CITY OF THE PLAGUE
Act I, Scene 4

The street. – A long table covered with glasses. – A party of young men and women carousing.

YOUNG MAN

    I rise to give, most noble President,
    the memory of a man well known to all,
    who by keen jest, and merry anecdote,
    sharp repartee, and humorous remark
    most biting in its solemn gravity,
    much cheered our out-door table, and dispelled
    the fogs which this rude visitor the Plague
    oft breathed across the brightest intellect.
    But two days past, our ready laughter chased
    his various stories; and it cannot be
    that we have in our gamesome revelries
    forgotten Harry Wentworth. His chair stands
    empty at your right hand – as if expecting
    that jovial wassailer – but he is gone
    into cold narrow quarters. Well, I deem
    the grave did never silence with its dust
    a tongue more eloquent; but since 'tis so,
    and store of boon companions yet survive,
    there is no reason to be sorrowful;
    therefore let us drink unto his memory
    with acclamation, and a ready peal
    such as in life he loved.

MASTER OF REVELS

                     'Tis the first death
    hath been among us, therefore let us drink
    his memory in silence.

YOUNG MAN

Be it so.

(They all rise, and drink their glasses in silence.)

MASTER OF REVELS

Sweet Mary Gray! Thou hast a silver voice,
and wildly to thy native melodies
can tune its flute-like breath – sing us a song,
and let it be, even mid our merriment,
most sad, most slow, that when its music dies,
we may address ourselves to revelry,
more passionate from the calm, as men leap up
to this world's business from some heavenly dream.

MARY GREY'S SONG

I walk'd by mysel ower the sweet braes o' Yarrow,
    when the earth wi' the gowans o' July was drest;
but the sang o' the bonny burn sounded like sorrow,
    round ilka house cauld as a last simmer's nest.

I look'd through the lift o' the blue smiling morning,
    but never ae wee cloud o' mist could I see
on its way up to heaven, the cottage adorning,
    hanging white ower the green o' its sheltering tree.

By the outside kenn'd that the inn was forsaken,
    that nae treedlc' footsteps was heard on the floor; –
O loud craw'd the cock whare was nane to awaken,
    and the wild raven croak'd on the seat by the door!

Sic silence – sic lonesomeness, oh, were bewildering!
    I heard nae lass singing when herding her sheep;
I met nae bright garlands o' wee rosy children
    dancing out the school-house just waken'd frae sleep.

I pass'd by the school-house – when strangers were coming,
    whose windows with glad faces seem'd all alive;
ae moment I hearken'd, but heard nae sweet humming,
    for a night o' dark vapour can silence the hive.

I pass'd by the pool where the lasses at dawing
    used to bleach their white garments wi' daffin and din;
but the foam in the silence o' nature was faing,
    and nae laughing rose loud through the roar of the linn.

I gaed into a small town – when sick o' my roaming –
    where ance play'd the viol, the tabor, and flute;
'twas the hour loved by Labour, the saft-smiling gloaming,
    yet the green round the Cross-stane was empty and mute.

To the yellow-flower'd meadow, and scant rigs o' tillage,
    the sheep a' neglected had come frae the glen;
the cushat-dow coo'd in the midst o' the village,
    and the swallow had flown to the dwellings o' men!

Sweet Denholm! not thus, when I lived in thy bosom.
    Thy heart lay so still the last night o' the week;
then nane was sae weary that love would nae rouse him,
    and Grief gaed to dance with a laugh on his cheek.

Sic thoughts wet my een – as the moonshine was beaming
    on the kirk-tower that rose up sae silent and white;
the wan ghastly light on the dial was streaming,
    but the still finger tauld not the hour of the night.

The mirk-time pass'd slowly in siching and weeping,
    I waken'd, and nature lay silent in mirth;
ower a' holy Scotland the Sabbath was sleeping,
    and Heaven in beauty came down on the earth.

The morning smiled on – but nae kirk-bell was ringing,
    nae plaid or blue bonnet came down frae the hill;
the kirk-door was shut, but nae psalm-tune was singing,
    and I miss'd the wee voices sae sweet and sae shrill.

I look'd ower the quiet o' Death's empty dwelling,
    the lav'rock walk'd mute 'mid the sorrowful scene,
and fifty brown hillocks wi' fresh mould were swelling
    ower the kirk-yard o' Denholm, last simmer sae green.

The infant had died at the breast o' its mither;
    the cradle stood still at the mitherless bed;

at play the bairn sank in the hand o' its brither;
    at the fauld on the mountain the shepherd lay dead.

Oh! in springtime 'tis eerie, when winter is over,
    and birds should be glinting ower forest and lea,
when the lint-white and mavis the yellow leaves cover,
    and nae blackbird sings loud frae the tap o' his tree.

But eerier far, when the spring-land rejoices,
    and laughs back to heaven with gratitude bright,
to hearken! and naewhere hear sweet human voices!
    when man's soul is dark in the season o' light!

MASTER OF REVELS
    We thank thee, sweet one! for thy mournful song.
    It seems, in the olden time, this very Plague
    visited thy hills and valleys, and the voice
    of lamentation wailed along the streams
    that now flow on through their wild paradise,
    murmuring their song of joy. All that survive
    in memory of that melancholy year,
    when died so many brave and beautiful,
    are some sweet mournful airs, some shepherd's lay
    most touching in simplicity, and none
    fitter to make one sad amid his mirth
    than the tune yet faintly singing though our souls.

MARY GRAY
    O! that I ne'er had sung it but at home
    unto my aged parents! to whose ear
    their Mary's tones were always musical.
    I hear my own self singing o'er the moor,
    beside my native cottage, – most unlike
    the voice which Edward Walsingham has praised,
    it is the angel-voice of innocence.

SECOND WOMAN
    I thought this cant were out of fashion now.
    But it is well; there are some simple souls,
    even yet, who melt at a frail maiden's tears,
    and give her credit for sincerity.
    She thinks her eyes quite killing while she weeps.

Thought she as well of smiles, her lips would pout
with a perpetual simper. Walsingham
hath praised these crying beauties of the north,
so whimpering is the fashion. How I hate
the dim dull yellow of that Scottish hair!

MASTER OF REVELS
    Hush! hush! – is that the sound of wheels I hear?

(The dead-cart passes by, driven by a Negro.)

Ha! dost thou faint, Louisa! one had thought
that railing tongue bespoke a mannish heart.
But so it ever is. The violent
are weaker than the mild, and abject fear
dwells in the heart of passion. Mary Gray,
throw water on her face. She now revives.

MARY GRAY
    O sister of my sorrow and my shame!
    Lean on my bosom. Sick must be your heart
    after a fainting-fit so like to death.

LOUISA *(recovering)*
    I saw a horrid demon in my dream!
    With sable visage and white-glaring eyes,
    he beckoned on me to ascend a cart
    filled with dead bodies, muttering all the while
    an unknown language of most dreadful sounds.
    What matters it? I see it was a dream.
    – Pray, did the dead-cart pass?

YOUNG MAN
                                    Come, brighten up,
    Louisa! Though this street be all our own,
    a silent street that we from death have rented,
    where we may hold our orgies undisturbed,
    you know those rumbling wheels are privileged,
    and we must bide the nuisance. Walsingham,
    to put an end to bickering, and these fits
    of fainting that proceed from female vapours,
    give us a song; – a free and gladsome song;

none of those Scottish ditties framed of sighs,
but a true English Bacchanalian song,
by toper chanted o'er the flowing bowl.

MASTER OF REVELS

I have none such; but I will sing a song
upon the Plague. I made the words last night,
after we parted: a strange rhyming-fit
fell on me; 'twas the first time in my life.
But you shall have it, though my vile cracked voice
won't mend the matter much.

MANY VOICES

A song on the Plague!
A song on the Plague! Let's have it! bravo! bravo!

SONG

Two navies meet upon the waves
that round them yawn like opening graves;
the battle rages; seamen fall,
and overboard go one and all!
The wounded with the dead are gone;
but Ocean drowns each frantic groan,
and, at each plunge into the flood,
grimly the billow laughs with blood.
Then, what although our Plague destroy
sea man and landman, woman, boy?
When the pillow rests beneath the head,
like sleep he comes, and strikes us dead.
What though into yon Pit we go,
descending fast, as flakes of snow?
What matters body without breath?
No groan disturbs that hold of death.

CHORUS

Then, leaning on this snow-white breast,
I sing the praises of the Pest!
If me thou would'st this night destroy,
come, smite me in the arms of Joy.

Two armies meet upon the hill;
they part, and all again is still.
No! thrice ten thousand men are lying,
of cold, and thirst, and hunger dying.
While the wounded soldier rests his head
about to die upon the dead,
what shrieks salute yon dawning light?
'Tis Fire that comes to aid the Fight!
– All whom our Plague destroys by day,
his chariot drives by night away;
and sometimes o'er a churchyard wall
his banner hangs, a sable pall!
Where in the light by Hecate shed
with grisly smile he counts the dead,
and piles them up a trophy high
in honour of his victory.
Then, leaning, etc.

King of the aisle! and churchyard cell!
thy regal robes become thee well.
With yellow spots, like lurid stars
prophetic of throne-shattering wars,
bespangled is its night-like gloom,
as it sweeps the cold damp from the tomb.
Thy hand doth grasp no needless dart,
one finger-touch benumbs the heart.
If thy stubborn victim will not die,
thou roll'st around thy bloodshot eye,
and Madness leaping in his chain
with giant buffet smites the brain,
or Idiocy with drivelling laugh
holds out her strong-drugged bowl to quaff,
and down the drunken wretch doth lie
unsheeted in the cemetery.
Then, leaning, etc.

Thou! Spirit of the burning breath,
alone deservest the name of Death!
Hide, Fever! hide thy scarlet brow;
nine days thou linger'st o'er thy blow,
till the leech bring water from the spring,
and scare thee off on drenched wing.

Consumption! waste away at will!
In warmer climes thou fail'st to kill,
and rosy Health is laughing loud
as off thou steal'st with empty shroud!
Ha! blundering Palsy! Thou art chill!
but half the man is living still;
one arm, one leg, one cheek, one side
in antic guise thy wrath deride.
But who may 'gainst thy power rebel,
King of the aisle and churchyard cell!
Then, leaning, etc.

To Thee, O Plague! I pour my song,
since thou art come I wish thee long!
Thou strikest the lawyer 'mid his lies,
the priest 'mid his hypocrisies.
The miser sickens at his hoard,
and the gold leaps to its rightful lord.
The husband, now no longer tied,
may wed a new and blushing bride,
and many a widow slyly weeps
o'er the grave where her old dotard sleeps,
while love shines through her moisten'd eye
on yon tall stripling gliding by.
'Tis ours who bloom in vernal years
to dry the lovesick maiden's tears,
who, turning from the relics cold,
in a new swain forgets the old.
Then, leaning, etc.

(*Enter an old grey-headed Priest.*)

PRIEST

O impious table! spread by impious hands!
mocking with feast and song and revelry
the silent air of death that hangs above it,
a canopy more dismal than the Pall!
Amid the churchyard darkness as I stood
beside a dire interment, circled round
by the white ghastly faces of despair,
that hideous merriment disturbed the grave,
and with a sacrilegious violence

shook down the crumbling earth upon the bodies
of the unsheeted dead. But that the prayers
of holy age and female piety
did sanctify that wide and common grave,
I could have thought that hell's exulting fiends
with shouts of devilish laughter dragged away
some hardened atheist's soul unto perdition.

SEVERAL VOICES

How well he talks of hell! Go on, old boy!
The devil pays his tithes – yet he abuses him.

PRIEST

Cease, I conjure you, by the blessed blood
of Him who died for us upon the Cross,
these most unnatural orgies. As ye hope
to meet in heaven the souls of them ye loved,
destroyed so mournfully before your eyes,
unto your homes depart.

MASTER OF REVELS

                              Our homes are dull –
and youth loves mirth.

PRIEST

                              O, Edward Walsingham!
Art thou that groaning pale-faced man of tears
who three weeks since knelt by thy mother's corpse,
and kissed the soldered coffin, and leapt down
with rage-like grief into the burial vault,
crying upon its stone to cover thee
from this dim darkened world? Would she not weep,
weep even in heaven, could she behold her son
presiding o'er unholy revellers
and tuning that sweet voice to frantic songs
that should ascend unto the throne of grace
'mid sob-broken words of prayer!

YOUNG MAN

                              Why! we can pray
without a priest – pray long and fervently
over the brimming bowl. Hand him a glass.

321

MASTER OF REVELS

Treat his grey hairs with reverence.

PRIEST

Wretched boy!
This white head must not sue to thee in vain!
Come with the guardian of thy infancy,
and by the hymns and psalms of holy men
lamenting for their sins, we will assuage
this fearful mirth akin to agony,
and in its stead, serene as the hushed face
of thy dear sainted parent, kindle hope
and heavenly resignation. Come with me.

YOUNG MAN

They have a design against the hundredth Psalm.
Oh! Walsingham will murder cruelly
"All people that on earth do dwell."
Suppose we sing it here – I know the drawl.

MASTER OF REVELS *(silencing him, and addressing the Priest)*

Why camest thou hither to disturb me thus?
I may not, must not go! Here am I held
by hopelessness in dark futurity,
by dire remembrance of the past, – by hatred
and deep contempt of my own worthless self, –
by fear and horror of the lifelessness
that reigns throughout my dwelling, – by the new
and frantic love of loud-tongued revelry, –
by the blest poison mantling in this bowl, –
and, help me Heaven! by the soft balmy kisses
of this lost creature, lost, but beautiful
even in her sin; no, could my mother's ghost
frighten me from this fair bosom. 'Tis too late!
I hear thy warning voice – I know it strives
to save me from perdition, body and soul.
Belovèd old man, go thy way in peace,
but curst be these feet if they do follow thee.

SEVERAL VOICES

Bravo! bravissimo! Our noble president!
Done with that sermonizing – off – off – off!

PRIEST
    Matilda's sainted spirit calls on thee!

MASTER OF REVELS *(starting distractedly from his seat)*
    Didst thou not swear, with thy pale withered hands
    lifted to Heaven, to let that doleful name
    lie silent in the tomb for evermore?
    O that a wall of darkness hid this sight
    from her immortal eyes! She, my betrothed,
    once thought my spirit lofty, pure, and free,
    and on my bosom felt herself in Heaven.
    What am I now? *(looking up)* – O holy child of light,
    I see thee sitting where my fallen nature
    can never hope to soar!

FEMALE VOICE
                  The fit is on him.
    Fool! thus to rave about a buried wife!
    See! how his eyes are fixed.

MASTER OF REVELS
                  Most glorious star!
    Thou art the spirit of that bright Innocent!
    And there thou shinest with upbraiding beauty
    on him whose soul hath thrown at last away
    not the hope only, but the wish of Heaven.

PRIEST
    Come, Walsingham!

MASTER OF REVELS
              O holy father! go.
    For mercy's sake, leave me to my despair.

PRIEST
    Heaven pity my dear son. Farewell! farewell!

(The Priest walks mournfully away.)

YOUNG MAN
    Sing him another song. See how he turns
    his eyes from you fair Heaven to Mary's bosom?
    The man's in love...

[The scene continues.]

Acknowledgements

I thank Alessandro Gallenzi for his confidence in commissioning me to prepare this translation and edition of Pushkin's completed dramatic works – a task that has only enlarged my appreciation and enjoyment of Pushkin and that will, I hope, do the same for others. I also thank my wife Elizabeth, without whose constant support and patience its achievement would not have been possible.

I am also grateful to Simon Blundell, librarian of the Reform Club in London, for his ever-willing help in securing for me the requisite volumes of Karamzín's *History* and other texts; to Professor Leonid Arinshtein of the Russian Cultural Foundation for his guidance and answers to my queries; and to Iwona Krasodomska-Jones for her advice on the spelling of certain Polish names.

-- Roger Clarke

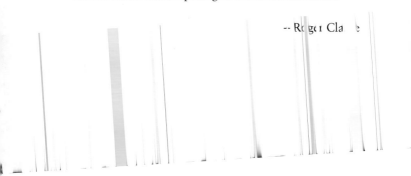

Made in the USA
Lexington, KY
16 May 2019